I1006612

Praise for *Our Search for Belonging*

"Howard Ross transformed our understanding of both bias and unconscious bias with his wonderful book *Everyday Bias*. Now he is transforming our understanding of why we have people in America both tribalizing and too often fighting each other in damaging and dysfunctional tribal ways. This book is a must-read for anyone who wants to understand the mess we are in today and what we need to do now to give us a better future for our organizations, our communities, and even our nation. This will be another iconic book."
—**George Halvorson, former CEO, Kaiser Permanente**

"*Our Search for Belonging* is a powerful statement of hope in a disquieting time. Our social divide is creating major challenges on college campuses, in workplaces, and in society itself. By helping us understand the reasons for the divide and the things we can do about it, Howard Ross has provided guidelines for a future that does not have to be limited by our past. A must-read!"
—**Dr. Kristina Johnson, Chancellor, State University of New York**

"Our field has an abundance of talkers, folks who have an opinion they feel obligated to share. We don't need more of either. We need more thinkers, more analysts of substance. In a world where national and tribal boundaries impose a defensive obsession with our differences, Howard has stepped in to fill that void. Legendary IBM CEO Thomas J. Watson, Jr., said, 'We serve our interests best when we serve the public interest.' In my own work I have focused on the thought, 'We talk to one another, not about one another.' In *Our Search for Belonging*, Howard is connecting those dots at a time when our societal survival is threatened. Global, national, local, or tribal—connect and respect are challenges we seem unable to execute. In this book, Howard is providing a mirror that makes us confront that picture and frames how we can navigate a treacherous road to higher, safer ground—a place where your place is not a bad place, and my place is not the only place for me."
—**J. T. (Ted) Childs, former Chief Diversity Officer, IBM**

"In a compelling narrative style that rests on a foundation of cutting-edge research, Howard Ross describes a paradox of belonging: a psychological need to be embedded in a group has produced an ideologically segregated America. To erase those tribal boundaries requires a deeper sense of belonging, which Ross suggests we might first achieve in an unexpected place: at work. At work, people see and experience difference as beneficial. And at work, people can learn behaviors that produce a more inclusive belonging."
—**Scott E. Page, PhD, Leonid Hurwicz Collegiate Professor of Complex Systems, Political Science, and Economics, University of Michigan, and author of *The Diversity Bonus* and *The Difference***

"The increasing polarization that exists in our society today can be a real impediment to producing the results we need and want in business and in politics. In this book, Howard Ross helps us understand the importance of breaking down those barriers and provides powerful tools for how to do it."

—Manny Chirico, Chairman and CEO, PVH Corp.

"In a nation with so much division, *Our Search for Belonging* is a much-needed read to educate us all on the importance of the inclusion of women and men across all distinctions of diversity both personally and professionally. Howard Ross explores and captures a broad range of topics and issues that I believe is crucial to uniting humankind and our divided nation."

—Dr. Sheila A. Robinson, Publisher and CEO, Diversity Woman Media

"*Our Search for Belonging* is a timely and wonderful gift to our national community as we struggle to find connection in the disparate views and feelings that divide us. It offers a guiding light of innovative and creative thinking grounded in impeccable research and scientific observation. This book is a necessary must-read to those wishing to further connect with the better in themselves regarding the isms and biases that we all carry as baggage in our lives. *Our Search for Belonging* is beautiful, powerful, and uplifting as it shares that goodness is latent in us all and how to achieve it."

—William H. "Smitty" Smith, EdD, Founding Executive Director, National Center for Race Amity

"If you are at all concerned about how we can pull our polarized nation back together, buy this book. Get copies for coworkers, friends, and especially your children. Howard Ross illuminates practical pathways for courageous leaders to shape a better future for us all."

—Bonnie St. John, Paralympic medalist and CEO, Blue Circle Leadership Institute

"Howard Ross has done it again! In *Our Search for Belonging*, Ross puts a human face on America's 21st-century conundrum and in doing so shows a path out of our current quagmire. He delves deeply into our psyche and neurobiologic drive to connect and shows how that drive to belong overshadows political or other external realities dividing us as a country into warring factions. And he shows us pathways toward healing the divide. This is must-reading for everyone across the political spectrum who really wants to make America great again."

—Robert Wm. Blum, MD, MPH, PhD, William H. Gates Sr. Professor, Department of Population, Family and Reproductive Health, Johns Hopkins University, and Director, Johns Hopkins Urban Health Institute

"Once again, Howard Ross has tackled the thorny divisive issues of our day—demographic diversity, politics, social justice—by shining the light of humanity on them. Through solid examples, he gives the reader space and context for understanding how and why we all have the potential to create 'us versus them' dynamics. His book serves as a road map that takes the reader on an empowering journey toward owning our part in creating inclusive cultures and helping others to belong."

—**Natalie Holder, diversity executive of a federal law enforcement agency**

"In this thought-provoking book, Howard Ross delves into one of the most important issues of our time, namely, how the human yearning for belonging can paradoxically sow the seeds of division. Drawing on evidence from a wide range of disciplines, the book delivers potential solutions for mending our fractured society. This book should be required reading for anyone wishing to chart a better course for humanity—in this regard, it could be one of the most important books of the year."

—**Sukhvinder S. Obhi, PhD, Director, Social Brain, Body and Action Lab, McMaster University**

"In this groundbreaking book, Howard Ross uses his keen insight and decades-long experience in the field of diversity and inclusion to explore how the human tendency to belong and include also leads to tribalism and exclusion. Calling the latter 'bonding against,' Ross uses research in behavioral and cognitive science to show how these 'us versus them' tendencies spring from our evolutionary heritage; in the modern world, they gravely threaten our civic and faith communities, our workplaces, our information ecosystem, and our politics. Unlike many books that diagnose the problems without providing solutions, Ross spends two chapters on how we can bridge our divides by focusing on mutual understanding and coexistence, both as individuals and, perhaps even more importantly, within institutions. From my perspective both as a scholar and consultant on emotional and social intelligence and effective decision-making, this book is a must for leaders who want to ensure that the institutions they lead avoid the disastrous consequences of bonding against."

—**Dr. Gleb Tsipursky, author of *The Truth-Seeker's Handbook*; President, Intentional Insights; cofounder of the Pro-Truth Pledge; Assistant Professor, The Ohio State University; and speaker**

"This is what the world needs now. Howard Ross articulates what many in the medley of humanity are feeling but struggle to process coherently—or, most importantly, act upon. I hope that the sound research and suggested action plans found in this book will inspire millions of butterfly wing flaps that generate a gentle wind bringing higher levels of harmony for generations to come."

—**Dennis W. Quaintance, cofounder and CEO, Quaintance-Weaver Restaurants and Hotels**

"Our contemporary conversations about discrimination often focus on individual bias but fail to show how those biases relate to our need for belonging. Howard Ross's accessible book makes this important connection. He examines current events, social science, and neuropsychology to explain this irony—how our 21st-century quest for community separates us from each other. But this isn't a dry academic survey. Ross offers insight gained from his rich experience, candor, awareness, and most importantly, realistic solutions for ourselves and our workplaces to address this paradox. This book should be read by organization leaders, professionals concerned about human relations, and anyone interested in building community consciously and carefully."

—Atiba R. Ellis, Professor of Law, West Virginia University

"Deep knowledge of the science behind unconscious bias and a rich tableau of experience working with the world's leading organizations leads to remarkable practical insight! That is the essence of this much-needed and timely new book by Howard Ross. A must-read for all of us as individuals who increasingly need to decode the complex implications and unintended consequences of our obsession with social media connectivity *and* for leaders and businesses seeking to build inclusive flourishing cultures that bind rather than divide us."

—Shubhro Sen, PhD, Director, School of Management and Entrepreneurship, Shiv Nadar University, and cofounder of Conscious Capitalism Institute

"The economic and political middle have been carved out of the United States. Now the cultural middle (the values and norms that hold us together as a society) is threatened. Howard Ross offers a compelling observation of how we associate with those most like us and how it's created a dangerous polarization. More importantly, he offers a different path forward."

—Brian A. Gallagher, President and CEO, United Way Worldwide

OUR SEARCH FOR BELONGING

OUR SEARCH FOR BELONGING

How Our Need to Connect Is Tearing Us Apart

HOWARD J. ROSS

with JonRobert Tartaglione

Berrett–Koehler Publishers, Inc.
a BK Currents book

Berrett-Koehler Publishers, Inc.
1333 Broadway, Suite 1000
Oakland, CA 94612-1921
Tel: (510) 817-2277
Fax: (510) 817-2278
www.bkconnection.com

ORDERING INFORMATION
Quantity sales. Special discounts are available on quantity purchases by corporations, associations, and others. For details, contact the "Special Sales Department" at the Berrett-Koehler address above.
Individual sales. Berrett-Koehler publications are available through most bookstores. They can also be ordered directly from Berrett-Koehler: Tel: (800) 929-2929; Fax: (802) 864-7626; www.bkconnection.com.
Orders for college textbook / course adoption use. Please contact Berrett-Koehler: Tel: (800) 929-2929; Fax: (802) 864-7626.

Distributed to the U.S. trade and internationally by Penguin Random House Publisher Services.

Berrett-Koehler and the BK logo are registered trademarks of Berrett-Koehler Publishers, Inc.

Printed in the United States of America

Berrett-Koehler books are printed on long-lasting acid-free paper. When it is available, we choose paper that has been manufactured by environmentally responsible processes. These may include using trees grown in sustainable forests, incorporating recycled paper, minimizing chlorine in bleaching, or recycling the energy produced at the paper mill.

Cataloging-in-Publication Data is available at the Library of Congress.
ISBN: 978-1-5230-9503-2

First Edition
25 24 23 22 21 20 19 18   10 9 8 7 6 5 4 3 2 1

Set in Granjon LT Std by Westchester Publishing Services.
Interior Design: R. Scott Rattray
Cover designer: Wes Youssi, M.80 Design

For Hannah, Mayah, Sloane, Penelope, Davis, and Audrey. May the world that you inhabit be a world of inclusion for all people, everywhere, all of the time.

For all of the healers, in so many forms, who are doing the good work of creating a world of belonging for all.

And for Jake. You touch, move, and inspire me every day with your courage and commitment.

Contents

Foreword

Over the many years that I have known Howard Ross, we have developed the kind of friendship that is rare in our divided country. Our friendship crosses differences of race, gender, religion, and age. We also have a history of working together and a shared commitment to social justice. And since I joined Cook Ross, the firm he founded in 1989, Howard and I are now close colleagues.

In this book, Howard describes how our need to connect with people who are like us is increasingly placing us at odds with people we view as "the other." This dynamic is threatening values that are fundamental to a democracy. Importantly, he proposes what we can and must do about this "us versus them" dynamic that is at the root of our deeply divided nation and world.

Drawing on Robert Putnam's work on bonding and bridging, Howard helps us understand that there is healthy bonding, like the bonding involved in raising a healthy family. But there is also what he calls "bonding against," that is, unhealthy bonding that can lead to exclusion, and ultimately to the kind of hatred and violence that has been openly expressed many times by white supremacists.

In this book, we learn that healthy bridging occurs when we are aware that our point of view is just that—a point of view. And we are willing to listen to and accept another point of view. Howard admits that even he sometimes finds it difficult to do what he is urging all of us to do. I have always found it difficult to engage in this kind of bridging when the other point of view challenges my rights and even my humanity as an African American and a woman. This challenge is even greater when certain individuals and groups are emboldened to openly express racism, sexism, heterosexism, anti-Semitism, anti-Islamism, ablism, and the range of attitudes and behaviors that are grounded in bigotry and hatred. In the current political climate in the United States, many people are struggling to engage in bridging in their workplaces and even in their families because of starkly different political views.

How, then, are we to engage in healthy bonding and healthy bridging? In this book on belonging, Howard's response to this critical question is similar to the approach he takes in his book *Everyday Bias*. He draws on the neurocognitive science that explains how bonding, like bias, is a natural process that all human beings engage in. He then explains how bonding, like our biases, can take unhealthy, destructive, and dangerous forms. And to avoid the negative consequences that can result from our biases *and* our bonding, we must be conscious of them. Of course, self-awareness is not enough. For when we do not mitigate against negative biases and unhealthy bonding, they feed bigotry and systemic oppression.

As difficult as it is to combat unhealthy bonding, we must do so if we are to ever experience in our personal lives, our work places, our communities, our nation, and our world the kind of peace and justice that we all deserve.

Johnnetta Betsch Cole, PhD,
President Emerita,
Spelman and Bennett Colleges

Preface

You are only free when you realize you belong no place—You belong every place—no place at all. The price is high. The reward is great.

—MAYA ANGELOU

We are living in a world of seemingly increasing separation. After what was arguably one of the most contentious elections in American history, the United States stands torn between two polarized views of the world that are so rooted in fundamental differences that some have compared it to the Sunni/Shia divide in Islam.[1] People are no longer merely disagreeing; instead they are disavowing each other's right to an opinion. The level of outrage seems to escalate and become a way of being, almost an addiction. The Brexit vote in the United Kingdom and the 2017 presidential election in France brought up the same kind of antipathy, and throughout the Western world this same mind-set creates an unceasing flow of polemic and a gap that widens into greater and greater divergence all the time. The rising visibility of white nationalism and white supremacy coincides with the rise of the Black Lives Matter movement. The increased visibility of and support for lesbian, gay, bisexual, and transgender people coincides with the attempt to make laws to exclude them from public bathrooms, the military, and other aspects of day-to-day life. Increases in participation by women in business and other aspects of life coincide with an increased awareness of deeply rooted patterns of sexism, misogyny, and sexual harassment.

As Sir Isaac Newton postulated in his third law of motion, "For every action, there is an equal and opposite reaction."

Our tribal nature seems to be emerging with more force all the time, and at an enormous cost to our sense of societal harmony, civility, and cooperation. I have been on this journey myself. As a social justice advocate for all of my adult life, and a diversity and inclusion specialist for more than thirty years, I have prided myself on working to listen to and understand different points of view. And yet, over the past couple of years, I have found myself being pulled much more deeply into the "us versus them" dynamic. As a result, I have been on a quest to understand why it is that people see the world so differently than I do. In the months following the November 2016 election I interviewed dozens of people who voted for Donald Trump and spoke with dozens of Democrats who supported either Hillary Clinton or Bernie Sanders. The interviews have been with some intellectuals, but far more everyday people: drivers in cars and cabs; people sitting next to me on airplanes, or standing next to me in lines; neighbors or people I have randomly come across through social media. The conversations have not constituted formal research, but they have revealed the vast diversity of people on both sides, and how the tenor of our culture drives that diversity toward the extremes.

That inquiry has led me to the exploration that I share with you in these pages. The fundamental question that I have asked myself, and that has guided the research I will be attempting to explore, is: *Why is it that we are drawn so strongly to identify with groups, how does that impact us, and what can we do about it?*

The purpose of this book is to explore the seemingly paradoxical manner in which our compulsion to connect with other human beings often creates greater polarity, leaving us deeply connected with some, yet deeply divided as a society. I will try to establish some of the ways this separation is occurring in our lives today. I will be focusing mostly on the United States, because that is the country where I live and which I know best, and because the confines of these pages make it challenging to go more broadly and deeply; however, the paradigms of behavior that I will be exploring are universal. To that purpose, I will begin by referencing some of the circumstances we find ourselves in at the time of my writing. We will look at how these patterns are occurring and how they are impacting behavior.

We will also look at some examples drawn from an immense amount of research that points to a seemingly undeniable fact: human beings are inherently social and tribal creatures. It is in our DNA to want to bond deeply with some people and not others. We will be exploring the question: *What is this thing we call belonging, and why is it so important to us?* We will look at the neurocognitive science behind our primary need to belong, to bond with others like ourselves, and how it motivates human behavior, and investigate how it is expressed in our daily lives.

The challenge, of course, is that if we only bond we are going to keep separating. We also have to work more on the ability to bridge across those differences if this great experiment of democracy is going to work. We also need to clarify the difference between how we feel about issues and how we identify and define ourselves by a particular point of view or group, and how that difference impacts our ability to think for ourselves and make wise decisions about issues and people.

I will also be exploring how politics, race, religion, and the media can foster healthy or unhealthy forms of bonding. Due to limitations of space, I have chosen these four domains with a full awareness that I might just as well have addressed gender, sexual orientation, generational differences, socioeconomic status, or other dimensions of diversity. This is not in any way to minimize how these dynamics show up, and I will attempt, where appropriate, to address the intersectionality of many of these distinctions as part of the inquiry into the four I will be focusing on.

Finally, we will explore ways to bridge the divide so that we can create greater harmony and cooperation in our personal, organizational, and civic lives. I will end with a discussion about the workplace environment because we live in a world in which, for many people, the workplace is the most diverse part of their lives. As we will see, our schools are more segregated now than they have been in generations. Our communities have increasingly become political enclaves. Our places of worship, social organizations, and exposure to media and social media all tend, more than not, to put us with people like ourselves. The workplace is the one place where most people have little choice about whom they sit next to and engage with on a daily basis. In that sense, the external environment creates particular challenges in today's workplaces, but it also may offer the best possibility of a place where people can come to terms with some of these issues and develop ways to bridge. I will be offering suggestions as to how to do that effectively.

I am acutely aware that I have my own limitations in this conversation. As a lifelong political progressive, I will always have a tendency to see the world from that point of view, even as I try to understand others' points of view. As a descendant of Holocaust victims and survivors, I started working on civil rights as a teenager, and spent time organizing for La Raza during the grape boycott of the late 1960s. I have led diversity trainings for hundreds of thousands of people, served as the first white male professor of diversity at a historically black women's college, and been the only heterosexual man on the diversity advisory board of the Human Rights Campaign. I've written two previous books on diversity and unconscious bias.[2] My whole life has been in the struggle for equal rights for all. Yet as a sixty-seven-year-old straight white male, I have lived with privilege my whole life, and despite actively working on understanding and mitigating that privilege for more than fifty years, I know better than to think that it no longer still impacts my worldview and my behavior. While my inquiry into these issues cannot help but be shaped by this, I have also worked to actively understand its impact on the way I and others who represent dominant groups see the world. The purpose of my writing here is not to provide a definitive answer to these questions, but rather to provoke inquiry.

I fully expect that people from both sides of the political spectrum will take issue with some of what I have written. And yet I also believe that there are many people who care about healing the divisions within our world—whether at a personal level, in the workplace, or in the community—and who will be open to my invitation. Please use this text as a catalyst for your own exploration into belief, emotion, and behavior. My deepest wish is that even if you completely disagree with me, you will be left looking for ways that you can personally work in your family, your community, your workplace, or beyond to bridge the differences that divide us. Our current security and the world we are leaving for our children, our grandchildren, and beyond require as much from us.

Let's get started.

Introduction

A Tale of Two Countries

It was the best of times, it was the worst of times, it was the age of wisdom, it was the age of foolishness, it was the epoch of belief, it was the epoch of incredulity, it was the season of Light, it was the season of Darkness, it was the spring of hope, it was the winter of despair, we had everything before us, we had nothing before us, we were all going direct to Heaven, we were all going direct the other way.

—CHARLES DICKENS

We are living in a society today that can feel at times like it is coming apart at the seams. For some this is mostly what they see on the news or on their social media platforms, because they live in environments that seem largely homogeneous. For others it is the day-to-day experience of living in communities that are torn between "them" and "us," or in workplaces in which there is a constant, underlying nervousness about what we can and can't talk about. Even within families, different political and social perspectives create tensions and separation.

The purpose of this book is to seek to understand these tensions and offer the hope that there are ways to address our differences that can bring healing. It is not impossible. In workplaces all around the country, people are beginning to engage in courageous conversations about difference, because the workplace may be our greatest hope for reestablishing connection between our different "tribes." Target sponsors a workshop to encourage dialogue between white women and women of color to generate greater understanding and mutual support, and pulls employees of all backgrounds together to talk about how the threatened ban on the issuance of visas to Muslims may impact their Muslim employees. General Mills conducts regular critical conversations in which employees come together to talk about their concerns and find common ground. Governmental agencies, the military, the intelligence community, and hundreds of corporations, schools, and other institutions engage in trainings to better understand how bias impacts their ability to work together. Starbucks attempts to create an opportunity for customers and baristas to talk about race. Some of these efforts have been more effective than others, for sure, but more and more organizations understand that the stresses that exist outside our work environment come to work with us every day and impact how we relate to our fellow workers.

As we will discover, it is natural for us to bond with people we identify with. Whether those groups are formed by family connection, race, gender, or other forms of mutual identity, we have a particular connection to people who are like us, in whatever way we define that. Most people, however, find that it is limiting to the fullness of our lives if we only relate to people with whom we bond. It is our ability to bridge with others that gives us new ideas, new insights, and a deeper, richer perspective on life. It is also very difficult to get the best out of people when they cannot be fully themselves. Organizations that want to thrive will be frustrated if they do not create a sense of belonging.

And most important for our society, the experiment that is democracy cannot work without bridging across differences.

Yet in our country today, those bridges are either in disrepair or burning.

For years, our political system has largely operated as a bell curve. While there were people on the extremes of both liberalism and conservatism, most politicians gravitated toward the middle, with many falling on one side or another depending upon the issues that were being discussed. During the days of the civil rights movement, northern liberal Republicans worked together with many Democrats; however, some southern Democrats teamed up with other Republicans to oppose landmark legislation. Anti–Vietnam War Democrats teamed up with some liberal Republicans to oppose the war, while some conservative Democrats and other Republicans supported it. The notion of politicians crossing party lines to support legislative action of one kind or another was more the norm than the exception. This is not to say there weren't plenty of other challenges: LGBTQ people were mostly resigned to living in hiding, the rights of people of color were barely being explored, and the rights of women were even more challenged than they are today.[1] Yet the divisions were not as stark as they are now.[2]

Now, however, we have devolved into what we might call a dumb-bell curve, in which everything is on the extremes and nothing is in the middle. The most conservative Democrats generally vote more on the liberal side than the most liberal Republicans, and vice versa. And the gap between the two is increasing, even in terms of where we live. We can see this clearly through analyzing what has been called the Whole Foods/Cracker Barrel divide.[3] Whole Foods Market and Cracker Barrel Old Country Store illustrate this polarization as much as any other example. Both companies exist throughout the United States and both emphasize connections to their local communities, yet when you look at the voting patterns of people who live around their franchises, you can see American political segregation in stark relief.

Whole Foods stores generally reside in more liberal/Democratic communities. Cracker Barrel restaurants, on the other hand, generally are in more conservative/Republican enclaves. In the 1992 presidential election, Bill Clinton won roughly 61 percent of counties with a Whole Foods Market in them and only 40 percent of those with a Cracker Barrel restaurant, a 21 percent gap. However, as you can see in Table I.1, that divide has increased every election since then. In 2012, Barack Obama won in 77 percent of the Whole Foods counties and only 29 percent of the Cracker Barrel counties, a 48 percent gap![4]

Year	Presidential Winner	Whole Foods Counties	Cracker Barrel Counties	Culture Gap
1992	Bill Clinton (D)	61%	40%	21%
1996	Bill Clinton (D)	66%	41%	25%
2000	George W. Bush (R)	43%	75%	32%
2004	George W. Bush (R)	39%	79%	40%
2008	Barack Obama (D)	80%	35%	45%
2012	Barack Obama (D)	77%	29%	48%

Table I.1 The Whole Foods/Cracker Barrel Divide

This is not to suggest that there are not counties that continue to have more political diversity, but the trend here is striking. A look at the electoral map bears this out, as does additional research.[5] The result has been that these extreme, homogeneous sides have cannibalized reasonable political discourse and shifted our sense of normalcy from an expectation that we will have to work together to a win-lose dynamic in which each side strives to win at all costs.

At an even deeper level, when we look at the 2016 presidential election totals through another lens, an even more troubling pattern arises. This polarization of voting doesn't only occur in political affiliation; it is a function of demographic identity.[6] People who voted for Trump overwhelmingly represent what we might call the dominant identity groups: 58 percent of whites, 53 percent of men, and 58 percent of Christians. Clinton voters represent the nondominant groups: 88 percent of blacks, 54 percent of women, 65 percent of Latinos, 65 percent of Asians, 71 percent of Jews, and 78 percent of LGBTQ voters. It was more than just a question of issues; it was a question of identity. And this is a critical difference. When we evaluate people based on issues, it is impersonal. When we evaluate people based on identity, we objectify them. It is no longer "I disagree with you on this point"; it becomes "I don't like who you are!" When the people we disagree with politically look different from us and have different cultural backgrounds, it is easier to demonize them as the "other." It also makes it easier for the power dynamics in society, between those in dominant cultural groups (e.g., whites, men, heterosexuals, Christians, people with higher incomes) to have their identity power manifest in the political process and therefore in public policy.

We are living in a time of increasing political segregation that threatens to tear us apart as a unified society. The result is that we are becoming increasingly tribal, and the narratives that we get exposed to on a daily basis have increasingly become echo chambers in which we hear our beliefs reinforced and those of others demonized.

This mind-set does not only impact our political lives. Communities in the United States are becoming more segregated than they have been in years. Racial segregation in public schools is at a rate comparable to the 1960s, and increasing movement to private and charter schools seems destined to make it more pronounced.[7] According to the Government Accountability Office, the number of high-poverty schools serving primarily black and brown students has more than doubled since 2000, and the proportion of schools segregated by race and class (in which 75 percent of children receive free or reduced-fee lunches and more than 75 percent are black or Hispanic) climbed from 9 percent to 16 percent during that period.[8]

The racial divide in the United States, though never resolved, has emerged more publicly again in response to the killing of numerous black men and women by police officers. African Americans continue to struggle with higher unemployment, poorer schools, lower-quality health care, and, on average, only one-seventh the accumulated wealth of the average white family. This has birthed the Black Lives Matter movement. Yet racial extremists have become more publicly emboldened, demonstrated by a rise in white nationalist and white supremacist organizations and activity. As I write this, the controversy about whether athletes should be allowed to protest is bringing the nation to its knees, as is the appropriateness of Civil War memorials in public places, and questions abound as to whether the 2017 hurricane damage in Puerto Rico is being treated differently because most of the U.S. citizens there are not white. Racial gaps in income and wealth continue to remain significant, and are even increasing as the tension around other societal issues continues to foment.

Fear leads to stronger anti-immigrant feelings throughout the West. Incidents of terrorism by radical Muslims lead to rampant Islamophobia and calls to keep "them" out. Anti-Muslim hate crimes are on the rise, as are those that are anti-Semitic.[9] Fear of difference regarding transgender people leads to transphobic reactions and laws to keep people from using the bathroom of their choice.[10] Attempts are being made to roll back some of the advancement of equal rights for LGBTQ Americans, under the guise of religious rights. Voter suppression laws are passed that will undoubtedly impact people of color and low-income people, at the same time as legal scholars assert there is, in fact, no real evidence of voter fraud for these efforts to "fix."[11] At almost every turn, we see an explosion of "us versus them."

The tension extends to our most fundamental relationships. Thousands of families canceled their usual Thanksgiving dinners after the 2016 elections because of the fear of confronting political divide within their own families, in effect feeling more bonded with their political tribe than with their families.[12] Businesses find it more and more difficult to avoid the tension that these dualities regularly create in the workplace. Studies show that this workplace tension causes not only generalized stress but an increased reticence to talk about "controversial issues," even when they impact the work.[13] Schools have seen a surge in bullying, some children returning home with the message from teachers and peers that their "families will be deported."[14]

At the heart of this division is fear: fear of the other, fear of exposing ourselves, fear of not having control over our own lives, fear for the safety and survival of our friends, our loved ones, and ourselves.

We do not have to accept this division as inevitable. In this book I will be attempting to help explain why we are so pulled to polarized positions, to explain why our demonization of each other is occurring, and to offer hope. There are numerous examples of people and organizations who are attempting to reach across the divide—to create bridges to belonging that can help us remember that it is possible to disagree without being disagreeable, and to remember that we have a shared destiny, whether we like it or not. These efforts are occurring in communities across the country and also in our workplaces. In fact, I will make the case that the workplace is one of the best vehicles we have for building healing and understanding by the very fact that it is one of the few places where people who are different from each other have to learn to work together. I will also offer suggestions as to how we can create that sense of belonging in our families, organizations, communities, and society.

Why Is the Divide So Painful?

Why do these tensions hit us so hard? Because at the same time as we are pulled apart by these political and social dynamics, we are learning at a deeper level that human beings have a strong need to belong, to feel connected to those around them. We have seen over the course of history how this need to belong can lead people to come together, especially during times of crisis, and achieve remarkable things, as in the mobilization of the United States as it entered World War II. We have also seen how that same need to belong has allowed people to engage in some of the worst events in human history: the Holocaust, slavery, the Rwandan civil war, et cetera. We have demonstrated a blind, and often terrifying, willingness to go along with the crowd, even when the crowd is doing evil. In today's world, the need to connect with those that we relate to, and at the same time stay away from *the other* is creating a degree of tribalism that we haven't experienced in centuries.

The 2016 presidential election, and politics in general, is just one way this divide is manifesting itself throughout our culture. The bigger issue, and the bigger question that underlies this book, is: *How does the inherent need to belong impact us as human beings?* And, perhaps even more important: *Why is this happening, and what we can do about it?*

I will be exploring why it is natural for human beings to feel more comfortable with people in groups to which we belong. It creates a kind of bond that has us feeling safer and knowing what to expect, what is considered normal, and how to relate. However, if we are to transcend the division that we now experience and move toward a more peaceful and equitable societal order, we will also have to learn better how to bridge across those bonded groups. Perhaps what is now seen as "us versus them" can, at least much of the time, be turned into collaborations in which we draw from the best of both.

I don't think that it is being hyperbolic to say that we are in a time of crisis. My hope is that this book will create a greater understanding of why that crisis is occurring, and chart a path that can help us build greater connection in our families, communities, and organizations. We'll start by getting a better understanding of what belonging is and why we need it.

It is natural for us to want to look for solutions, and we will get there. Yet my thirty-five years of professional experience in creating sustainable change has taught me that over the long term, transformational change occurs *only* when we understand why we do the things that we do. In this case that means exploring why it is that human beings are so driven to live in and be influenced by the groups that they identify with.

It is no accident that people demonstrate a universal desire to fit into groups. The need for belonging is an inherent survival mechanism. We will start by exploring why that is, how it impacts us, and how both the human brain and the mind are geared toward belonging, even at times when it separates us from others.

Chapter 1

Wired for Belonging

The Innate Desire to Belong

The essential dilemma of my life is between my deep desire to belong and my suspicion of belonging.

—JHUMPA LAHIRI

A Tale of Three Colleagues

The annual holiday party at Munchester Industries is a raucous event. The company has about seven hundred employees, and for the holiday gala they all gather with their families in tow. The party has a huge buffet, an open bar, people dancing to the sounds of a DJ's music, and a clown making balloon animals for the children. People are gathered in small clusters, either at tables or standing around chatting. On the surface this looks like any number of company parties we have all seen before. However, this year the party has a different tone, coming just six weeks after the 2016 presidential election. The room is abuzz with conversations about politics, mostly people celebrating or commiserating with their friends. Waiting for drinks, three employees stand together in awkward silence, their countenance seemingly different from most of the people around them, suggesting politeness but not much more. A tall, blond-haired white woman, with two children at her side, shifts from foot to foot, her eyes looking around the room, almost as if she wants to escape. A shorter, darker-skinned woman stands quietly by the side. The third person, a tall white man, appears friendly, even gregarious, alternating between trying to make conversation with the two women and making side comments to a shorter, brown-skinned man who stands behind him. Who are these people? What's going on?

To answer these questions, let's rewind the clock to that morning. . . .

CASE STUDY

Joan Smith woke up at 7:00 AM, as she usually did on a workday. After her morning rituals, she proceeded to one of her regular patterns: looking at her smartphone. Joan checked for any emails and then went directly to her news feed, where she saw the morning headlines from some of her usual sources: *Breitbart*, the *Daily Caller*, and the *Drudge Report*. Her newsfeed was still humming with a sense of victory and celebration over the surprising results of the election. She checked her Facebook page and her Twitter account, where she found articles posted by several of her friends, including an interesting one on religious suppression, posted by one of the women in her church's book study group. Almost all the posts agreed with her politically. She then wandered down to her basement to put in some time on the treadmill, while watching the morning news on *Fox and Friends*.

Joan has been working at Munchester Industries for the past two years in a clerical position. She was able to get the job after her marriage ended following several years of stress that were triggered by her husband's layoff from his job of sixteen years at the local processing plant. The divorce has been hard on her because of her strong religious values and belief in keeping families together, but her husband's work challenges resulted in changes in his behavior that made staying together untenable. He is still looking for full-time employment. Though he does make some money as an Uber driver, he has very little to contribute to Joan and their twelve-year-old son and nine-year-old daughter. Joan is fortunate that she has benefitted from both material and emotional support from her church community, which has helped her get through these hard times.

At the encouragement of her family, Joan has started dating again. She went out with a man she met at a friend's dinner party, however, the conversation was somewhat limited because Joan quickly realized that he was a Democrat and she didn't want to get into any political arguments. As it is, she doesn't talk about her politics at work; most of the people who work at Munchester tend toward the liberal side.

After finishing her exercise, Joan showered and got ready for work. Today is the company party, and the office would be closed in the late afternoon for the festivities, which would go into the evening. Just last night she was getting her mother's advice, because she was feeling nervous about the party, not wanting to find herself in a position of having to defend her political stance. She planned on having her friend drop the kids off at the party. Given all of the alcohol that they have at these events, she has mixed feelings about them being there, but she received a lot of pressure from her coworkers that this was a must-attend event, family included.

CASE STUDY

Barry Jones sat at the breakfast table with his husband, Sam, and their eighteen-year-old daughter, Jennifer. Jennifer is Sam's birth daughter from his previous marriage, and she has recently come to live with them. Barry and Sam have been together for almost sixteen years, and last night they celebrated their third wedding anniversary with Jennifer and a small group of family and friends. The event was very pleasant, although family gatherings have been considerably more muted since the election. Most of Barry's family are Republicans, and most of Sam's are Democrats. In addition, Sam's father is a Mexican immigrant, having come to the United States more than twenty years ago; he became a naturalized citizen in 2006. The tension somewhat limited conversations to superficialities and pleasantries, which was just fine for Barry and Sam—they didn't want a repeat of the incident that occurred at Thanksgiving, when Sam's sister and Barry's father got into a political debate that was so heated it threatened to ruin the holiday dinner.

The family was watching the morning news on MSNBC as they ate, but Barry was, as usual, multitasking between breakfast conversation, watching the news, and looking at his news feed, mostly articles from *BuzzFeed*, the *Huffington Post*, and the *Daily Kos*. The news seems increasingly bothersome to Barry, who voted for Hillary Clinton, though he was a Bernie Sanders supporter in the 2016 primaries. He had no problem making the switch because he was so offended by Donald Trump's comments about Mexicans, Muslims, immigrants, and women, not to mention the Republican platform positions on LGBTQ rights. Being Jewish and having had family members who were lost in the Holocaust, Barry is highly sensitive about examples of what he perceives to be bigotry. He also didn't want their daughter to have a president who would speak and act the way he perceives that Trump did about women. As a result, watching the news over the last month or so has felt like a living nightmare to Barry, and he has been spending a lot of time with a community organizing group of late, trying to figure out how to get more Democrats elected to Congress.

At 7:45 AM, Barry and Jennifer said goodbye to Sam and got in the car. Barry planned to drop Jennifer off at school and then drive about twenty minutes to his job at Munchester Industries, where he is the director of human resources. He plans to see Sam and Jennifer this evening at the company holiday party, although for many of his fellow employees, the mood lately has been more funereal than celebratory.

CASE STUDY

In another part of town, Fatima Mohammed, having completed her morning prayers, was also getting ready for work, with the morning news from the BBC playing on her television set in the living room. Her eighteen-year-old son, Malik, is about to head off to school. It has been more difficult lately to get him out the door, as he has experienced some taunting by his fellow students, one of whom "jokingly" asked him whether his family was going to get deported now that Trump was elected. In addition, because of the recent killings of young black men by police officers, Fatima is always concerned about Malik's safety when he is out driving. Fatima was born in the United Kingdom to parents who had immigrated years before from Afghanistan. She came to the United States on a student visa in 1992 and met her husband, Daanesh, in school. Daanesh was from a family of Somali immigrants who had come to this country when he was just a boy. They were married in 1996 and she officially became a U.S. citizen the following year.

Daanesh graduated from the University of Maryland in 1996 and then went to medical school at the University of Michigan. He has been practicing medicine for more than ten years, but recently has encountered some difficulties due to interactions with several patients who questioned whether they wanted to be treated by a Muslim, especially one with very dark skin.

Fatima watches the news every day with apprehension, because her brother Rashed, who followed her to the United States as a student eight years after she came, decided to enlist in the U.S. Army after he graduated from college, and is now stationed in Afghanistan. Rashed was excited about serving his country and was well received by army recruiters, who thought that somebody with his maturity and knowledge of language and culture would be a valuable asset. He has been trained in mediation and conflict resolution, which often puts him in sensitive situations. He plans on retiring from the military after he completes twenty-five years, and then going to graduate school. Fatima not only worries about Rashed's safety but also is frightened by the anti-Muslim political rhetoric that she is constantly hearing on the news.

Fatima has worn an abaya and hijab for most of her life, in keeping with her family's religious traditions; however, at her mother's request, of late she has decided to go with more typical Western dress when she goes to her job as an engineer at Munchester Industries. On the weekends, and when she goes to her mosque—which she has been attending more frequently lately because she feels comforted being with "her people"—she still wears her traditional dress, but she became tired of being looked at suspiciously and has also read too many articles about Muslim women being harassed, and so she has decided it is safer and easier to "when in Rome, do as the Romans do."

As they stand in line at the party, the inner world of each of these three individuals is present in the way they are relating. There is not all that much in the buffet for Fatima, because she follows halal practices and avoids alcohol. Not wanting to bring attention to herself, she eats what she can and drinks a bottle of water. Joan has her children with her, and is somewhat uncomfortable with what feels to her like the public display of affection that Barry is showing toward Sam in front of them. She had heard rumors that Barry was gay from others in the company, but feels somewhat like he is rubbing it in her face, and she doesn't like her children being exposed to it. Barry, on the other hand, is aware that he and Sam may make people uncomfortable at times, but frankly he thinks that's their problem. After all, company policy is very clear, and Munchester even recently received a high score on the Human Rights Campaign Corporate Equality Index.[1] Fatima knows Joan fairly well, given Joan's clerical position in the engineering department; however, she has recently noticed a chill in their relationship, especially during the presidential campaign. While Fatima seems nice enough, the "Muslim thing" still makes Joan feel uncomfortable. Both of them met Barry when they came to work at the organization, and they also attended a human resources training he gave a couple of months ago, talking about new employee practices that have been instituted.

As is often the case these days, the conversation quickly turns to the daily news. Barry is quite outspoken in his views, but both Joan and Fatima find themselves increasingly uncomfortable even being in the conversation. Joan has learned to not discuss her political views at work, because employees of the company are, more often than not, judgmental about conservative views like hers, and she is not interested in getting into debates or being judged by her colleagues. Fatima, on the other hand, finds that any discussion of politics leaves her feeling very vulnerable. She definitely does not feel comfortable talking about her faith in public. The social interaction on the surface is superficial. The silence underneath the conversation is deafening.

The characters depicted above are not real, although they could be. They are a composite of traits, all drawn from people with whom I have met. Most of us can relate to the situation they find themselves in at the party. Questions abound in their minds: *What's normal anymore? What is it safe to say? How much can we disagree without being disagreeable? Will my job be in jeopardy if people find out what I believe in?* And often, *How quickly can I get back to my people so that I can feel comfortable just being myself?*

Most of us like the feeling of belonging to groups around us. Whether it is being accepted by our friends and neighbors or being part of the in-group at work or school, there is something safer and more secure about being accepted and included. The need to belong is essential to human survival. In his landmark 1943 paper, "A Theory of Human Motivation," Abraham Maslow introduced his now ubiquitous "hierarchy of needs."[2] In it, Maslow postulated that "human needs arrange themselves in hierarchies of prepotency. That is to say, the appearance of one need usually rests on the prior satisfaction of another, more pre-potent need. Man is a perpetually wanting animal."[3]

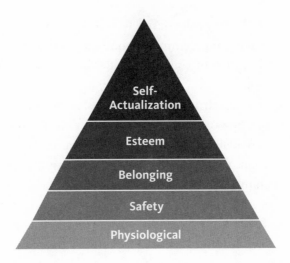

Figure 1.1 Maslow's Hierarchy of Needs

Anybody who has taken a basic Introduction to Psychology course is probably familiar with Maslow's model, often depicted as a pyramid (Figure 1.1).

According to Maslow, our physiological needs are the first that must be satisfied, followed by our needs for safety, belonging, self-esteem, and finally self-actualization. While Maslow's model has been challenged for representing a predominantly individualistic cultural model, it has remained a bedrock of the study of human development for more than seventy years.[4]

Within American culture, this is consistent with our tendency to place a high value on individualism.[5] In 1831, Alexis de Tocqueville, in his historic study of American culture, *Democracy in America*, identified individualism as a fundamental distinguishing characteristic of democracies, and the capitalist American democratic model in particular. Tocqueville recognized the essential role that individualism plays in separating people from society: "Individualism is a considered and peaceful sentiment that disposes each citizen to isolate himself from the mass of his fellows and to withdraw to the side with his family and his friends; so that, after thus creating a small society for his own use, he willingly abandons the large society to itself."[6]

According to Maslow, the desire to fulfill our personal physiological and safety needs are preeminent, and breed a certain sense of individualism that has each of us seek to get what we need to be fulfilled in those dimensions.

More recent research indicates that Maslow may have missed the mark. There may be no greater human need than the need to belong. Human beings no doubt have remarkable survival skills, and yet we rely on our social groups to survive. Throughout human history, we evolved to live in cooperative societies that have grown larger and more diverse all the time. For most of our history, we have depended on those groups to help us satisfy both our basic physiological needs and our social and psychological ones. Just like our need for food or water, our need for acceptance emerged as a mechanism for survival. For most of our history, it was rare that a solitary individual could survive living in jungles, in forests, or on vast plains. We needed others in order to get our physiological needs met.

Every human being starts life in total dependency. A newborn baby is incapable of meeting its own physiological needs or needs for safety and will survive days, at most, if it "belongs" to nobody. The first imprint that we have on our core psyche is "I exist because you exist."

This inherent need to belong has created, particularly in more individualistically oriented Western countries, an inherent tension between an ethos of individualism and the need to connect, belong, and rely on others to survive. Many people, even psychologists, have underestimated the impact of social exclusion on the individual experience, even as it contributes to all manner of negative societal behavior, including sociopathic behaviors such as murder.

How does this group connection manifest in our lives?

Bonding and Bridging

In his landmark study of social capital, *Bowling Alone,* Harvard sociologist Robert Putnam identified two fundamental ways that we form social connections and identify our sense of belonging that are distinct

PUTNAM: FORMS OF SOCIAL CAPITAL

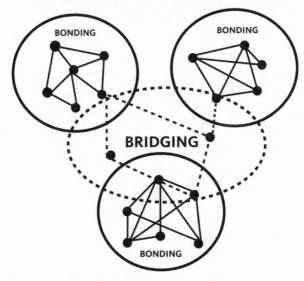

Figure 1.2 Bridging and Bonding

when we are connecting with in-groups or out-groups; he refers to them as *bonding* and *bridging* (Figure 1.2).[7]

Bonding is generally present in the fundamental connection between members of in-groups, especially homogeneous ones. Because members of a group share cultural norms and values, and because we are naturally more empathetic toward people in our own groups, bonding can be valuable as a sort of social safety net that can protect us from outside groups. In many societies, the maintenance of relationships of family and tribal identification can even help provide basic survival needs, especially when the larger social structure is in breakdown. There are some circumstances in which the decline in trust in the existing leadership structure or political system can encourage people to rely more on their in-groups than at other times.[8] This can be especially true when a group is marginalized or oppressed by another group. The networks of support within African American churches in the United States, for example, have provided a necessary social safety net against racism and segregation for generations, as did the NAACP, the National Organization for Women

(NOW), and charitable organizations that formed to help support Jewish, Mormon, and Catholic communities. We bond with those we feel we share the greatest and most important connections to, and with whom we have a common perceived fate.

Bridging, on the other hand, generally occurs when people form connections in socially heterogeneous groups. Bridging can be critical to mutually beneficial relationships between groups, as between different countries in a global sense, between a group and its allies in an identity sense (e.g., LGBTQ and heterosexual people; men and women; whites and people of color), or between different individuals in a personal sense. Bridging facilitates the sharing and interchange of ideas, information, and innovation and can be an important factor in building agreement and consensus among groups representing diverse interests.

Bridging can broaden and extend social capital by increasing what has been called the "radius of trust" that people experience.[9] This is a particularly important part of a healthy, diverse, and inclusive environment, as well as in an increasingly global world order. Bridging usually occurs as a result of some perceived shared interest or goal that creates something larger or more important than the differences that exist between the bridging parties, and most often includes some expectation of general reciprocity—"If I'm there for you, I expect that you'll be there for me."

Bridging often occurs in coalitions that form situationally in order to deal with a common challenge. For example, when apartheid was still in place in South Africa, Mangosuthu Buthelezi's Inkatha Freedom Party (IFP) worked closely with Nelson Mandela's African National Congress (ANC) to fight the common enemy of the apartheid government. At that time their destiny was shared, they needed each other in order to win the fight, and they shared the values of democracy over oppression. However, shortly after apartheid fell, they returned to their bonded groups and were back in opposition to each other.

Bonding generally occurs because of a perception of understanding other people and of being understood, whereas bridging is generally formed out of mutual need and desire. Belonging is fundamentally based in bonding; however, bridging can be a way of creating belonging. The challenge, though, can be that one person or group's bonding can be another's bridging.

This often happens in relationships between people who are members of dominant and nondominant groups. As a general rule, people in nondominant groups are more likely to maintain an awareness of their group identity and to be seen by people as a member of their group. The perpetrators of the 9/11 attacks, the San Bernardino, California, shootings, the Fort Hood, Texas, shootings, the Boston Marathon bombing, and other terrorist acts are often referred to as "radical Islamist terrorists" (a term that often has racial overtones as well) in the parts of the Western world in which Muslims are a minority group. On the other hand, the white perpetrators of the Oklahoma City bombing, the Charleston church shootings, the attack at the Sikh temple in Wisconsin, or the attack at the synagogue in Kansas are almost never described as "radical terrorists," and the Christian ones are rarely, if ever, described by their religious affiliation. This often plays out in media coverage.

This dynamic is fluid rather than fixed. When members of different groups interact, this movement between bonding and bridging can sometimes be confusing and upsetting. White women, for example, often see themselves mostly as women, without a particularly strong focus on their racial identity. As members of a nondominant gender group, they feel connected to all women.

My colleague Rosalyn Taylor O'Neale, an African American woman, describes it this way:

> African American women, on the other hand, tend to relate from both of their nondominant group identities and are usually very aware of race as a distinguisher. The impact can often be a presumption of more connection on the part of white women in the relationship than is experienced by black women. White women, as a result, can occur as being presumptuously intimate in their connection with black women, who still may see them as "the other." While the white women think they are bonding, the black women can experience the same exchange as bridging. When people openly discuss these differences, it can ease some of the related social pain.

A similar example occurred after the Pulse nightclub in Orlando, Florida, was attacked by Omar Mateen, a Muslim, on June 12, 2016, and forty-nine of the mostly LGBTQ attendees were killed. In the aftermath, many conservatives who had taken anti-gay positions in the past found themselves in the uncomfortable position of deciding whom to align with or against: the gay community, about whom they had expressed homophobic judgment for years, or the "Muslim terrorist" who committed the murders.

These dynamics are occurring today across political parties. It seems profoundly irrational for families to be unable to sit at the same holiday table with their closest family members; however, each has bonded with his or her political brethren, and now they are all faced with bridging with people they have known their whole lives. At that moment the question seems to be "Where do I really belong?" and, even more important, "Where will I be safe?"

It is important to understand that bonding and bridging can be both positive and negative, both healthy and unhealthy. As a general rule, positive bonding and bridging are directed *for* something. We bridge with another group to get things done or to establish people's rights, as in the case of the ANC and IFP. Negative bonding and bridging are often *against* something, as in the coalitions of white supremacist groups that have bonded around their common efforts to suppress people of color, Jews, Muslims and others who are not white Christians.

In either case, we strive to connect because the pain of separation is a prime threat to our sense of survival.

Social Separation Syndrome and Addiction

Brandeis professor George N. Appell has described a sense of isolation as *social separation syndrome*.[10] Consider your own experience. Can you remember a time when you were not invited to a friend's birthday party or other social event? Or times when you felt like your friends were ganging up on you or teasing you? It's not hard to recall how insecure these circumstances can make us feel. We often begin to question ourselves and our worth because of the reactions of others. The same feelings can emerge when we find ourselves to be the "only": the only woman in a group of men, the only person of color in a group of whites, the only lesbian or gay person in a group of heterosexuals, and so on. There is an increased sense of conspicuousness and a vulnerability to this kind of isolation that almost anybody can relate to.

One of the places where social separation has been found to be particularly powerful is in its impact on addiction. For some time, addiction has been characterized as primarily a chemical dependency. To combat such addictive tendencies, counselors have used counteracting chemical agents (such as methadone for heroin addicts) to reestablish normalcy to our altered neurotransmitters, opioid receptors, and mesolimbic pathways.[11] While it would be foolish to ignore the role physical dependency plays in catalyzing addictive tendencies, it appears equally foolish to ignore the role that social connectedness can play in moderating the likelihood of engaging in such addictive practices to begin with.

How many people do you know who have tried to curb addictive behaviors such as overeating, laziness, too much TV, drug use, or drinking and found it much easier when doing it in partnership with somebody? How much easier is it to get out of bed to exercise when you know somebody is meeting you at the gym or waiting outside for you to go for a run? How much harder is it to eat that thing you shouldn't when everybody at the table with you has jointly committed to eating healthier?

Social environments impact addiction. Canadian psychologist Bruce Alexander and his colleagues Robert Coambs and Patricia Hadaway started by getting laboratory rats hooked on morphine.[12] For fifty-seven consecutive days, the rats would have access to only a morphine solution to consume in order to meet their need for water. Once they were addicted, a second option of unlaced tap water was introduced, giving the rats an opportunity to choose between the new, drug-free water or the water laced with morphine. Addiction models that rely on the theory of drug-induced addiction would have predicted that rats would continue to indulge in the morphine solution regardless of their social circumstance, but Alexander and his team questioned this traditional view.

In their studies, the researchers divided the rats between two distinct social environments: a small, barren cage where a rat would be housed by itself, or Rat Park (Figure 1.3), a large, open space where rats were housed among many others and had access to a variety of toys, tunnels,

Figure 1.3 Bruce Alexander's "Rat Park"

and opportunities for stimulation. They then observed the rats to see how those who had become addicted in the solitary confines of a small, cramped cage would react when placed in Rat Park.

The findings were stunning. While rats who remained in cages continued to opt for the morphine cocktail, the addicted rats who were transitioned to Rat Park overwhelmingly chose the plain water over the morphine solution. It appeared that addiction depended heavily on social variables. For rats confined to a small, cramped cage, a morphine kick might be a way to cope with the otherwise bleak nature of their lives. However, for rats afforded the luxury of Rat Park, such a coping mechanism proved unnecessary. These findings are not unprecedented. Drake Morgan, an addiction specialist at the University of Florida College of Medicine, and his colleagues conducted a similar study with macaque monkeys.[13]

The same can be true for human beings. Forced separation can be devastating to the human psyche. Researchers at seven medical schools collaborated to study the impact of solitary confinement on a group of recently released prisoners and found that they were two and a half times more likely to show post-traumatic stress disorder (PTSD) symptoms than prisoners who were not in solitary.[14] There was also an increased number of suicide attempts among the group. Dr. Aaron Fox, associate professor of medicine at Montefiore Medical Center and one of the lead authors of the study, said, "If exposure to solitary confinement causes PTSD, then it may be harmful and dangerous and something we should think twice about. If people with PTSD are placed in solitary confinement, that's also a problem, as it's exacerbating their mental health problems." Robert King, a prison reform activist who himself was wrongly incarcerated for thirty-two years, including twenty-nine years in solitary confinement, said, "I can tell you from experience: If you've done time in solitary confinement, you've been damaged. Even if you survive it, it has an impact on you."[15]

During the Vietnam War, a large number of soldiers became addicted to heroin. While many still struggled with addiction when they returned home, a remarkable percentage of them simply stopped using.[16] From a traditional viewpoint of addiction as a purely chemical dependence, this seems exceptionally peculiar, but when viewed through the lens of the rat and monkey studies, it makes perfect sense. These soldiers were regularly exposed to horrific atrocities, immense stress, and extended periods of anxiety while in Vietnam. They were thrown into an environment with people they didn't know and for whom the normative behavior included drug abuse. Their social environments were often nightmarish, so they sought refuge in the temporary fix afforded by drug use. When they returned home to social environments devoid of such carnage and despair and were back with people they had known and loved all of their lives, the need for such a coping mechanism dissipated. In fact, it wasn't just addiction that was impacted. Lt. Col. Angel Lugo, of the U.S. Air Force, shared this example with me:

> Early in my enlisted career, I was an Airman Leadership School instructor. As part of our program, we invited a few of our local "living history" icons (POWs, Tuskegee Airmen, etc.) to speak to the students from time to time. I soon became good friends with one retired officer who was a Vietnam POW for more than seven

years, including time at the notorious Hanoi Hilton during his ordeal. He talked about the tap code that prisoners used to communicate with each other. He highlighted the tap code methodology and greatly emphasized how the communication system soon became the lifeline for the prisoners. It established their sense of community; they taught each other different languages, mathematics, and other subjects. But the next words out of his mouth blew me away. He soon realized it wasn't the beatings and torture that drove some prisoners to their demise; it was their hopelessness and loss of faith and ultimate decision to unplug from the tap code system. They literally isolated themselves, crawled up in a corner, and died.

One of the greatest examples of the benefits of social support in addressing addiction are twelve-step programs, particularly Alcoholics Anonymous. AA was founded by Bill Wilson (or "Bill W." to those in the program) and Dr. Bob Smith in Akron, Ohio, in 1935. Wilson had joined the Oxford Group, a nondenominational movement that had been created to help members get and stay sober. Wilson had felt a "kinship of common suffering" that drew him to the group, and he put himself into an alcohol rehabilitation program just days after attending his first meeting, never to drink again. After focusing more on the "science" of sobriety, rather than solely on religion, he was able to achieve his first success at helping another to achieve sobriety with Smith, another member of the Oxford Group. By 1937, Wilson had separated from the Oxford Group and formed what is now AA.

Over the years, AA has become the best-known sobriety network in the world. Including the original program and other spin-offs for drug abuse, overeating, and other issues, millions of people every year use the program, largely because of the sense of belonging that it gives them. Consider these testimonials from participants I interviewed in the program:

Lydia: Before coming into the program, I felt lonely in general. I always had a group of friends with common interests, but I didn't know what a genuine connection was. I come from a single-parent family and was raised where everybody else seemed to have Mom, Dad, and the white picket fence, so I felt like an outsider. I drank to numb the feelings of loneliness. When I came into my first meeting, I found so many different kinds of people who didn't fit in. People from sixteen to their eighties, representing all races, creeds, and economic walks of life. The ease of knowing that they know exactly where I'm coming from is such an important part of it. Not being judged makes it easier to open up to things that are challenging for me. I know I have people who will be there anytime, day or night, for anything I'm going through.

Emily: In every way, shape, and form the alcoholism tried to make me alone. Before, I always had a support group, my mom and dad and friends. It was never a lack of support; it was a lack of me using it. The way my mind played me was by convincing me that I was so different that nobody would support me. But when I was drunk, I wasn't miserable anymore. Alcohol gave me a break from me. People were trying to get me to stop but I wouldn't, so I decided to try to find another group of people who wouldn't try to stop me. They were more hard-core. I didn't feel lonely at that point because I had finally found people who acted like me, so finally I wasn't alone or rejected because of my behavior. I could feel like I was normal. AA for me is the home that I never knew I was missing. Now I have a safe place. We can share about anything. We laugh about stuff that other people wouldn't be able to hear. I now see that I'm a small part of a large community. The relief I get for myself now is by supporting other people.

The message comes across loud and clear: belonging keeps them sober.

The same can be true about people who join gangs as a means of protection, as a way of dealing with the torment and threats from other gangs, or if their friends or family members belong. In order to fit in with other gang members, they may also begin to wear certain colors, distinctive hairstyles, or other types of clothing. They may use gang terminology and get involved with gang activities. And they often may find themselves engaging in behavior that would be considered inappropriate, illegal, or insane in other circumstances. Belonging, it seems, brings rules of normalcy of its own making.

In many workplace environments, employee resource groups (ERGs) can play a similar role. An evolution of what we use to call "affinity groups," ERGs (sometimes called business resource groups) provide a way for people in underrepresented groups (women, African Americans, LGBTQ employees, etc.) to bond and create mutual support networks that can help them function more effectively within the dominant environment.

The Power of Social Groups

Our relationships with our social groups, either through social isolation or through blind belonging, can contribute not only to outward acts of violence but also to violence against oneself. A study conducted at San Francisco State University found that LGBTQ teens who experience high levels of rejection from their families during adolescence (when compared with young people who experienced little or no rejection from parents and caregivers) were more than eight times as likely to have attempted suicide, more than six times as likely to report high levels of depression, more than three times as likely to use illegal drugs, and more than three times as likely to be at high risk for HIV or other STDs.[17]

It is also important to recognize that the more threatened we feel, the more we pull back into our most core group identities. It is no coincidence that hate crimes or other rampant discriminatory behaviors tend to occur with far more frequency when people are in times of high stress and insecurity. Think about the rise of intolerance in Nazi Germany, Mussolini's Italy, after the Taliban took over in Afghanistan, and so on. During times of upheaval, it's all too easy to find a scapegoat to blame for our discomfort. Our current indictment of Muslims and immigrants clearly follows this same pattern.

This threat dynamic is exacerbated by the increased diversity in the world around us, and especially by increased worldwide migration. There is substantive scientific research showing that humans benefit tremendously from diversity in domains such as decision-making, problem-solving, and creativity.[18] But we also know that sudden increases in diversity can present challenges to social cohesion. When diversity expands rapidly, and in especially visible ways, it causes people of all races to withdraw into their own groups and disengage from social institutions that we generally think of as community-building, such as civic associations, PTAs, and bowling leagues, creating a "turtling effect," as if people were proverbially pulling back into their shells.[19] This effect may be motivated by different stimuli, depending upon the group, but it is generally driven by some manifestation of fear of the other, real or imagined.

What Is Belonging?

We define ourselves by the groups we are a part of and are accepted in. Those groups might be at our very core (family), or they might be social, religious, political, identity, cultural, and/or economic groups that share some sense of common purpose, experience, or goal.

The Merriam-Webster dictionary defines *belonging* as "close or intimate relationship." My experience is that in terms of our experience of groups, belonging has five major qualities:

- A sense of shared identity, in that we see people in the groups we belong to as "us"
- A shared destiny: the belief that what happens to you might also happen to me
- A sense of interdependence, in that we rely on each other in some way, either directly or indirectly
- A general sense of shared values: we may not agree on everything, but we generally share a set of overall values that connect us
- An ability for people to feel fully able to be themselves

The last is probably the most important of all because it distinguishes a true sense of belonging from those times when we feel like we have to go along with the crowd in order to be accepted. It requires permission for people to bring their full selves to the group, and doing so takes enormous courage and vulnerability for most human beings.

Belonging tends to build a feeling of security in which members may feel included, accepted, and related, and generally conform to some agreed upon way of being, thereby enhancing their sense of well-being and security. In more simple terms, people who experience belonging feel less alone and less isolated, and they experience a greater sense of well-being. This doesn't mean that we don't disagree; however, in groups of belonging, those disagreements do not alter our shared identity.

Brené Brown has emphasized that belonging is built on our ability to experience and share our sense of shame and our vulnerability, and certainly most of us think of the groups we are most deeply bonded with as places where we can safely expose those parts of ourselves. In that sense, our feeling of belonging is deeply tied to our feeling of self-acceptance, because without self-acceptance we are more likely to be more tentative as to how much of ourselves we share with others.[20]

When we do not belong, it is significant, and the impact can be dramatic. Isolation is a complicated topic, primarily because there are multiple ways in which it can be conceptualized. We can think of *objective* social isolation as a definitive state of being, where one is physically cut off from social contact. Individuals in solitary confinement or on a deserted island would qualify as isolated, as they literally have no sources of connection available to them. However, social isolation can occur in a subjective manner as well: we may *experience* ourselves as isolated, even while we are surrounded by people and opportunities to connect.

In his 1994 autobiography, *The Long Walk to Freedom,* the late South African president Nelson Mandela wrote about his twenty-seven years in captivity under the apartheid government. "I found solitary confinement the most forbidding aspect of prison life. There is no end and no beginning; there is only one's mind, which can begin to play tricks. Was that a dream or did it really happen? One begins to question everything."[21]

Yet even Mandela, deprived of his freedom and locked away in objective isolation, refused to internalize his experience of being a prisoner. "I have never regarded any man as my superior, either in my life outside or inside prison," he said in a letter to the South African commissioner of prisons in July 1976, while he was still incarcerated.[22] Knowing that he was in the right and that his imprisonment was the fault of an immoral system actually gave him the strength to maintain himself, even in the face of unbearable conditions. Even while isolated, he remained connected, psychologically and spiritually, to his community.

So how do we ensure that people feel connected? Contrary to what many cynics have abrasively suggested, ensuring that people feel included is not simply a matter of unnecessary coddling or indicative of a generation plagued by weakness and entitlement. We now have a litany of studies that demonstrate the profound negative repercussions of ignoring our fundamental need to belong, to be part of a group that we identify with. What's more, it's not *objective* social isolation that's fueling the majority of these findings, but rather *subjective* social isolation; simply *feeling* lonely leads to dramatic health deficits. Although loneliness is an inherently mental construct, its implications for our health are by no means limited to simply our mental health; loneliness also manifests in serious physical symptoms.

The three people in the opening scenario of this book all live and work in environments with many people around them, yet Fatima feels isolated at times because of her religion, Joan because of her political views, and Barry because of his sexual orientation. Isolation and loneliness can be more about our experience than whom we are with.

Loneliness can impact health at all levels, and a wide range of scientists have been proving it for years. One study found that individuals with fewer social ties were at a significantly higher risk of dying from cancer and heart disease.[23] The subjects with the fewest social connections died at more than twice the rate of their well-connected peers during the course of the longitudinal study. John Cacioppo and William Patrick cite scientific evidence to show that it only takes feeling lonely to produce chronic health issues.[24] In another study, researchers identified a variable that in terms of being a risk factor for illness and early death was comparable to better-known dangers such as smoking, obesity, and high blood pressure. That variable? Social isolation.[25]

When we feel like we don't belong, we also experience a dramatic reduction in our cognitive performance. University of Virginia researchers found that children from schools with elevated rates of bullying perform significantly worse on tests than children from more tolerant, inclusive schools.[26] And if you think that the students' cognitive impairment had something to do with their young age, think again. Roy Baumeister, professor of Psychology at Florida State University, and Jean Twenge and Christopher Nuss, from San Diego State University, had two groups of healthy adults complete a GRE-style test, with the only difference being that one group was told, following a fake personality test, that their results indicated they were more likely to be alone in the distant future, while the other group was provided with neutral feedback. The results were stunning: adults simply made to *imagine* being lonely in the future answered, on average, 39 percent of the test questions correctly, while the control group averaged 68 percent accuracy![27]

Feeling socially rejected can also sap our motivation and willpower. Dealing with social pain for long enough can sometimes lead us to throw in the proverbial towel, and empirical evidence supports this claim. Researchers have found that socially excluded individuals are less likely to "stand up to challenges" and instead respond to obstacles with pessimism, apathy, and avoidance.[28] If you've ever coped with loneliness by seeking refuge in comfort foods, you're not alone: disconnected individuals have dramatically poorer health habits, including being 37 percent *less* likely to exercise but significantly *more* likely to eat a diet high in fats.[29] While people may sometimes say, "I'm sick and tired of being lonely," the evidence suggests that it might be more accurate to say, "I'm sick and tired *because* I'm lonely."

Most of us have any number of groups to which we belong. Our family is, for most people, our most basic source of belonging (and, as we all know, families can be fraught with all kinds of dysfunction). We might also be defined by belonging to a particular racial, ethnic, or national group, a religious or spiritual group, a workplace, an interest group, or a social organization. Our level of belongingness to each group varies, but these places of connection fill a critical need nonetheless.

Though our desire to connect may be a universal impulse, to whom we are wired to connect is far more constrained. Through much of our evolutionary history, we lived in small, often isolated tribes. Being considered a member of a tribe was critical, as membership conferred benefits such as the right to share in communal resources and the luxury of group protection. An individual typically could not belong to different tribes simultaneously. The distinction was a simple one: you were either in our tribe, and hence one of "us," or out of our tribe, and consequently one of "them." Survival during this period depended heavily on our ability to differentiate members of our own tribe, who represented safety and security, from members of competing tribes, who represented danger and uncertainty. Tribalism has equipped humans with a hypersensitivity to signals of group membership and a reflexive urge to favor those whom we deem members of our own tribe over out-group members.

Though most of us rarely traverse a landscape as physically treacherous as the ones our ancestors did, the thick residue of tribalism continues to obscure our view of the world. For those hoping to promote untethered connectedness that supersedes racial, ethnic, and geographic barriers, it is crucial to understand that such a goal is, in many ways, counter to our biological predispositions. We have not evolved to facilitate unconditional connection between any and all groups. Extensive research in multiple cultures around the planet has determined that we are likely to experience less empathy for people who are in different racial groups than we are.[30] This dynamic happens in all areas of our lives. In schools or workplace environments, it may occur as cliques that include some and exclude others.

This is not to say that there aren't groups in which people actively try to build connection across differences. In cases such as that, what can unite us is our common desire to connect despite our differences.

The implicit need to categorize individuals into in-groups and out-groups—"us versus them"—is so fundamental to our nature that we automatically do so even when categorizations are purposely trivial. Polish social psychologist Henri Tajfel divided individuals into groups based either randomly or on incidental differences (such as what kind of chewing gum they liked).[31] Participants were then given opportunities to anonymously allocate money to other individuals within the study. Logically, favoring a stranger about whom you know absolutely nothing aside from his or her preference in chewing gum doesn't make a great deal of sense, but this is precisely what Tajfel found. When provided with minimal information about those around them, individuals instinctively looked for even benign signals of group membership they could latch onto. The result is people disproportionately giving money to strangers with whom they share an unimportant characteristic. Our penchant to favor members of our own tribe prevails even when the identity under which our tribe is constructed is inconsequential.

This dynamic can lead to situations when an incident, a statement, or a circumstance can cause a relatively sudden shift in the perception of whether someone is in an in-group or an out-group. Whether we look at past events, like the O. J. Simpson trial, or more recent ones, like the shooting of Michael Brown in Ferguson, Missouri, or the Colin Kaepernick–inspired protests by football players and other athletes, black and white people who had felt connected before the incident often found themselves suddenly feeling different from each other afterward, knowing that there were two completely different reactions based on race, the level of trust they had in the police or justice system, and how it impacted them personally.[32]

Out-Group Homogeneity

We also relate to groups differently, depending on both their in-group/out-group status and their dominant/nondominant status in our societal structure. For example, in the United States, whites, men, heterosexuals, and Christians are dominant cultural in-groups based on their prevalence and power. Once people have been labeled as members of an out-group, they tend to be stripped of their individuality. This has been labeled the *out-group homogeneity effect*. We tend to see the groups to which we belong as a collection of diverse and unique individuals while other groups are perceived to be a uniform assortment of clones and sycophants: predictable, derivative, and otherwise unoriginal. Taken to the extreme, deindividualization leads to dehumanization, which has obvious large-scale consequences, as proven throughout history.

Think about how much easier it is to distinguish people of one's own race versus distinguishing those of a different race. All of the statements that we have heard about how "all of them look the same" bear this out. Studies have consistently shown that we attribute greater personal variability to the members of our own in-group while seeing members of out-groups as largely similar in their personalities, tastes, preferences, and motivations.[33] In one study, ninety sorority members were asked to judge the degree of differences among their own sorority sisters and two other groups. Every single participant judged their own sorority members to be more dissimilar than the members of the other groups.[34]

Let's think of this relative to how racial groups are seen in the United States. Who is more likely to see the differences between African Americans, Caribbean-born blacks, and African-born blacks—people from those groups or people from other racial groups? The same is true for Hispanics or Latinos from Cuba, Mexico, and Puerto Rico; Asians from China, Vietnam, Korea, or Japan; and whites who are Jewish, Mormon, or Catholic and from completely different cultural backgrounds. From the outside, many of these groups seem homogeneous, but from the inside we know that significant differences can exist.

An unfortunate consequence of the out-group homogeneity effect is that it makes it easier and more automatic to stereotype groups of which you do not consider yourself a member. If we already tend to view members of out-groups as being homogeneous, deploying stereotypes becomes not only easier but in a sense a logical (though problematic) labeling device. As I wrote in my book *Everyday Bias,* this stereotyping contributes dramatically to conscious and unconscious biases that impact not only our beliefs but our behaviors as well.[35]

Even if you are a member of a group, your survival isn't guaranteed, especially if your identity is aligned with a nondominant group. People who are in out-groups societally have to pay more attention to group identity in order to survive than do people who belong to in-groups. If you are a woman in a predominantly male environment, it is more necessary for you to pay attention to the gender dynamics of the group in order to be safe and successful in it. This concern is exacerbated by public examples of misogyny or sexism, as we have seen with Bill Cosby, Roger Ailes, Bill O'Reilly, and Harvey Weinstein, and as we saw during the 2016 presidential election with Donald Trump. The same is true for race. People of color are more likely to be aware of dynamics of race than whites are because they need to be in order to survive and thrive in a white-dominant culture. It can even impact the way one perceives oneself. If you are heterosexual, for example, how often do you think about your heterosexuality? However, if you are LGBTQ, you probably include that in your thinking in various ways on a regular basis (for example,

"Whom do I tell?" "How much do I tell?" "Are they reacting to me the way I think they are?"). On the other hand, imagine if you were the only straight person in a large group of LGBTQ folks. All of a sudden, your heterosexuality is in the forefront of your thinking. You have never felt more straight in your life!

Our identity brings with it a whole set of expectations. Because we belong (or are assumed to belong) to a particular group, we are expected to go along with that group in terms of beliefs and behaviors, and we often do. In the period following World War II, social scientists conducted hundreds of experiments designed to help us understand how the Nazis were able to turn one of the most cultured countries on the planet into a genocide machine virtually overnight. Some of these experiments are well known. In 1951 Solomon Asch's conformity experiments showed that people will tend to conform to a group's viewpoint, even when they see that the evidence against it is obvious.[36]

Other experiments by Stanley Milgram and Philip Zimbardo demonstrated how our identification with a group, and particularly authority within our group, can lead to behavior that goes beyond the irrational to downright deadly.[37] Once we have identified with a group, their behavior begins to seem "normal" to us, and the behavior of others therefore seems "abnormal," "sick," or "evil." This is especially true when our group is the dominant cultural group, because our view of ourselves then becomes the prevalent view in the broader culture. When faced with a conflict between what we know is right and our desire to go along with the predominant group behavior, we tend to go along. It simply *feels* like the right thing to do.

Our tendency to identify ourselves by group keeps us safer: we know who our friends and enemies are very quickly and easily. But it is not only about safety, and it starts very young. According to Sarah Gaither, a social psychology professor at Duke University:

> If you build your identity around a group, it's important to define what that group *isn't*. That's what really ends up pushing kids to be more exclusionary to other kids. Over the course of elementary school, physical aggression is replaced by tattling, and then eventually by gossip—both ways of drawing boundaries, and of

keeping an errant peer in their place. The act of shutting people out, then, doesn't necessarily have much to do with the ones on the outside; more often, it's an act of self-preservation.[38]

This is a great example of what I described earlier as "bonding *against*." Our group identity is clarified and strengthened by knowing that "we're not one of them." We ultimately rely on "us versus them" thinking in order to define ourselves, define the other, and figure out how to be safe and successful in our lives. By doing this we allow ourselves to be clear about the norms of group behavior that we are expected to follow; to be clear about whom we should be afraid of and protect ourselves from; to know whom we can trust and whom we must distrust; and to know whom we can harm and whom we must keep safe. Our understanding that we can feel more comfortable when one of the people outside of our group is harmed than we do when one of our own is harmed is the reason we eschew fraternizing with the enemy. It is harder to defeat a foe when you identify their humanity than when you assign them to objectified groups and dehumanize them (e.g., "Japs," "gooks," "Islamic terrorists," "socialists," "racists," or "fascists"). We define ourselves by who we are *not* just as much as we do by who we *are*, and sometimes even more.

We have a strong pull toward dualism. It is very natural, and sometimes even automatic, for human beings to choose sides. In fact, we have a strong tendency to create either/or, right/wrong, them/us dynamics in our lives. Think about how many times things that are really more along a continuum are divided into two parts so as to increase our ability to deal with them: day becomes night and night becomes day at a moment. The same can be said about hot and cold. We even do this where people are concerned. People or "for us" or "against us," "one of us" or "one of them." We have a tendency to want to separate the world into dualities.

This imposed simplicity makes it easier to deal with life at some level, but it also blurs the nuance and complexity of life. This is the case with our tendency to see the world as "us versus them."

But how do we decide who is "us" and who is "them"? Given our previous look into the world of politics, let's start there.

Chapter 2

The Politics of Being Right

I think people involved in politics make good actors. Acting and politics both involve fooling people. People like being fooled by actors. When you get right down to it, they probably like being fooled by politicians even more. A skillful actor will make you think, but a skillful politician will make you never have to think.

—DONNA BRAZILE

In September 1894, a French housekeeper who was working in the German embassy found an unsigned and undated letter, torn into six pieces, that was addressed to the German attaché. The letter seemed to indicate that confidential French military documents were about to be sent to a foreign country. The housekeeper took the pieces of the letter and gave them to the French counterintelligence agency. The letter found its way to the French minister of war, General Auguste Mercier, who had been roundly criticized by the media for being incompetent. General Mercier immediately initiated two separate investigations of the matter.

A suspect was quickly identified: Captain Alfred Dreyfus, a Jewish artillery officer who was the only Jewish officer on the General Staff. As the investigation continued, the pall of anti-Semitism, as well as rumors about Dreyfus's personality and character, led to a biased and one-sided analysis of the "evidence." Despite objections by some about the reliability of the evidence, the case proceeded with fanfare. Dreyfus's home was searched, his background was investigated, and any specious piece of information became woven into the fabric of the case against him.

In October 1894, Dreyfus was interrogated with the intention of eliciting a confession, which he refused to produce. The judicial police officer even suggested suicide, leaving a loaded revolver within Dreyfus's reach; however, Dreyfus insisted on proving his innocence. He was imprisoned and illegally placed in solitary confinement, where he was interrogated day and night to attempt to gain a confession.

In the months leading up to his trial, Dreyfus was subjected to a notorious propaganda campaign, lead mostly by the publisher of a well-known anti-Semitic newspaper. Any evidence, or lack thereof, was manipulated to make Dreyfus appear guilty. When nothing was found in his home, the newspapers and prosecutors said this was proof of his guilt, as he was hiding things. The fact that he had a good memory and language skills was said to show that he had trained himself to be a spy. In December 1894, Dreyfus was arraigned by a military court and charged with treason.

The newspapers had a field day in the weeks leading up to the trial. Mercier declared Dreyfus guilty in a newspaper interview. Others asserted that, as a Jew, he could not be trusted. False letters were introduced into evidence. Questionable testimony was elicited, all to prove the assumed truth that Dreyfus was guilty.

On December 22, seven judges unanimously convicted Dreyfus of collusion with a foreign power and sentenced him to military degradation and lifetime exile on Devil's Island in French Guyana under the harshest of conditions—he was often confined to bed with his ankles chained, unable to move. Dreyfus's brother mounted a sustained campaign to prove his innocence, which was countered by a virulent campaign to maintain his imprisonment. Military officials forged documents and hid evidence that suggested his innocence, even when the real culprit surfaced. Riots broke out across the country between those who supported Dreyfus and the anti-Semitic fringe.

On January 13, 1898, Emile Zola, the great French intellectual, published an extensive article naming all the people who had framed Dreyfus. The article spread across the country, reaching 300,000 people the first day. By accusing specific people, Zola intentionally made himself the target of a trial for defamation of character. He was acquitted, and

Dreyfus was retried and eventually acquitted in July 1906, after which he was reinstated in the army and his rank restored. He retired the following year and lived until 1935.

The Dreyfus Affair is one of history's greatest examples of *motivated reasoning* and *confirmation bias*. Historians almost universally agree that Dreyfus was innocent, and most believe that the conspiracy to convict him came not so much from people consciously framing an innocent man, but more likely because their inherent anti-Semitism led them to believe that he was guilty. They used that belief when they processed information, including whether or not to believe witnesses and documents, and generally found the evidence to support a case they believed to be true.

Nothing better describes the way most people respond to politics in America today. Treading into the world of politics is fraught with challenges. Politics by its very nature is a fluid, contradictory, and emotional domain. It is difficult to discuss politics without being driven by biases, both conscious and unconscious, that shape what we see and how we interpret it. Our three Munchester Industries employees, Fatima, Joan, and Barry, for example, each have a very clear political perspective, influenced by the media they're exposed to, the people they talk to, and the people they avoid. Politics is also one of the major battlegrounds in which we seek the support of groups of people around us and in which we demonize those of other groups. In that context, it is the perfect place to continue our discussion of how our desire to belong is pulling us apart.

I do not claim to be devoid of my own political point of view, nor am I immune to the tendency at times to be pulled into the "us versus them" political discourse. I will consciously try to step outside the fray and look at the dynamics of belonging in our politics today with the intention to understand the undercurrents at play, rather than arguing for a particular point of view.

How Do We Choose?

To discuss our political system and the way people choose their leaders, we have to understand that we are not as rational and reasoned about voting as we think we are; we may not be rational at all. Dozens of research studies have demonstrated that votes are cast on anything but a rational basis. Let's look at the 2016 election as an example. Hillary Clinton was touted by her supporters as being the "most qualified person to ever run for the office of the presidency." After all, she had just served the country as secretary of state, and before that as a senator. Between her own years of service and the role she played in the administration of her husband, Bill Clinton, she had literally decades of public service. But do qualifications really matter?

How many presidential elections have been won by the "most qualified" candidate? If qualifications were the only criterion, Richard Nixon would have beaten John F. Kennedy in 1960. After all, both had served in the House and Senate, but Nixon also had been vice president for eight years. Certainly Gerald Ford would have beaten Jimmy Carter in 1976. Carter was a one-term governor from Georgia, while Ford had served in Congress for twenty-four years, including eight years as minority leader, then as vice president and then president for two and a half years. In 1992 Bill Clinton, governor of Arkansas, never would have beaten George H. W. Bush, a sitting president who had also served in Congress and as ambassador to the United Nations, ambassador to China, director of the CIA, and vice president before that. Certainly George W. Bush, who served barely more than a term as governor of Texas, could not have beaten Al Gore, the sitting vice president and before that a congressman and senator for more than sixteen years, in 2000. Barack Obama, the freshman senator from Illinois, would never have beaten Hillary Clinton for the Democratic nomination in 2008, nor defeated John McCain, a war hero who had served in the House and Senate for twenty-five years, in the general election.

We choose our political leaders the way we choose most other things in our lives—by using our fast or intuitive brains. Reason has very little to do with it. We tend to gravitate toward candidates whom we like, whom we trust, or whom we associate with qualities that look "more presidential."

What is "more presidential"? Gregg R. Murray, associate professor of political science at Augusta University, studies how evolutionary theory explains some of the choices we make in politics. For example, Murray has found that since 1789, the taller candidate has won the election almost

60 percent of the time and the popular vote almost two-thirds of the time. In one experiment, Murray and his colleagues asked almost five hundred students to draw pictures of a "typical citizen" and an "ideal national leader," and 64 percent of the time they drew the leader as taller.[1] One can only imagine the impact this might have on women candidates in elections, given that women are generally shorter than men. Did the current president's height "trump" Hillary Clinton's experience?

Or was it general appearance? We know that certain aspects of appearance affect voters dramatically. Franklin Roosevelt was careful to conceal his disability, lest the voters see him as "too weak" to serve. Richard Nixon's famous loss to Kennedy in the televised presidential debates of 1960 was largely attributed to his "five o'clock shadow" and perspiration visible on the screen, even though by some accounts he fared better in the radio broadcast of those same debates. Gerald Ford is said to have suffered because of an image that he was clumsy, the result of a couple of incidents for which he was mocked on *Saturday Night Live*, even though he was one of the greatest athletes to ever serve as president.

People vote for candidates for a myriad of other reasons, many having nothing to do with their policy positions. People often vote for candidates because they think they will win, rather than because they think they would perform better in office.[2] In fact, there is even evidence that the College of Cardinals does the very same thing when electing a new pope.[3]

Perception outplays reality. In the 2016 election, Clinton was largely seen as less trustworthy, and many of Donald Trump's supporters said their trust in him was the reason they voted for him.[4] This is in stark contrast to findings by independent fact-checking organizations that Clinton told the truth far more often than Trump.[5]

Some of this is as a result of a fascinating phenomenon known as the *illusory truth effect*. In 1977, researchers from Temple University and Villanova took a group of college students and showed them three lists of sixty statements that they were unlikely to know anything about (e.g., "The first Air Force base was launched in New Mexico"), distributed two weeks apart, with some statements true and others false. Twenty statements occurred on all three lists. The students were asked to report how confident they were that the statements were true. The ratings on the statements that were not repeated remained constant, but the students' confidence about the statements that were repeated rose each time.[6] In other words, there is validity to the old saying "A lie repeated becomes the truth."[7]

Whatever you may think about him or his campaign, Donald Trump brilliantly exercised this principle in the 2016 election. While critics lambasted him for the simplicity and dishonesty of his language, he simply repeated the same phrases over and over again ("Crooked Hillary," "Lyin' Ted," "Low-Energy Jeb," "Little Marco") until they were imprinted in the minds of his followers; in the age of mass media, repetition is not a challenge. Clinton, on the other hand, was praised by many of her supporters for her deep understanding of the issues, yet was criticized by others as coming across as too "wonky." Her message often was perceived by many to be too complex and to be "over the heads" of some voters.

I live in a geographical area (the northwest suburbs of Washington, D.C.) that is very liberal. Most of the people I work with and live around follow that pattern. I have been involved in hundreds of conversations that demonstrate that there was a wide range of reasons people voted for Hillary Clinton and that some people struggled with that vote, even if they eventually pulled the lever for her. Clearly, to many people she was an inspiring choice, and to others she was the "lesser of the evils." However, relatively few of the people I interact with on a daily basis were open Trump voters, and as a result, I found myself falling into the out-group homogeneity effect of stereotyping Trump voters. I decided to find out what they really felt, and I started by meeting Jacob Rascon.

Rascon, not a Trump supporter, is an NBC News reporter who was assigned to cover the Trump campaign. Here is what he told me about the people he met:

> Over the course of nine months or so I was assigned to follow the Trump campaign. This gave me the opportunity to not only talk to people at his rallies who were most passionate about voting for him, but also the protesters, who may have hated him the most. I got a different sense from them than the people I met at the Hertz counter, or Uber drivers. Those people didn't

necessarily know that I was a journalist, and they were speaking more honestly.

In a lot of cases people were more willing to give this new guy, Donald Trump, a shot because they were desperate to see significant changes in Washington, D.C. The overwhelming number of people did not trust the media and did not watch a lot of news. I realized that more on the campaign trail than I had realized before. They cared about issues they dealt with and actually mattered to them. Many of them really cared about factories closing down and the difficulty in finding decent paid jobs. Trump talked about jobs and was more in tune with their concerns. The same was true about immigration. There were a surprising number of Hispanics and others and many, in their own minds, were not racist at all. They wondered why when it was so hard for them to get jobs, and it was so easy for people to come in illegally. The same was true about people from Muslim countries. When it came to attacks against the country, the issues were bubbling and candidate Trump tapped into them. The media freaked out that he would say, "I would ban all Muslims," but in their minds they weren't racist and didn't have anything against Muslims; they just didn't feel safe and could go along with the ban since, in their perception, most attacks were seen to be by Muslims. The way that they talked among their friends and at work or over coffee about what they were concerned about was the way Trump talked about it. He spoke their language. He promised to keep them safe. I heard this sentiment everywhere. Finally, somebody was talking about their concerns.

The greater fear was Hillary Clinton. They preferred a political novice, even if they hated some of the things that he said on the trail. They were not happy with recent decisions by the Supreme Court, like the legalization of gay marriage [and] more accessibility to abortion, and [they were] concerned that Clinton would appoint more liberal judges. I spoke to one woman who was an orthodontist who talked about how much debt she went into and how excited she was that Trump would change the tax code. She was highly educated, and that was the only thing that inspired her.

Trump's followers were able to reject the accusations toward him from the media. I really saw how deep the distrust is of the national media, and how it had lost credibility for most of the people I talked to, so it didn't matter if they said that Trump lied about something. There were actually times when I was at the rallies and saw that things he was saying were taken out of context on the news that evening or the next day. People who already distrusted the media took those examples and said, "Look they're lying to you." All they needed was one or two good examples of that. That was just no credibility, and that was a major problem.

Rascon's experience was not very different from what I heard from the forty-eight Trump voters that I interviewed. These people were cab drivers or Uber drivers, people standing next to me in airports or sitting next to me on planes. Some connected with me through social media, or were people in the companies I work with who happened to let on how they voted. Eighty-five percent were white. Thirty were men, eighteen were women. They ranged from twenty-one years old to seventy-four, and they came from all over the United States.

Some interviews lasted ten minutes; others went on for more than an hour or during days of emailing back and forth. I started each conversation by telling the interviewee that I was writing a book about polarity in our society and was surrounded by Clinton voters, so I just wanted to better understand why people voted for Trump. I assured them that it was not my intention to try to change their minds; rather, I wanted to get their point of view. Everyone I asked save for one person was willing to talk.

The results were intriguing. About one-quarter of the people I spoke to were very partisan in their responses. They matched some of the louder voices you might have seen on television. In those cases, I mostly tried to listen and understand. However, as Rascon discovered, most of the people talked about specific issues. Forty-six percent said that Obamacare was a significant issue for them, largely because of cost, although when asked to be specific, very few could provide details. Others talked about abortion, gun control, or national defense. Ten specifically mentioned that they were tired of political correctness forcing us to not make smart decisions, especially when it came to proposals for barring entry to Muslims. One young woman said that she couldn't vote for Clinton because she home-schools her children and Clinton didn't support homeschooling. Several said that they thought it was good to have a businessperson rather than a politician at the helm. When asked if they were offended by the lan-guage Trump used in the campaign in reference to women, people of color, or a disabled reporter, the sentiments of many were expressed by one limo driver who said, "I personally think the guy is a jerk, but some-times jerks get stuff done!"

Perhaps the two most telling themes echoed Rascon's. When I asked whether they felt more like they voted *for* Trump or *against* Clinton, twenty-six of the forty-eight (54 percent) said they voted more against Clinton. And when I asked whether they believed the news, thirty said no, and another thirteen said they weren't sure. Less than 10 percent believe the news they listen to! The feeling I was left with was that these were, for the most part, normal people who struggled with their vote. This is not inconsistent with many more-sophisticated studies of this vot-ing population.[8]

We also know that voters tend to vote along party lines, especially when they are not clear on what they are voting for. One study showed that when given versions of the Democratic and Republican health care bills with the party names switched, 70 percent of voters chose something they probably didn't believe in, simply because it had their party's name on it. Similarly, studies have shown that more voters were opposed to Obamacare (46 percent) than to the "Affordable Care Act" (37 percent), even though what people call "Obamacare" *is* the Affordable Care Act.[9] And more supported "gays in the military" than "homosexuals in the military," even though both statements are talking about the *same* group of people![10] Even people who say they are independent voters generally do not vote as independently as they would have you believe.[11]

We clearly do not vote rationally; but why is this more of an issue today than at other times in our recent history? In order to understand that better, we have to consider the underpinnings of how we see politics today.

We are living in more-segregated political enclaves than we have in the past, and our political leaders have become more segregated. Since the signing of the Civil Rights Act in 1964, when President Lyndon Johnson purportedly said, "I think we have turned the South over to the Republican Party for the rest of my life and yours," the country has become increasingly divided into conservative Republican and liberal Democratic enclaves.[12]

There have been structural changes that have contributed to this separation. The increasing costs of running for office have caused politicians to focus a high percentage of their time on fundraising.[13] Funding organizations and lobbying groups generally tend to represent a strong political point of view and therefore tend to influence the candidate accordingly. Elected officials spend less time socializing with those across party lines than ever before. The daughter of a long-term Republican senator told me, "We used to socialize with people from the other party. Joe Biden was one of my father's best friends. Now it's very rare." In addition, gerrymandering has turned congressional districts into single-party enclaves that offer the more extreme elements of both parties a greater chance of being elected, instead of more moderate representatives. And the primary system gives greater power to people with stronger political views, who are more likely to vote than those who do not feel as strongly.

The lines between our tribal groups are more clearly drawn. While in the past we may have had a significant amount of interaction with people from "the other side" and were far more likely to work across party lines to get things done, now people tend to interact more with people who are like them. In order to belong, rejecting the other side becomes part of the price of admission. Compromise becomes a dirty word, as *60 Minutes* host Lesley Stahl found when she was interviewing incoming Speaker of the House John Boehner in 2010:

> Boehner told Stahl that it wouldn't involve compromising, but instead finding "common ground":
>
> **Stahl:** But governing means compromising.
>
> **Boehner:** It means working together.

Stahl: It also means compromising.

Boehner: It means finding common ground.

Stahl: Okay, is that compromising?

Boehner: I made it clear I am not going to compromise on my principles, nor am I going to compromise the will of the American people.

Stahl: What are you saying? You're saying, "I want common ground, but I'm not gonna compromise." I don't understand that. I really don't.

Boehner: When you say the word "compromise," a lot of Americans look up and go, "Uh-oh, they're gonna sell me out." And so finding common ground, I think, makes more sense.

Stahl noted that Boehner compromised his position on the Bush tax cuts to get a deal with Obama last week, noting that he had wanted all the Bush-era tax cuts extended permanently but only got a two-year extension. Boehner again said it wasn't a compromise. "Why won't you say you're afraid of the word?" Stahl asked. "I reject the word," Boehner said.[14]

When we eschew compromise, it leaves us to dig in and try to win. *Our* morality becomes *the* morality. In order to better understand how this affects us, we must understand how our morality develops.

Moral Foundations Theory

Let's imagine that you dislike broccoli. You find the taste disgusting, the texture strange, and the smell unappetizing. You'd be perfectly content never crossing paths with this unsavory vegetable again.

Suppose that someone was confident that she could change your mind. Being a reasonable person, you decide to give this broccoli advocate an opportunity to make her case. She proceeds to list the myriad nutritional benefits that broccoli provides, describes the expert consensus among dietitians about its weight loss benefits, and tells you how many doctors credit the consumption of vegetables like broccoli with increased longevity. As you walk home, you reflect on this encounter. You find yourself with a greater appreciation for broccoli, and you're even willing to concede that, despite its shortcomings, broccoli may have its benefits. Unfortunately, chances are you still won't like the taste of broccoli, and no matter how good it is for you, you are unlikely to eat it.

We're all born with particular palates that dictate our tastes. While such an explanation is pretty easy to swallow (excuse the pun) in the domain of food, we also possess *moral* palates that determine our sensibilities in the domain of morality. These moral palates underlie our political ideology, with liberals and conservatives showing dramatically different neuroreceptors. It is more and more evident that we may have a neuro-cognitive inclination to morality.[15] Much as with broccoli, researchers are finding that no matter how coherent a political adversary's argument may be, and even though we may understand its logic and recognize its merit, it *still doesn't taste quite right*. Additionally, because voting patterns today are driven by identity, perceptions of racism, sexism, homophobia, and xenophobia all make it more difficult to embrace others' points of view.

Jonathan Haidt is a professor of ethical leadership at New York University. Haidt is considered one of the foremost thinkers in the field of moral psychology and has studied extensively not only how we think politically but why we think that way. Haidt has spent years exploring why we react the way we do when we are confronted with deep moral issues in politics and religion, and has found that there are patterns in the way human beings have evolved morally that give us a window into understanding why good people can disagree so vehemently.

Along with his colleague Jesse Graham from the University of Southern California, Haidt has postulated that all human morality rests on a set of broad foundations that serve to determine our reactions to political issues, almost like the way the taste buds on our tongues combine to produce a particular experience of eating. These moral foundations form the basis of our political tribal connections. As we discovered in earlier chapters, human beings are naturally tribal. We are unlike virtually all other animals that form themselves into groups in that we form tribal alignments with people outside of blood connections. As a result, our moral code has become the core of our sense of belonging.

Think about it in terms of almost any group of which you have been a part, whether it was an organization, a fraternity or sorority, the Scouts, a movement, or something else. We almost always have a set of spoken *and* unspoken rules by which we live. We might imagine these rules as normative beliefs and behaviors that provide a boundary that allows for safe interaction within that group, and makes it clear that there are certain things that we can expect from each other so that we can feel a sense of belonging. Without the boundary that these rules provide, we are liable to stray in directions that might create contention within our group or even harm the group. We lose the sense of belonging that is so key to our comfort and our survival. We can see this very clearly when we think about cultural patterns among various peoples around the world. We can also see it in our response to politics.

Building on the work of anthropologist Richard Allan Shweder, Haidt and Graham identified five of these moral foundations in their initial studies, and Haidt later added a sixth in his book *The Righteous Mind*.[16] We might think of these foundations as a set of taste receptors for right and wrong. All people are born with moral palates that have varying sensitivities to these six foundations—that is, they believe some of these foundations to be more important than others, and a deeper look at the foundations gives us a fascinating view of how distinct patterns in such sensitivities inform the divergent palates of liberals versus conservatives. We might describe the six foundations in these terms, listed here with their opposites:

- **Care/harm** is related to our ability to feel (and dislike) the pain of others. It underlies virtues of kindness, gentleness, and nurturance.
- **Fairness/cheating** is related to the evolutionary process of reciprocal altruism. It generates ideas of justice, rights, and autonomy that may differ in interpretation. Liberals might think that it is not fair for some people to have more money than others; conservatives might think that it is not fair to take money that one person has earned and give it to somebody else.
- **Loyalty/betrayal** underlies virtues of patriotism and self-sacrifice for the group. It is active anytime people feel that it's "one for all and all for one."

- **Authority/subversion** was shaped by our long primate history of hierarchical social interactions. It underlies virtues of leadership and followership, including deference to legitimate authority and respect for traditions.
- **Sanctity/degradation** was shaped by the psychology of disgust and contamination. It underlies religious or moral notions of striving to live in an elevated, less carnal, more noble way. This can apply to deeply moral issues such as abortion or climate activism, in which people feel categorically *right.*
- **Liberty/oppression** is about the feelings of reaction and resentment people feel toward those who dominate them and restrict their liberty. It is often in tension with those of the authority foundation.[17]

These moral foundations become especially interesting when one sees them in relation to our political "tribes." Haidt suggests that one might think about this as the controls on a music equalizer board. Based on research with hundreds of thousands of people, Haidt and his colleagues have identified clear patterns that demonstrate a fascinating insight into the ways the different tribes think. We can see in Figure 2.1 how differently liberals and conservatives (this is not to say Democrats and Republicans, who may or may not actually align with these labels) view the world in the context of these moral foundations.

Any discussions about groups must be done archetypally (common practices of that group are identified, but it is acknowledged that not every member behaves the same way) and not stereotypically (all members of a group are assumed to behave in the same way). Liberals seem to reflect beliefs that are predicated on a three-foundation construction: they overwhelmingly base their moral systems on considerations of care and fairness, with a relatively high level of concern for liberty. As such, liberal morality is primarily concerned with protecting others from harm and ensuring that justice is preserved, especially for the weak and disadvantaged. The fairness aspect, in the case of liberals, seems to center on equity. Hence the Clinton campaign's motto, "Stronger Together." Within this construct, the core underpinnings of liberals are reflected in the movements toward equality for women, people of color, LGBTQ

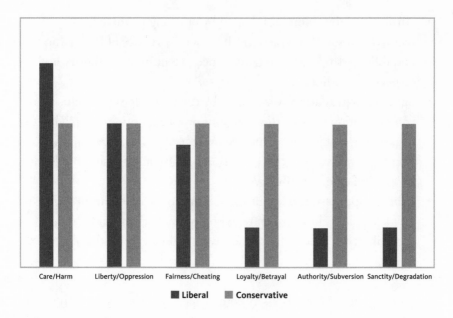

Figure 2.1 Foundations of Moral Authority
Adapted from an interview with Jonathan Haidt by Bill Moyers, *Moyers & Company*, February 3, 2012.

citizens, religious minorities, and so on. We might say that these have been the sacrosanct aspects of modern liberalism since the middle of the twentieth century. Because of that, it is virtually impossible for most liberals to look past statements made during the campaign by Trump about women, immigrants, people of color, Muslims, and others. Those statements violated the core foundational morals of liberalism. Liberals also tend to be less attached to the notion of "America first" and to consider themselves as "global citizens" (coinciding with their low scores on the loyalty foundation); the frequency with which one sees RESIST AUTHORITY bumper stickers on their cars coincides with liberals' low scores on the authority foundation; and the attitude of "Do your own thing" can be seen as violating the sanctity foundation that conservatives tend to value.

Conservatives, though possessing a reduced sensitivity to care and fairness as compared with their liberal counterparts, have values that typically incorporate elements of all six foundations relatively equally. While liberal morals show sensitivity almost exclusively to care and fairness, conservative morals also possess metaphorical receptors for in-group loyalty, respect for authority and hierarchy, and the maintenance of purity, both in terms of cleanliness and within domains of the divine. They are more likely to resist change and want order and simplicity, and they more readily hold aspects of their beliefs as sacred. Hence, studies indicate that conservative students generally have more cleaning supplies and organizational items and that they lean toward more self-discipline and structure, while liberals like to travel more, including to more exotic places, and like fewer restrictions and more novelty items.[18] The Trump campaign slogan, "Make America Great Again," speaks to these concerns, as do the emphases on the perceived threat of immigrants taking jobs away from citizens, the influx of Muslims with their "strange" religion and ties to "terrorism," and the demonization of "welfare cheats." All of these messages focus on the need for group loyalty (the loyalty foundation), a harking back to the simpler values of the past (the sanctity foundation), a desire for more order and control (the authority foundation), and a greater sense of *proportional* fairness—for example, that people should have means proportional to their ability to create them (the fairness foundation).

These different views of the world create a form of tribal epistemology, a fundamental theory of knowledge that is different from one group to the next. Each group has a completely different way of determining truth, which makes it difficult, if not impossible, to come to a shared understanding. The problem is that if our moral palates determine our political ideologies, and such palates—similar to our taste palates—cannot really be influenced by strong arguments, how are we to reconcile our differences and find opportunities for compromise? Can someone learn to like the taste of broccoli?

If we look at these dynamics in the context of the themes we have discussed earlier, it is easy to see the dilemma in which we find ourselves. Given the segregation that we are experiencing politically, the separated access to information that the segmented media is providing to people, and the need and desire to fit into the groups that we identify with, it is not hard to see how our tribes are becoming more separate. Since the mid-1970s, political party membership/identification has become a better predictor of voter decisions than it was previously, and while the notion that "people are leaving political parties" may show up in polling, it is clear that it does not show up in voting patterns.[19] People are less likely to split their ticket—that is, select candidates from both sides of the political spectrum.[20] There is also evidence that people are becoming more segregated in terms of socioeconomic status, educational level, religious affiliation, and race.[21] This is significant because we know, for example, that white people who live near people of color tend to be more comfortable with racial equity than are those who live in homogeneous environments.[22]

As these party loyalties and identities solidify, there is an increasing dislike for those in the out-groups among party members, as we have begun to evaluate those on the other side of the aisle with increasing negativity.[23]

Politically, we have formed ourselves into camps that are more separated geographically, socioeconomically, educationally, and in other ways than they were before. Because of this segregation, the perspectives that we hold start to become like religion: sacred and absolute. Rather than seeing our differences as points of view on issues, we now see our view as truth and as something that is morally right. It is easy to see how this makes the other view "wrong," "bad," "stupid," or "evil," rather than just simply different. Once we have classified people in this way, they become objectified and stereotyped. Clinton voters are no longer just "people who voted for Clinton"; they are "naive," "libtards," or "leftists." Trump voters are no longer just "people who voted for Trump"; they are "racists," "idiots," or "white supremacists." While there is no question that some in each group may align with those stereotypes, when we see those who voted for the other candidate as separate from us, the out-group homogeneity syndrome has us beginning to act as if they are all the same. The sources of information that they represent can then be easily ignored. One Trump voter I spoke to who has a PhD in philosophy from Princeton said, "I don't believe anything the *New York Times* prints," and dozens of liberals I know just as easily dismiss everything on Fox News as "propaganda." Obviously it strains credulity to think that *everything* on any given news program can be false.

Once we objectify people, it is easier to treat them as less human, or "immoral," and therefore justify any action to defeat them. This leads to incredible hypocrisy, whether on the part of Republicans who minimize Russian influence in the 2016 presidential election or who continue to assert that voter fraud is an issue and therefore justify voter suppression techniques, despite all evidence to the contrary, or Democrats who believed that Trump's unwillingness to say that he would stand by the results of the election would bring down the republic but then were out marching on "Not My Presidents Day" on February 20, 2017, one month after the inauguration.[24]

In a polarized culture, the extremes set the tone, and tend to take over. Polarity leads people to justify the unjustifiable.

Let's go back to the story of the Dreyfus Affair and the concepts of motivated reasoning and confirmation bias. We tend to accept information that confirms our prior beliefs, and we ignore or discredit information that does not. In the words of Jonathan Haidt, our minds are designed to act less like scientists (evaluating all information with an equal degree of scrutiny) and more like trial lawyers (selectively highlighting information that supports our views while ignoring or dismissing evidence to the contrary).[25] Or as Atiba Ellis, professor of law at West Virginia University, has said, "People are more invested in their world view than their view of the world."[26]

The challenge is that once we have objectified the "other," we move from an issue orientation, in which we can talk about what is best for our country, to an identity orientation, in which we choose to believe what our tribe believes because we think that is what we are supposed to believe. At that point we are no longer thinking—we are being programmed.

Building Bridges across Politics

We are far better served as a country when people from both sides work together to generate solutions. Our Pledge of Allegiance ends with the words "with liberty and justice for all." As a rule, conservatives tend to focus on liberty, and liberals tend to focus on justice. But either one, left unchecked, can create problems. Liberty unchecked can lead to massive disparities in society. We have determined as a society that there are times when we have to be sure that people do not sell meat with maggots in it, or paint schools with lead-based paint. We understand that it serves us to have a common agreement to drive at certain speeds or otherwise limit people's freedom. Yet at the same time, a focus on justice without a consideration of people's liberty can lead to excessive governmental influence on people's daily lives. The challenge is, how do we get the best of both? How do we create healthy bridging with people who are on the other side of the political divide?

History has taught us that the kind of moral tribes that we see being formed can be dangerous. They can give us war, justify genocide, cause political upheaval, and stoke hatred and bigotry, especially when they are contained and exclusive. On the other hand, when our tribal consciousness is broader and belonging is more inclusive, our shared identity can lead us to greatness. How do we get the latter and eschew the former?

It is important to realize that there are certain people you may never reach. This is not to suggest that you should ignore concerns about personal safety if, for example, someone has threatened violence against people like you. However, when we feel there is a chance to reach across the aisle to make a connection, here are some things that can help.

Start by understanding your own biases. If we are going to make conscious choices to become more civil in our society, we have to develop a deeper understanding of our own biases. Are we thinking or reacting? In *Everyday Bias*, I wrote extensively about ways that we can learn to manage our biases.[27] Like with any other bias, being aware of our political biases is the first step in helping us manage them. That requires slowing down our thinking a bit and avoiding knee-jerk reactions. We have to develop *constructive uncertainty* and consider the possibility that there may be another point of view or other information that we are not aware of. I am not suggesting that we cannot have a strong point of view, just that we remember that *it is a point of view.*

Work from a set of principles, not just what justifies you in feeling "right." All too often, once we have made our own point of view sacred, we lose our moral center. If people on the other side are "evil" instead of just having an opinion that's different from ours, it is easy to justify almost anything. For example, I believe fervently in freedom of speech. My life experience has taught me that the same process that I might use to stifle somebody else can later be used to stifle me. I am troubled when I see excessive political correctness, or people saying that certain groups should not be able to march peacefully.[28] I remember all of the marches for civil rights, for women's rights, against the Vietnam War, and for other causes. Work from a core foundation of principles, *even when it doesn't suit you!* Remember, the more we can define ourselves as a larger tribe (Americans), the more our need to belong will engender civility.

Get to know the other point of view. As we know, we are deeply influenced by the informational echo chambers we live in. Take the time to really understand where others are coming from on both sides of the issue. It is critically important that, rather than focusing only on *what* people on the other side of the political divide believe, we focus on *why* they believe it—and that we apply the same inquiry to ourselves. Are we being true to our own beliefs, or are we just stuck in the desire to be right? Author George R. R. Martin has said, "Nobody is a villain in their own story. We're all the heroes of our own stories." If we can get to know their point of view, from their framework, we may have ways to find common ground that we cannot see when we are more committed to being right.

Don't conflate a voter with everything his or her candidate believes or stands for. Just because somebody voted for a candidate doesn't mean that person supports everything about the candidate. Nor does it mean that person supports everything the candidate believes in. It may make you feel better and more righteous to say, "Well, if they can vote for _____, then . . . ," but for the people I interviewed, on both sides of the political divide, in most cases their vote was not a 100 percent decision. It may often have been the lesser of two evils. If we can avoid objectifying people as, for example, "Trump supporters" or "Clinton supporters" and start to interact with them as individuals, we are far more likely to avoid stereotyping and at least open the possibility of finding common ground.

Move from position-taking to problem-solving. If we really want to work on solving problems, we have to focus on issues, not personalities. Sometimes personality can become an issue, but health care, taxation, gun control, and other similar issues are not personalities. Paying attention to times when you are getting triggered by personality rather than focusing on ideas is a critical part of the process. When we get fixated on the person we are dealing with rather than his or her ideas, we are far less likely to be able to hear something with which we can agree.

Take "the other" to lunch. Begin to reach out to individuals who represent the other point of view and create a structure for getting a better understanding of what each other is thinking and feeling. One model that I have adapted and found to be very effective was originally created by author Elizabeth Lesser. I have used this four-step process in some pretty intense mediations. Start by inviting someone to get together, and agree on a set of ground rules: "We are not here to persuade, defend, or interrupt. We are here to be curious, to be authentic, and to listen." Then take turns answering these five questions, giving each person the same amount of time:

1. *What is something that you admire about the other person?*
   This may seem like a stretch, but if you really couldn't see anything positive in the person, then chances are that you would not be talking to him or her. Beginning with that acknowledgment honors the relationship and enhances the listening on both sides.
2. *What are some of your life experiences that have led you to feel the way you do?*
   Really listen and try to understand not only what the person believes but *why* he or she believes it. This can help as you seek common ground.

3. *What issues deeply concern you or even scare you?*
   This is critical. As I discussed in earlier chapters, most human reactiveness is fear-based. If you can get under the reaction and share your fears, you will be much more likely to connect than if you focus on the strategies you have developed to protect those concerns.
4. *What have you always wanted to ask someone from "the other side"?*
   So often we are working on assumptions that may or may not be accurate. Ask the questions you've always wanted to ask, and answer the other person's.
5. *Is there anything you would like to say to "clean up" the past?*
   After having actually listened to each other, we can see that we may have said or done things that dishonor the other person. Take responsibility for those things so that you can move forward without that baggage.

Try to disagree without being disagreeable. There is no denying how difficult this is, particularly in the light of our current cultural dissonance. The more we can keep the conversation in a civil tone, however, the greater the chance we have of understanding each other and finding common ground. Some of the relationships I value the most in the world are people with whom I can disagree and still be very connected.

Get engaged and work on sustainable systemic change. Work to support organizations that are trying to change structural and systemic factors that contribute to our societal discord. This may mean for some, ensuring voting rights, or developing a better system to control money in politics, or whatever you think creates a more equitable system. Don't be a bystander.

You can also work with organizations that are trying to open dialogue and break away from the intense "us versus them" nature of our political world. That might include organizations such as Citizen University (www.citizenuniversity.us), No Labels (www.nolabels .org), and the National Institute for Civil Discourse (http://nicd

.arizona.edu), among others. Support the efforts of politicians who are trying to work together across the aisle, like the forty members of the House's "Problem Solver" caucus, which is being cochaired by current Reps. Tom Reed (R-NY) and Josh Gottheimer (D-NJ).

Be willing to forgive and apologize. Be willing to admit when you are wrong. This may be the greatest flaw in our current situation. People have gotten so attached to being right that they refuse to even consider admitting when they've made mistakes. If you messed up by becoming overly aggressive, getting caught up in the emotions of the moment, or whatever, apologize. And also be willing to forgive. As Nelson Mandela said, "Courageous people do not fear forgiving, for the sake of peace."

Leave room for change. Perhaps the only certainty of life is that things will change, both within each of us and in the world around us. As John F. Kennedy said, "Change is the law of life. And those who look only to the past or present are certain to miss the future."[29] It's so important to keep an open mind, keep reevaluating the current realities, and not let your politics define you. When politics becomes an identity, we start looking for ways to justify and stop looking for ways to learn.

The political realities we are dealing with are troubling, but it is our responsibility as citizens to pull ourselves out of the quagmire of it.

Politics may divide us, but often politics is the extension of our more deeply held beliefs and values. In Chapter 3 we'll be looking at the source of some of those beliefs and values.

Chapter 3

Why Do We See the World
the Way We Do?

If you're treated a certain way you become a certain kind of person.
If certain things are described to you as being real they're real for you whether
they're real or not.

— JAMES BALDWIN

I have established how important belonging is to human beings. One of the most important ways that we form these connections is through a common morality, a common set of values. How we see ourselves and determine what is important to us and the groups to which we belong is a fundamental part of our orientation to life. Questions of moral choice, such as how we decide between right and wrong and how we make some of life's hardest decisions, are undoubtedly some of the most intricate, multifaceted problems we are likely to come across, and they are deeply rooted in our relationships to the groups to which we belong. Our morality plays such an important role in connecting us to others that it is important for us to look at how our morality shapes the world we see.

Let's consider one of the most famous thought experiments in human ethics, the Trolley Dilemma.[1] You see a trolley car coming down the track at a high rate of speed. When you look down the track in the direction the trolley is heading, you see five workers whom you have no way of warning about the oncoming trolley. Assume that they will be killed if the trolley is not diverted. However, you are standing in front of a lever that you can pull to turn the trolley onto a different set of tracks on which there is only one worker. Is it acceptable for you to pull the lever and redirect the trolley onto the track where the one worker is standing, knowing that this worker will consequently be killed?

Most people will have little difficulty making this choice. The equation is painful, but pretty simple. Should I save one life, or five? We might still feel bad that somebody had to die, but the death of one is clearly preferable to the death of five.

Let's now consider the most notable variation of the original experiment, which poses a similar question but with a small yet very meaningful twist.[2] The same runaway trolley is barreling down the same track toward the same five workers who will be killed if nothing is done. In this version, rather than standing by a lever next to the track, you are standing on a footbridge that overlooks the track. Also on the footbridge is another large person whose body, hypothetically, could stop the trolley if he were being pushed off the bridge onto the tracks, but he would be killed. Assume that there would be no possible negative legal ramifications. Considering these altered circumstances, what would you do now? What *should* you do?

The scenarios are arguably identical from a utilitarian perspective, in that the choice is between one life being lost or five lives being lost. However, if you are like most people, you may have experienced the two situations very differently. While the overwhelming majority of people would easily pull the lever to save five people, far fewer feel comfortable *pushing* somebody off a bridge and killing them, even though they lead to the same consequences.

Now consider one other question: Would your answer have been different if there was nobody there to see you make the decision or to know about it afterward?

What's so interesting about these hypotheticals is that they confront us with one of life's great questions: What are our values, and how do they dictate our behavior? There may be no real difference in consequences between the two choices, but there is *something* about having to actually perform the action ourselves that calls up a different question: *What am I actually willing to do?* Is there a difference between doing something physical versus doing something less directly, such as pulling a lever? Is there a difference between having to do something yourself or letting somebody else do it? The question of how directly we ourselves have to act impacts decisions we make every day, as well as broader societal decisions.

The late Brandeis University sociologist Philip Slater identified this phenomenon as the "Toilet Assumption":

> The notion that unwanted matter, unwanted difficulties, unwanted complexities and obstacles will disappear if they're removed from our immediate field of vision . . . Our approach to social problems is to decrease their visibility: out of sight, out of mind. This is the real foundation of racial segregation, especially in its most extreme case, the Indian "reservation."
>
> . . . Prior to the widespread use of the flush toilet all of humanity was daily confronted with the immediate reality of human waste and its disposal. They knew where it was and how it got there. . . . As with physical waste, so with social problems.[3]

If our adherence to our values is impacted by whether or not we have to observe the impact of our choices, as Slater suggests, does anonymity also impact our choices? Is there a difference between being seen or being anonymous? Think about how you deal with homeless people when you encounter them. Do you give them money? If not, do you still acknowledge them, or do you avoid interacting with them in order to avoid having to say no?

Furthermore, our sense of right and wrong is influenced by our sense of belonging, as we'll explore in the next section.

The Social Theater

We are social creatures, and one of the most potent yet fragile weapons for a social actor is his or her reputation. Reputations are of such immense importance because they signal whether an individual is trustworthy and could prove to be a valuable friend or a deceitful manipulator whom we would do best to avoid, all before we even have the opportunity to interact with that person. Our reputations are like our social resumes, and people are constantly reviewing them. Humans spend up to 65 percent of their conversation time discussing the triumphs, failures, and dalliances of other humans—in other words, gossiping.[4]

Although it is commonly thought of as a frivolous waste of time, gossip actually has a great deal of evolutionary significance. As Harvard psychologist Joshua Greene notes, gossip is a critical mechanism for maintaining social control because it encourages individuals to treat each other fairly (or at least to be sure that they appear to do so publicly) in the hopes of cultivating positive reputations.[5] If I develop a reputation as a trustworthy and cooperative partner, people will be far more likely to interact with me, allowing me to build connections and grow a healthy social network. If I develop a reputation as a liar and a cheat, people will avoid engaging with me, leaving me socially isolated, vulnerable, and ultimately at a significant competitive disadvantage.

Does the way others see us determine our sense of right and wrong and how consistent our actions are with our values? The inquiry into this question takes us back centuries to Plato and his older brother Glaucon. In Plato's *Republic*, Glaucon raises the question through contemplating a magical artifact called the Ring of Gyges.[6] The ring gave its owner the power to become invisible at will. Through the story of the ring, Plato and Glaucon debated whether people would act more or less morally when they were being watched. Plato argued that invisibility would not make people act less morally, while Glaucon disagreed, arguing that being watched by others plays a large role in our willingness to engage or avoid engaging in immoral acts. It appears Glaucon was right: our public perception is another way that our need to belong influences our behavior.

Due to the tremendous survival impact of maintaining a strong reputation, humans are far better behaved when they know that they might be watched. *Impression management,* a concept first introduced by sociologist Erving Goffman, is the attempt to regulate behavior so that you may be judged more favorably by potential onlookers.[7] What's remarkable is that impression management strategies not only are deployed when we consciously recognize that we have caught the eye of onlookers but also are activated by subconscious triggers that may suggest the possibility of being judged. Studies have shown that people are less likely to cheat in a well-lit room as opposed to a dimly lit one, that people are more likely to offer to help a stranger in the presence of a security camera, and that children are less likely to steal Halloween candy when the bowl is placed in front of a mirror.[8] Each of these manipulations has one thing in common: making our deeds more visible to interested onlookers. Duke University behavioral economist Dan Ariely cites an experiment in which his students were more likely to honestly grade their own exams after they had been simply asked to read the Ten Commandments before the exercise.[9] Even the potential of "heavenly oversight" impacted their behavior!

We are so attuned to the potential of social judgment that impression management can be activated by even the subtlest of manipulations. Psychologists utilize an economic exercise known as the Dictator Game to study social interactions and economic exchanges.[10] The game is simple: the participant (the "dictator") is given a certain amount of money and is permitted to allocate as much (or as little) to his or her partner as they see fit. Some give nothing and take everything, most give a little bit, and very few give most of their allotment. In one experiment, there was a very slight manipulation: some participants saw three dots arranged in the shape of a triangle as they were deciding how much to give, while others saw three dots arranged in the shape of an upside-down triangle (see Figure 3.1).[11] If you were to look at the two shapes, you would notice the one on the right bears the faintest resemblance to a face, with the top two dots representing eyes and the bottom a nose or a mouth. Surely something this subtle couldn't activate impression management, could it? It absolutely could, and did. People exposed to the upside-down, face-like triangle were three times more likely to give to their partners than those exposed to the neutral, non-face-like triangle.

It is easy to see how bonded relationships reinforce the impact of social judgment. If I am relating to people with whom I deeply identify, I will naturally want to align my moral code with theirs so that we can

Figure 3.1 The Dictator Game

coexist more easily. In fact, because we are bonded, the very things that encouraged the development of their moral code were probably similar to those that developed my own. It is much easier to develop a different moral code from those that I do not feel a strong connection to; indeed, that may be the very factor that gets in the way of our bonding.

The (Not Really) Blank Slate

If our ability to make moral decisions is based on our exposure to the impact of our decisions and to our visibility to the people around us, how then do our moral foundations form? Though the trajectory of our moral, social, and cultural development is largely influenced by *how* we are raised, it is also significantly impacted by *who* we are, that is, by our genetic makeup. While nurture undoubtedly plays a defining role, the impact of nature—and especially genetics—has been obfuscated for quite some time. Despite the fact that it often is uncomfortable to acknowledge, the concept of the human being as a tabula rasa, or blank slate, is largely a myth that has been overturned by scientific research.[12]

What's fascinating about our aversion to acknowledging the role genes play is that it is typically aroused only when referenced in relation to our brains, as opposed to any other part of our physiology. People willingly admit that a couple who both stand over seven feet tall would be more likely to have a tall child than a couple who both fail to reach five feet. If we were to ask similar questions about, for instance, political orientation, many would be hard-pressed to admit that a child born to two ultraconservative parents would be more likely to be born with a predisposition toward conservatism than a child born to two extremely liberal parents. This is, however, exactly what scientists have found to be true. Our moral code may well be somewhat genetically programmed to have us align with those with whom our sense of belonging is essential.

The best methodology for assessing nature-versus-nurture claims is examining differences between sets of identical and fraternal twins. Fraternal twins share 50 percent of their DNA—the same as any other siblings—while identical twins share 100 percent of their genetic material. Due to this, any differences that emerge can likely be attributed to environmental influences. If genetics played no role in our cognitive dispositions, identical and fraternal twins should be equally similar in personalities, temperament, and things like political orientation. But is this the case? Decidedly not.

Not only do identical twins have more similar political preferences than fraternal twins, but their political outlooks will continue to correlate strongly even when they are raised apart.[13] The same cannot be said for fraternal twins.

While many understandably attempt to sustain the blank slate doctrine due to fears of legitimizing prejudicial attitudes or horrific practices like eugenics, or perhaps simply as a well-intentioned attempt at political correctness, the blank slate doctrine itself can also serve to justify some of the social, economic, and racial inequality that plagues our society. A blank slate mentality is often used to dilute notions of systemic injustice, because if we all (ostensibly) started off the same, then one can more easily argue that "*my* position in society is simply a product of my effort and *yours* is simply a reflection of your lack of ambition." In fact, multiple factors lead to a person's success, and many of them are out of our control. For example, I am six feet five inches tall. Research as well as personal experience suggests that being tall is an advantage not just in our society but in societies all over the world. People attribute strength, leadership, and confidence to height. One study showed that an inch of height is worth almost $800 per year in corporate America.[14] And yet I had nothing to do with my height.

Development of Moral Values

Evolution has often tended to favor ruthless, competitive strategies, although that does not preclude it from promoting selectively cooperative strategies as well. Individuals who were willing to cooperate, and who were discerning regarding the people they chose to cooperate with, stood to gain a tremendous tactical advantage during our evolutionary past. The question we might explore is, who are people more likely to support: people they identify as being a part of their group, or people they identify as the "other"?

If we look at all of this from an ontological perspective—that is, from the perspective of our way of being—we can see how the human mind develops this sense of perspective. We encounter a vast array of "rules to live by" over the course of our lifetime. As we are exposed to these, we create our own internal "book of rules." It makes perfect sense that the rules we will tend to adopt are those that are part of the social system around us, beginning with family and culture, because understanding and living with those rules will put us in a more harmonious relationship with the people who are most essential to our survival.

We internalize some of these rules into our fundamental personality structure, the component that Sigmund Freud called the *superego.* The superego functions as an ongoing bench of judges, almost like an internalized Supreme Court, which holds the voice of our parents, our culture, and society ingrained in our psyche.[15] This inner court holds the laws, both conscious and unconscious, that include our ideal ways of being, our spiritual goals, and our conscience. It is pretty easy to identify the superego. Think about a time when somebody cut you off on the highway. My guess is that, if you're like me, some part of you considered reacting with a particular finger on your hand. But the superego probably stepped in at the moment and whispered, "Remember road rage," preventing you from taking that action.

This internalized book of rules actually helps create the way we interact with the world. In order to keep us safe, it begins to create a schematic framework that shapes what we need, what we see and what we don't see, what we seek and what we find. The collection of these schemas results in a filter that shapes the world we experience. UC Berkeley philosopher John Searle referred to this as our *background.*[16] Our background is shaped by a set of abilities, capacities, tendencies, and dispositions that each of us has developed over the course of our lifetimes, influenced by our cultures, our personal experiences, our group experiences, and the various institutions we have been exposed to. All of these things shape the world that we see, and how we react to that world.

I am a musician, and my wife is a painter. If we are listening to a piece of music, my wife may say, "That's a great song!" However, with my musical background, I may be paying attention to the way the bass beat corresponds to the percussionist, or how the voices are harmonizing— things that she may not even notice. On the other hand, if we are in an art gallery looking at a painting, she may talk about how "the brushstrokes blend into each other. And look at the colorization the artist used along with the shading," when all I see is "pretty picture." People's backgrounds are influenced by their race, gender, generation, sexual orientation, socioeconomic status, and any number of other identities or experiences.

All of these influences combine to shape what Swiss psychologist Carl Jung referred to as our *persona,* the word coming from the Latin word for "mask."[17] Goffman saw the theater, in this sense, as a powerful metaphor for our interactions with other human beings. Each of us dons a mask that we use for interacting with the world. Each of us shapes our persona(lity) in whatever way allows us to feel safer, more secure, and more effective in accomplishing our goals. Some of this is conscious, but by far the larger portion is unconscious. It becomes our way of being in relation to the world.

However, very few people can exist with personas that are completely distinct from those of people around them. Our natural compulsion to act like the people around us leads to *emotional contagion*, the tendency to automatically mimic and synchronize facial expressions, vocalizations, postures, and movements with those of another person and, consequently, to converge emotionally.[18] In other words, emotional contagion involves "catching" another's emotions, similar to how one can catch another's cold. This emotional contagion helps us connect with others. The ripple effects of emotional contagion have been observed in individuals, groups, and even dogs.[19] It is as if we were biologically encoded to fit in.

What's perhaps even more intriguing is that science is starting to show that similar contagion-style phenomena are not limited to emotions. Nicholas Christakis and James Fowler have demonstrated that our physical health is profoundly impacted by those with whom we choose to surround ourselves.[20] In a striking series of studies that took place over decades, they simultaneously mapped individuals' social networks alongside their fluctuations in weight and found an extraordinary relationship between the increases in weight of our peers and our own weight gain. Specifically, Christakis and Fowler discovered that an individual's chances of becoming obese increased by 57 percent if he or she had a friend who became obese during the same period. These results could not be attributed to variables such as shared environment or geographic distance; rather, they were specific to the social bond shared by the pairs. The researchers hypothesized that the weight gain of a close friend may act to alter an individual's social norms concerning the acceptability of obesity, therefore permitting the person to gain weight with a reduced fear of social repercussions. Similarly, being in direct contact with an individual undergoing weight gain (presumably via a change in lifestyle) might lead to corresponding shifts in an individual's lifestyle that could contribute to similar trends toward obesity (e.g., alterations in eating habits or exercise schedules).

Most of us have had an experience of this desire to fit in. Perhaps it was the first day at a new school or on a new job. The first thing we often do is, in effect, conduct a social scan of the environment we are in. How are people acting? How should I act in accordance with the way they are acting? What is expected of me?

We can see how these internalized rules might impact the three coworkers we met at the beginning of Chapter 1: Joan, Barry, and Fatima. Joan's internal book of rules is undoubtedly impacted by her Christian faith and her conservative politics, Barry's by his more liberal politics and his relationship with the gay community, and Fatima's by both her cultural background and her Muslim faith. They may agree on some things and disagree vehemently on others. It is possible, for example, that Joan and Fatima may align on their views regarding sexual orientation but disagree on political issues. Barry may agree with Fatima about some political values but disagree around sexual orientation. Joan may perceive Barry as "another American," despite her feelings about his sexual orientation, but see Fatima as an "other." The dynamics are very fluid.

We pick up standards and norms of behavior from people around us, and these can change over a very short period of time. The Nazis were able to change a highly developed culture into a killing machine by consciously and strategically shifting the definition of what was considered "normal." People who saw themselves as good, decent people turned in their Jewish neighbors and in some cases then took their property or moved into their houses. The same happened in 1994 in Rwanda, seemingly overnight. Vital Akimana, a Rwandan refugee, describes his chilling experience as an eleven-year-old as his country turned from a "normal" place into a genocidal state in which 800,000 Tutsi and moder-

ate Hutus were killed and 2 million more had to flee, all within an as-
tonishingly short period of time. His story begins in 1991, when he was
eight years old:

> The change didn't happen at once. It was iterative over a few
> years. The first conflict I experienced was in 1991. People in the
> country had been coexisting pretty happily up to that point, but
> then the radio started to report things like, "We have to stamp
> out the cockroaches who are invading from the mountains" in
> reference to the Tutsis, who made up a large part of the then
> RPF [Rwandan Patriotic Front] guerrillas. I was raised in a
> mixed-tribe home, with a Hutu father and a half-Tutsi mother.
> At first I thought they were really talking about bugs. The me-
> dia started demonizing these groups. There were a series of
> roundups that began in 1991 or 1992, including a friend of my
> dad's who was arrested. At first you saw more and more mili-
> tary buildup, which made people feel some uneasiness about
> their neighbors. When you started to see houses being raided,
> you really didn't know what people had done. There was a com-
> munal fear that took over. Soon they became associated with
> political parties [which were strongly associated with tribal af-
> filiation]. All of a sudden, you had to wear your party's colors
> boldly if you were in the president's party, then the other side
> wore their colors so that people knew whom they could trust.
>
> At some point my dad said we had to leave the house, because
> it wasn't safe. As people were fleeing, we had to be careful who
> we were even walking next to. In 1992–93, due in part to interna-
> tional pressure, the country became a multiparty system, as the
> president was forced to recognize other political establishments
> like the RPF and my mother's party, PSD [Social Democratic
> Party]. Then communities really started to segregate more
> overtly. Near my mom's home area, dissident groups, sanctioned
> by the establishment, held rallies in front of prominent Tutsis'
> homes to intimidate them. You were told that you have to choose
> sides. Our house was initially targeted due to my mother's af-
> filiation with the Social Democratic Party, but when groups like

the CDR [Coalition for the Defense of the Republic] and MRND [Movement for Revolutionary National Development] caught wind that we were half Tutsi they had a field day, holding a rally for over a month. At first when the rallies would happen our neighbors would go shopping for us, bring back food, et cetera. They would also try to protect the house. Tutsis were called "implants" or a "false group" trying to take over the country. Weapons were distributed by the authorities to far-right Hutu groups like the Interahamwe, which was the deadly youth wing of the then MRND. People were aligned by the colors they were wearing. We quickly learned to fear the Red, Black, and Green. Eventually neighbors would shy away, especially when a big show of force was made. It became too dangerous for them and they could be targeted as collaborators.

In 1993, my mother [a leader in the agriculture ministry and a chapter president for the Social Democratic Party] realized it was dangerous. There were a number of assassinations of friends and associates, and neighbors were saying that they couldn't protect us anymore. Supporters were being intimidated. They would change almost overnight. People needed to look like they were part of the people in power. Soon it became about how people looked [e.g., "your nose isn't flat enough" or "you're too tall to be Hutu"]. The radio constantly sent out messages demonizing Tutsis.

In 1994, when people were too intimidated, things really fell apart. Reasonable voices had been silenced. Communities were told, "Produce somebody who is an enemy or we will burn down the community." If you didn't refer to Tutsis as "cockroaches," you were seen as being on the wrong side.

Flat tires and broken car windows, et cetera, started to happen with greater frequency. Hutu government leaders were tacitly supportive of the vandalism. The extremist wing of the political party that the president was a part of, the Interahamwe, were emboldened and more and more prominent with every assassination.

By March 1994, almost all of the leaders of the party that my mother was affiliated with had been assassinated. You could see the change in the strength of the parties by the colors that people were wearing, proudly. By that time the streets were mostly filled with variations of Red and Black. Almost like people wearing swastikas. People became more and more emboldened. As early as this, we heard stories of mixed families that were forced to perpetrate acts of violence against their own family members in order to survive. "Kill your Tutsi wife and half children or you will all die." Tutsis started to hide their family members or send them away.

April 6, 1994, the president's airplane went down and it was like a signal went out for the genocide to begin. If people were harboring Tutsis, they could either join the murder or die themselves. By that time, it became "normal" and commonplace for people to come in with machetes, grenades, and guns and force people to declare their allegiance. We hosted so many families who were on the run from 1993 to early 1994 before the genocide, but after the airplane went down, overnight everything fell completely apart. People were vanishing. For two weeks we were trapped in the house with bullets hailing down. The radio was saying that "any Tutsis you run into should be killed or turned in." The radio was telling people to tear down shrubberies around houses to take away hiding places. A neighbor came to the door and told my father that there was a convoy looking for us, and they couldn't keep them away any longer. That was the last message we got from our neighbors. I don't think they wanted us to be harmed, but they couldn't take the risk of protecting us.

My dad put us in the oldest clothes we had, we covered ourselves with mud and dirt so we didn't look like we were of higher income. Dad took off his glasses so he didn't look intellectual. As we walked down the road, we were stopped at checkpoints. If you were taller and your nose was more European, then you were in trouble because you looked like a Tutsi. My brother was identified as not looking like a Hutu and was sent to the line of people who were going to be killed. My dad took out a bag of sugar, his watch, and money and bargained for my brother's life.

People were told that they had to demonstrate their loyalty by going out and finding a Tutsi to kill, in order to save their own family members. Even if they thought they were wrong in doing this, they still couldn't stand up for their neighbors, so their minds started to come up with justifications so that they didn't have to feel like cowards. It was almost like the more they could make us wrong, the more they could justify their own inability to save us. Having no safe harbor in the capital city nor my mother's home city, we made our way over fifty miles on foot to hide in the countryside with my dad's family. Later we would find out that we were less than twenty miles from one of the largest mass graves.

The entire structure of society had shifted, and what was right became wrong and what was abnormal became normal.

Perhaps the most striking sentence in this tragic story is the final one. This is the power that norms have over our lives. They shape what we see as "normal." They create a schema for us to interpret life through. This schema shapes the behaviors we engage in, the styles we adopt, and the symbols we embody with meaning in virtually any intact group, whether it is the hats that Shriners wear, the frayed jeans and tie-dyed shirts of the 1960s, hairstyles, fads of the day, or belief systems that we adhere to in order to fit in with our group. It occurs in the popularity of certain internet memes today. Notice how quickly we tend to adapt to the norms of the cultures we find ourselves a part of. In the ghastliest of circumstances, behaviors that we would otherwise consider "inhuman" and obviously "wrong" can become normalized. Think about things that have been "normal" at one time or another: slavery, distributing smallpox-contaminated blankets to Native Americans to "control population growth," denying women the right to vote, removing organs to "cure" mental illness, Jim Crow laws in the South, lobotomies, and homosexuality being officially classified as a mental illness by the American Psychiatric Association. "Normal" is what we define it to be, based on what we expect, what we see the most of, and what serves our overall group needs.

Consider Matthew Heimbach and Alvin Bamberger, for example, who were charged with physically assaulting anti-Trump protesters at a campaign rally in Louisville, Kentucky, during the 2016 presidential campaign. Both later sued Trump himself, suggesting that they never would have participated in such acts had they not been encouraged by Trump and his crowd.

> Heimbach claims he was relying "on Trump's authority to order disruptive persons removed," according to documents filed in federal court. Alvin Bamberger is also being sued for allegations he shoved a woman who was protesting Trump. Bamberger filed a counterclaim on Friday stating he had taken action in response to Trump's "urging and inspiration."[21]

> In his filing, Bamberger cited other Trump rallies, saying the president and his campaign "repeatedly urged people attending [the rallies to] remove individuals who were voicing opposition to Trump[']s candidacy" and promised to pay the legal fees of those who removed protesters.[22]

Groups can encourage positive behavior, and they can also justify negative behavior. And because we are social animals, they help determine our sense of right and wrong.

The types of relationships we have with the people in our lives have a large say in how those people's attitudes, beliefs, and behaviors influence us. We are, for example, far more likely to be influenced by people who have power over us, professionally, socially, or in other ways, than by those who are less powerful; more by people whom we bond with more than by those we bridge with; more by those we see or communicate with often than by people whom we rarely see or talk to. What we see flashed before us in the media or through social media impacts us as well.

Our need to fit in can lead us to engage in behavior that shows support for the group perspective. We sometimes call this phenomenon *groupthink*. It occurs when group members irrationally or dysfunctionally make decisions in order to get along in the group, thereby stifling alternative points of view. Some of the earliest research on groupthink used occurrences such as the Bay of Pigs disaster and the attack on Pearl

Harbor as primary case studies; later research looked at the *Challenger* disaster and the Iraq War.[23]

We can quickly see how these different frameworks of thinking play out in some of our biggest controversies. Let's consider, for example, the Black Lives Matter movement. Most people have a viewpoint about this movement, which some call a "black nationalist movement" and others label a "new civil rights movement," depending on the side they're on. However, we are not even arguing over the same words. We may think we are disagreeing about those three words: *Black Lives Matter.* In reality, however, we are arguing over a fourth, invisible word that is different for each side. For some, the four words are "Black Lives Matter *Too!*"—a statement affirming that the rights of African Americans are as important as the rights of anyone else. For others, the four words are "*Only* Black Lives Matter!"—an expression of the narrative that protesters put African American lives above those of others. As long as we are not even arguing about the same thing, there is little chance that the argument can be resolved.

While we often focus on these kinds of differences, we are much more connected than we realize. It is no accident that the same archetypal stories occur in cultures all around the world. A vast body of study in a wide array of fields is proving that we are all connected through various forms that we may not even realize. Carl Jung called this the "collective unconscious," a term he first coined in his 1916 essay, "The Structure of the Unconscious."[24]

Biologist Rupert Sheldrake referred to it as "morphic resonance."[25] Biologist E. O. Wilson discussed what he called "eusociality," the dynamic among certain species (including humans) that creates a "hive" mentality.[26] Scientists from Albert Einstein and Max Planck to those of the present day have talked about universal connections in physics. It seems very clear that the human species is connected at a level that is not always visible, and so we are not always aware of it.

Our patterns of moral development, and our patterns of emotional connection to others are all deeply ingrained in our ability to feel a sense of belonging. Let's explore how this impacts perhaps the greatest source of our social discord: race.

Chapter 4

Power, Privilege, Race, and Belonging

I imagine one of the reasons people cling to their hates so stubbornly is because they sense, once hate is gone, they will be forced to deal with pain.

—JAMES BALDWIN

The past is never dead. It's not even past.

—WILLIAM FAULKNER

Our Munchester Industries trio, Joan, Barry, and Fatima, represent the intersectionality of our identities in a powerful way. Joan is white, and also a woman and Christian; any one of these identities might predominate, depending upon the circumstances she finds herself in. The same holds for Barry's white, Jewish, gay, and male identities, and for Fatima's Muslim and female identities, as well as her status as a woman of color. All of them are significant, but none more so than race.

Much has been and will be written about why Donald Trump was able to pull off one of the greatest electoral upsets in history, but underneath all the very complex narratives that one can tell about the election, there is a very simple one that is inescapable: this election was a testament to how race is an aspect of our lives that simultaneously generates a profound experience of belonging and is the essence of "us versus them." It also is a reflection on the dynamics of power and privilege that exist within our historical racial hierarchy. What do the voting patterns that we saw in the 2016 election, patterns that have been relatively consistent for almost forty years, tell us about belonging in America by race? Are we even one country when it comes to racial attitudes? It's fair to say that race in America has historically been a domain where our sense of bonding and bridging has been more unhealthy than healthy.

Race has served as a point of separation since the creation of the United States as an entity, and it continues to this very day. As I write this chapter, it has been a little over a week since a young white female protester was murdered by a white supremacist in Charlottesville, Virginia, after one of the larger and more visible white supremacy/white nationalist rallies in recent U.S. history.

Racial disparities are nothing new to the American experiment. In 1831, when Alexis de Tocqueville came to the United States to study the relatively new democracy, he made the following observations:

> The human beings who are scattered over this space do not form, as in Europe, so many branches of the same stock. Three races, naturally distinct, and, I might almost say, hostile to each other, are discoverable among them at the first glance. Almost insurmountable barriers had been raised between them by education and law, as well as by their origin and outward characteristics; but fortune has brought them together on the same soil, where, although they are mixed, they do not amalgamate, and each race fulfills its destiny apart.
>
> Among these widely differing families of men the first that attracts attention, the superior in intelligence, in power, and in enjoyment, is the white, or European, the MAN preeminently so called; below him appear the Negro and the Indian. These two unhappy races have nothing in common, neither birth, nor features, nor language, nor habits. Their only resemblance lies in their misfortunes. Both of them occupy an equally inferior position in the country they inhabit; both suffer from tyranny; and if their wrongs are not the same, they originate from the same authors.[1]

This is the story of the American experience, and the differences in the treatment of racial groups have maintained themselves in every aspect of American life since its inception. One hundred and thirty years after Tocqueville published his thesis, African American writer James Baldwin wrote:

> It comes as a great shock to discover that the country which is your birthplace and to which your life and identity has not, in its whole system of reality, evolved any place for you. The disaffection and the gap between people, only on the basis of their skins, begins there and accelerates throughout your whole lifetime. You realize that you are 30 and you are having a terrible time. You have been through a certain kind of mill and the most serious effect is again not the catalogue of disaster—the policeman, the taxi driver, the waiters, the landlady, the banks, the insurance companies, the millions of details 24 hours of every day which spell out to you that you are a worthless human being. It is not that. By that time, you have begun to see it happening in your daughter, your son or your niece or your nephew. You are 30 by now and nothing you have done has helped you escape the trap. But what is worse is that nothing you have done, and as far as you can tell nothing you can do, will save your son or your daughter from having the same disaster and from coming to the same end.[2]

Over time, the demographic patterns of the country have changed. The genocidal annihilation of the Native Americans has left them far smaller in number. Immigration by Asian Americans, beginning with thousands coming to work on sugar and pineapple plantations and building the railroads in the nineteenth century, and Hispanics, many coming originally as farm workers and domestic laborers, have changed the racial makeup of the country from Tocqueville's time. Similar patterns of immigration impacted other racial groups as well. But those changes in demographics have not changed the most fundamental aspect of understanding belonging, or a lack thereof, in America: that the American dream has been built upon the platform of *white supremacy*.

What Is White Supremacy?

I know that the two words *white supremacy* trigger an intense emotional reaction from many people. One cannot talk about the American experience, and certainly one cannot talk about belonging in America, without recognizing race as a factor in how we bond, how we bridge, and especially how we have elements of our culture that rarely connect with each other at all.

The Merriam-Webster dictionary defines the term *white supremacy* as "the belief that white people are superior to those of all other races, especially the black race, and should therefore dominate society." This has been the case throughout our history. The indigenous population of the continent was not only moved from the lands they had occupied for centuries but also devastated by European diseases and an active policy of genocide for hundreds of years. Africans were brought as slaves and treated as such until being legally emancipated in 1863, but they were not declared equal citizens under the law in every sense until more than a hundred years later. Others have come for various economic and political reasons over time. Still, the question of which race is on top of the social structure has remained unchanged since the beginning.

The reason many people react strongly to the term *white supremacy* is that they assume the term implies intention on the part of all white people to hold people of other races as less than them, and an assumption that it implies that every white person has it easier than every person of color. Neither is necessarily the case. The reality that white supremacy exists doesn't mean that all white people are white supremacists. White supremacy is a system and an ontological framework even more than a structure of beliefs. It defines our way of being about race. It involves the systemic advantage of one group over others and is carried out in various ways on a daily basis throughout the culture of the country.

The great narrative of America has always been the "melting pot," the notion that different people have come and gotten all mixed together into one homogeneous kind of person and culture. This is a myth. For the most part, people came to this country and formed various communities that reflected their "home" culture. Colin Woodard suggests that we actually have formed ourselves into eleven distinct regional cultures in North America, and that doesn't even include the different subcultures that occur within those regional cultures.[3] Many people who come from large cities, especially on the coasts, know that cities have had, and in many cases still do have, neighborhoods that were famously segregated: various areas called "Chinatown," "Little Italy," "Polish Town," or "Japan Town," and parts of cities that were Jewish, black, or Hispanic. Most people in major population centers experience these enclaves.

Throughout it all, the dominant operating culture of the country has remained white. When we look at the system that has been created, most of the patterns of immigration of people of color have supported the development of that system of white supremacy. Not only did African slaves support the development of the plantation culture of the South, but African Americans also supported northern industrial development, as well as building many of the most famous attractions in the United States, including the White House. Mexican American immigrants, as well as others, provided the labor to develop orchards and farms on the West Coast and southern crescent. Asian workers helped build the railroads, as did the Irish, and on and on. The American story is a story of race, and inside that story, the plot is one of the supremacy of white people over all of the others who were here before and since the arrival of white Europeans.

This is where the Faulkner quote at the head of this chapter comes into play. The past is not dead in America. It is played out every day in the narrative that we have about each other as groups and individuals, and in the way our separateness affects how we deal with issues ranging from legislation to statues and monuments. It forms the basis of how each of us, regardless of our group, projects that past into the present through the way it guides our interpretation of the things that are happening around us and to us. It creates barriers to healthy bridging across race. Because, as the historian George Santayana purportedly said, "Those who cannot remember the past are condemned to repeat it," it is worth considering how our present has been informed by the past.

The overall "mainstream" narrative that has shaped the United States has not aligned with the actual lived experience of many people in our country. Virtually everybody who was raised in the United States has been exposed to the narrative of the American dream—the grand experiment of a country and a culture formed by the combining of many different cultures into one, and in which anybody can be successful if he or she is willing to work hard enough for it. The narrative was further enhanced by things like the stories written by Horatio Alger Jr. after the Civil War that told tales of impoverished people "lifting themselves up by their bootstraps" and finding happiness and success. The motto of our country, "E pluribus unum"—Latin for "out of many, one"—was deeply ingrained in our collective belief system, even as the truth of the experience has been so different from that for so many. This has created an inherent conflict between the spoken narrative and those who have benefitted from it, on one side, and the lived experience of so many people who have not benefitted, on the other. We live inside our narrative, but because the narrative hasn't always aligned with the truth, and because many people buy the myth more than the reality, a dissonance gets created, both internally and among groups of people. When we don't fully know our story, we can't truly own it. And when we don't fully own our story, our story owns us.

This is both an individual experience and a collective experience. One part of the story is what has happened to each one of us over the course of our lives. Another part, just as important, is the part of our story that is shaped by our collective experience. A black man does not need to have the personal experience of being shot by the police in order to have a flash of fear when encountering police, because he is aware that it has happened disproportionately to other black men. White people, on the other hand, may be aware of and sympathetic to that history, *but they can never experience it in the same way.*

Part of the development of any system is the development of a set of rules that governs how we are supposed to act. That includes not only behavioral but also moral guidelines. As a country, we have been challenged by the fact that those rules have been different for white people and people of color, and even as the rules have been legally realigned in an attempt to eliminate most of the instances where they were different, they still have been internalized differently by both groups, influencing how the other group is perceived.

Our view tends to occur to each of us as *the* view. The more we are a part of the dominant group in any culture, the more we believe that our view is the "right" one. This "right" view is generally taught in schools. Leaders typically share this view. Those very same dynamics contribute greatly to the development of blind spots on the part of people in the dominant group when it comes to the difficulties and challenges that people in nondominant groups face in having to live with the impact of those rules. As a result, we're torn further apart.

Bias

There are many ways that cultures maintain their sense of belonging within groups and of separateness between groups. Two of the most powerful are bias and privilege. If we think about how our cultural narratives are acquired and maintained, only a small percentage of that is conscious. We don't have to think about what is "right" on a daily, action-by-action basis because we have been habituated to act and think in particular ways: these *are* the *right* ways to be, to do, and to act as part of our group. Some of these are cultural norms that have been handed down from one generation to the next. Certain aspects of language become commonplace. The way we look, act, dress, and wear our hair is part of what it is to be a member of *our* group. When groups are living in closer proximity, with more and more interaction between them, these can lead to conflicts that show up in puzzling and sometimes difficult ways—for example, a Sikh employee of a fast-food restaurant being terminated for not being willing to shave his beard, which in his religion is a symbol of devotion.

Our unconscious narrative naturally leads to the formation of unconscious bias. As I wrote about extensively in *Everyday Bias,* bias in and of itself is neither good nor bad. We know from studying the neuro and cognitive science behind bias that the brain learns to make very quick decisions about situations that we are in, primarily to keep us safe. It also conserves energy, which is critically important because the brain consumes such a huge part of the body's energy. Bias gives us the ability not to have to deal with every situation in life as if it were brand-new and therefore required research, speculation, or testing. We know that if somebody is coming toward us with a glowering expression and hands balled up in fists, that person is likely to be angry and thinking of causing us harm. Making that determination quickly might save us from being harmed.

When we grow up in a culture of white dominance, it is understandable that many of our biases would support that culture—for example, by assigning positive thoughts and feelings to white people and negative thoughts and feelings to people of color. Hundreds of studies over the past two decades have established that this is true. We are mostly unaware of the assumptions that we make about others. Our lack of consciousness about such associations does not prevent us from demonstrating behaviors that reflect such biases. Our actions, in many cases, really do speak louder than our words.

A research team at the University of Pennsylvania's Wharton School of Business emailed 6,500 professors in eighty-nine academic disciplines at the top 259 schools in the country, pretending to be students. The emails were identical except for the names of the students in the email. The names were chosen by their association with certain ethnic, racial, and cultural identities—for example, Brad Anderson, LaToya Brown, Juanita Martinez, Sonali Desai, Mei Chen. They then followed the responses to determine if there would be any difference between the responses of the professors relative to the groups associated with the names in question.

The results were clear. Names that would be normally associated with white men (e.g., Brad Anderson) were 25 percent more likely to get a response to their request than those that reflected names that would be more generally associated with women or people from other racial groups.[4] In addition, the study showed that professors in private universities, in business schools, and in higher-salaried subject areas outside the humanities showed a higher level of bias than the norm. The highest level of negative bias was found to exist toward Asian students, despite the tendency of many people to think of Asians as the "model minority."

Another study sponsored by the National Bureau of Economic Research found significant differences in how people of different races are treated by the police.[5] White police officers were found to be 17 percent more likely to use their hands with blacks, 18 percent more likely to push them into walls, 16 percent more likely to use handcuffs, 19 percent more likely to draw their weapons, 18 percent more likely to push them to the ground, 24 percent more likely to point a weapon at them, and 25 percent more likely to use pepper spray or a baton.

Researchers at Yale University and Central Connecticut State University discovered that both Asian American and black medical students were less likely to be chosen to be members of Alpha Omega Alpha, a medical student honor society. Even when controlling for other factors (such as community service activities, test scores, and leadership experience), the researchers found that Asian Americans were about one-half as likely and blacks less than one-fifth as likely as whites to make the honor society; Hispanics were only 79 percent as likely.[6] Since many medical school residency programs use membership in this honor society as a criterion for acceptance, this type of bias is career-impacting.

In almost twenty years of researching and observing bias in action, I can definitively say that the results of these studies are more the norm than an aberration. There have been hundreds of studies that show the same thing: we tend to be more positive toward in-group members and more negative toward those who are in groups outside of our own. Some members of nondominant groups may even have been socialized to favor the dominant culture. When one group has more people, more power, and more authority than others, this dynamic serves to keep the social structure in place by imposing a huge imbalance. And while biases affecting a person's career trajectory are serious, nothing becomes more serious than when biases and dynamics like this actually impact whether people live or die.

A University of California, Davis study found that there is "evidence of a significant bias in the killing of unarmed black Americans relative to unarmed white Americans, in that the probability of being black, unarmed, and shot by police is about 3.49 times the probability of being white, unarmed, and shot by police." The study also found that "there is no relationship between county-level racial bias in police shootings and crime rates (even race-specific crime rates), meaning that the racial bias observed in police shootings in this data set is not explainable as a response to local-level crime rates."[7]

Externalized bias causes people of color to lose jobs, housing, their health, and their lives. To support the notion that we are better than another, and especially for us to abuse, enslave, or discriminate against another, we have to dehumanize that other. My wife and I have a small farm. One of our neighbors with a smaller piece of property asked if he could keep some cows on our land, a request to which we readily agreed. When we asked him if the cows had names he laughed, as if it were a city-slicker question. "These are beef cows," he said. "You don't name something that you'll be eating."

As insignificant as that may sound relative to cows, it actually is true of people as well. Just as it is harder to kill and eat a cow when you have anthropomorphized it by giving it a name, it is also harder to oppress people when we acknowledge their full humanity. This is precisely why the military rule about not fraternizing with the enemy ensures that soldiers learn little or nothing about the personal lives of the individuals they are fighting. It is much harder to kill Mark, who has a wife, two children, and enjoys golfing on the weekends, than it is to kill unnamed "enemy combatants." When we stereotype people, it helps us remember how our respective places in the social order are constructed. If "those people" aren't perceived as being as smart, talented, friendly, or safe as we are, then the social constructs of "us versus them" are easier to follow.

One of the most pernicious ways that this happens is through the development of internalized bias. When people live in a society that does not value them equally, and that message is reinforced almost constantly, it is not unusual for those messages to become internalized. A classic example of this was the doll study conducted by Mamie Phipps Clark and Kenneth Clark that became central in the *Brown v. Board of Education* case that legally desegregated American schools. The Clarks created an experiment based on Mamie Clark's master's thesis. Children were presented with two dolls that were virtually identical, except in skin color, and asked to choose one. Virtually all the children, including the black ones, chose the white doll. The experiment was one of the first that specifically demonstrated internalized racism on the part of black children. (An interesting footnote: Even though the studies were inspired by and mostly conducted by Mamie Phipps Clark, most historians refer to it as the "Kenneth Clark study." A true irony that this landmark study of race relations shows gender bias in the way it is historically referenced.)

Similar studies have shown that this phenomenon of internalized bias can lead to *stereotype threat,* in which the awareness of stereotypes about "people like me" can cause a person to perform at a lower level. This is actually a pervasive problem among people who are in nondominant groups. If I get enough negative messages about "people like me," I may, consciously or unconsciously, start to believe them. Sometimes those messages may even be unintentionally reinforced.

I once conducted a public workshop in which a sixty-something African American woman was one of the participants. The woman had a PhD in social work and had written books on the subject. She was eminently qualified and very successful in her field. When we were doing some work around "self-messaging," she shared that when she was little, her parents had communicated the same mantra that many of my black friends heard growing up: "You have to work twice as hard to be able to be half as successful." This had left her with a drive to always have to do more. Nothing she did was ever enough for her. In the workshop, she realized an even deeper truth: that as a child, she had heard that message and made it mean that she was only half as good! No matter what she did, that inner voice kept criticizing her. Only by becoming aware of that inner critic was she able to appreciate her accomplishments.

Race and the Self-Fulfilling Prophecy

Earlier I discussed the impact of confirmation bias on our perception of people and circumstances. Our perceptions of people based on race are especially susceptible to this bias. The distressing spate of fatal exchanges between police officers and African Americans that have made headlines in the last few years might very well be the result of the dark side of expectations and self-fulfilling prophecies. With a better understanding of how expectations profoundly affect our interactions, we can see how exchanges that start as routine can quickly escalate. Due to the myriad of negative stereotypes attached to young African American men (e.g., that they are aggressive, violent, etc.), an officer is likely to expect resistance and aggression. The officer is consequently likely to adjust his or her approach—consciously or unconsciously—to adapt to this expectation, perhaps by being more directive, authoritative, or suspicious. In turn, a young African American male—who has his own expectations about how police officers treat people who look like him—is more than likely going to respond with anxiety, mistrust, and agitation. These responses only serve to confirm the beliefs of the others, creating a feedback loop that can often have lethal consequences. It is as if both parties experience simultaneous fear reactions. The very notion that these fatal exchanges seem "unprecedented" may be another example of the same phenomenon, because, sadly, African Americans have endured countless examples of these fatal interactions, but white Americans were not societally sensitized to see it, and people did not regularly carry cell phone cameras to record it.

Some may argue that such escalations would never even have the chance to take place were the alleged perpetrator not doing something to garner the attention of an officer in the first place. Increased vigilance in low-income, predominantly minority neighborhoods itself represents a self-fulfilling prophecy. The more an area is monitored, the more likely police are to find something illegal. Even a great driver will likely give an officer a reason to pull him or her over if the officer follows for long enough. Once police make arrests in a given area, their expectations feel justified, their surveillance and vigilance increase, and more arrests are made. Research is now showing that you don't even have to be an actual police officer to be influenced by stereotypic expectations: simply donning the uniform of one will suffice.

Since Trayvon Martin was killed on February 26, 2012, the hoodie has been symbolic of the treatment of young black men. Sukhvinder Obhi and Ciro Civile have shown that students who were asked to wear police uniforms while completing reaction time tasks demonstrated significantly more biased attention to symbols of low socioeconomic status (e.g., a person wearing a hoodie). When students wore the uniform, the presence of the hoodie-wearing individual substantially affected reaction times in a manner that symbols of high socioeconomic status (e.g., a person in a suit) did not. These results were different when students were asked to wear mechanic overalls, indicating there is something specific about dressing like a police officer that affects the way we think and what we notice.[8] This is not unlike the findings from the now famous Stanford Prison Experiment. In 1971 Philip Zimbardo created a simulated prison in the basement of the Stanford University psychology building and chose students to randomly play the roles of prisoners and guards. Zimbardo found that everything from the uniform to the mirrored glasses that the "prison guards" wore affected their behavior in similar ways, encouraging the "guards" to become more violent and abusive and the "prisoners" to become more docile and depressed.[9]

Even at a very young age, children can be "typed" in this way. Researchers at the Yale Child Study Center asked preschool teachers to watch a video of four children, two black and two white, in a preschool environment. The teachers were told, "We are interested in learning about how teachers detect challenging behavior in the classroom. Sometimes this involves seeing behavior before it becomes problematic. The video segments you are about to view are of preschoolers engaging in various activities. Some clips may or may not contain challenging behaviors. Your job is to press the enter key on the external keypad every time you see a behavior that could become a potential challenge."

The teachers were not aware that their glances at the screen were being traced with laser technology that could identify where they were looking. The results were astonishing, and deeply troubling. Despite the fact that there was no actual "challenging behavior" demonstrated in the video, researchers found that the teachers "watched" the black children more and, not surprisingly, found more "challenging behavior" among the black children! Is it any surprise, then, that black preschoolers are 3.6 times more likely than white preschoolers to receive one or more suspensions, or that despite the fact that black children make up only 19 percent of preschoolers, they account for 47 percent of preschoolers suspended?[10] The combination of bias and the discretionary power of the preschool teacher can contribute to a lifetime of learned helplessness (which I will discuss more in Chapter 7), educational failure, and reinforces the dominant cultural biases toward blacks.

Our Own Narratives

People in different areas of the United States have been raised in very different narratives that shape the way we see race. In my first book, *Reinventing Diversity*, I shared the following experience I had when I was conducting a diversity workshop for a newspaper in a small town in Louisiana. It was an old-style southern town with old-style southern attitudes. Ku Klux Klansman David Duke had carried the parish during his run for governor, a campaign considered by most to be a throwback to the old "segregation today, segregation forever" southern attitude.

> The two-day training included a mix of people: reporters who had come from all over the country, as well as some local ones, and others who worked for the paper who generally were from the town and its surrounding environs. The first day we got into the normal kinds of dialogues. People shared their experiences, argued points with each other. People of color, mostly African American at this particular training, talked about the pain of racism, how it had impacted them in their lives. Whites in the group were all over the place. Some understood, and some resisted. One man sat virtually silent the whole day, clearly listening, clearly engaged, but not speaking except in minimal comments in small groups. He was a pressman, dressed in a flannel shirt and jeans. White, probably in his mid-thirties, he could have fit the stereotyped picture of a local "Southern boy." His demeanor was pleasant, even friendly. He smiled a lot and seemed to interact easily, though quietly, with people at the breaks.
>
> During the morning discussion on the second day of training, a couple of the African American participants shared much more openly then they had been about their life experiences, the challenges they had faced, and their fears for their children. It was deep and emotionally moving. Finally, out of nowhere, the man who had been silent said, "I have something to share."
>
> His speaking surprised me, and I think others as well, and I have to say I remember feeling curious and a bit apprehensive about what would come out of his mouth. He leaned forward

on his chair and started to speak, looking down mostly. I don't recall it word for word, but when he spoke he said something like this:

"I've been sitting here listening to what folks have to say and I feel a little confused and pulled in two directions. I can understand the kind of upset that people are talking about. I haven't really heard black folks talk about it in quite this way ever before. I guess I haven't wanted to. But I know some of these folks and they seem like nice folks. I also know that the kinds of things that they are talking about that have happened in these parts, particularly when I was a kid, were pretty scary for them. But I grew up right around here, on a farm not far outside of town. I've lived here my whole life. I know folks in this town, white and black. I grew up with them. There are good people in this town. It is hard for me to believe that those people did some of the things that you folks are talking about . . . but I know enough from what I've heard, and I believe you when you say they happened."

He paused for a few minutes and looked down at the ground. He stayed that way for what seemed like a long time, long enough so that the rest of us wondered whether he was finished. I remember that just as I was about to ask him whether he was finished, he looked up and he had tears in his eyes. I think everybody in the room was surprised.

"Here's my problem," he said. "My father and grandfather were the most important people in my life. They're both gone now, but they taught me everything I know. They took me hunting and fishing from the time I was this high." He motioned with his hand. "They were leaders in our community, helped people. My grandfather was the pastor of my church. They taught me to be a good father . . ."

And then he dropped the bomb.

"But they were both members of the Klan. It wasn't talked about that much, but it wasn't hidden that much either. I don't know what they did, and I don't want to know, but as I sit here I feel the conflict inside of me. I know that what you have all been saying makes sense. Nobody should have to feel the way you're saying you feel. But I feel like when I say that, I reject the two people who were the most important people in my life, and I know, as well as I know anything, that they were good people."

The room was dead silent. I noticed that I had very little to say to the man. . . . I asked him a few questions and then, after a short time, we decided to break for lunch. As the group dispersed I sat in my chair, processing what had happened. I noticed one of the most outspoken African American men in the group approaching the man, and they pulled up chairs and ate with each other engrossed in conversation.

Even at that moment I realized that something profound had happened within myself. In all the years I had dealt with the issue of race, worked on social change, and conducted trainings, my perspective had been clear: there are good people in the world who are open, accepting, nonbiased, and inclusive. Then there are bad people, who are biased, racist, sexist, anti-Semitic, homophobic, and so on. The lines, in my mind, were pretty clearly, and from my understanding today, naively drawn. Yet as I looked at the two men talking, and as I thought about what had transpired, I realized that this was a good and decent man, an honest man, even a courageous man. And I couldn't help but think that there is something else here to consider.[11]

Power and Privilege

One of the ways our different narratives impact us is that they give us a different sense of power and privilege. Power has a startling impact on people in many ways and can be greatly affected by stereotypes. This ability to have and use power can be subtle. It is also closely related to the level of privilege people experience, based on their race. When we have been consciously or unconsciously raised to see ourselves as higher in the social order, this affects how we relate to others and how we see ourselves.

The United States is a culture of white privilege. I know that the words *white privilege* are often wildly misunderstood and bring up defensiveness on the part of white people, but they are nonetheless true. When people hear the term, it is misunderstood to reflect personal privilege. A white person once said to me, "What are you talking about? I grew up in a low-income family and had to work from the time I was twelve years old. I didn't have any privilege!"

Privilege does not mean that people in the dominant group do not confront challenges; it means that the nature of the challenges they face is different from that in the nondominant group. When we have had personal experiences that are counter to the very thought of privilege, the term is a hard pill to swallow. But the term *white privilege* is *not* personal. It describes a shared group experience. The term was likely first articulated by Peggy McIntosh, a senior research associate at the Wellesley Centers for Women. McIntosh stated her case in her 1988 piece "White Privilege: Unpacking the Invisible Knapsack."

McIntosh established that privilege is not necessarily intentional and sometimes not even consciously known by the people who are part of the groups that receive it. It includes things like:

- I can swear, or dress in secondhand clothes, or not answer letters, without having people attribute these choices to the bad morals, the poverty or the illiteracy of my race.
- I can be pretty sure that if I ask to talk to "the person in charge," I will be facing a person of my race.
- If a traffic cop pulls me over or if the IRS audits my tax return, I can be sure I haven't been singled out because of my race.
- I can go home from most meetings of organizations I belong to feeling somewhat tied in, rather than isolated, out-of-place, out-numbered, unheard, held at a distance or feared.
- When I am told about our national heritage or about "civilization," I am shown that people of my color made it what it is.

Very few white people I know would choose all of the privilege they have. Most people would like to feel like they have earned what they get in life, and they may have to some degree. But when we are not aware of the many ways that other groups have it harder, we just assume that we are living by the same rules. One of the most self-justifying aspects of privilege is that being oblivious or unaware of where you experience privilege, or even arguing against it in denial, is in itself a part of being privileged. That white people don't have to think about or be aware of their privilege is itself part of our privilege. Our privilege lives in the absence of the kinds of challenges that others face. Even though we largely didn't choose these privileges doesn't mean that we don't benefit from them, and that they don't affect our sense of self and our sense of belonging. The real question is, are we willing to become aware of how privilege affects us?

For example, I have four sons, all of whom have their driver's licenses. When they were learning to drive, I never had to have a conversation with them about how to behave if stopped by a police officer, *in order to stay alive.* It just never occurred to me. On the other hand, virtually every black parent I know has had the "driving while black" conversation with their teenagers, and for good reason. Study after study shows there is greater risk for black drivers than white ones.[12] Not having to worry about that is an example of white privilege, and also a great example of why we don't often notice it. It is hard to notice something when you don't have to pay attention to it.

My colleague Peter DiCaprio describes how white privilege plays out in these ways:

> People of color, as well as HUD [the Department of Housing and Urban Development] and other institutions, report that class and financial means being equal, people of color will be funneled to neighborhoods where the economic class is on average lower than in the neighborhoods where white people are funneled. In other words, people of color often cannot find housing in areas that they can otherwise financially afford. And though there are certainly people who espouse explicit white nationalist philosophies in all spheres of U.S. society, most of this happens without conscious awareness or intention. Certainly, many whites who are real estate agents, property managers, owners, etc., hold earnest beliefs in equality but don't see the ways they are contributing to the process.[13]

Although we are explicitly talking about white privilege here and the profound societal impact of that privilege, it's important to note that almost everybody experiences privilege in some way. Privilege can and does come from many directions. Race, gender, sexual orientation (before marriage equality became the law of the land, did you have to build a case to have your partner covered by company health insurance?), class, education, citizenship, religion (do you have to worry that somebody will think you are a terrorist because you are wearing some artifact or clothing that represents your religion?), or almost any other identity can be associated with privilege when one aspect of that identity group is seen as better than another, even if a person still lacks privilege in another of his or her identities.

White Fragility

The awareness of white privilege and the related biases it produces often creates a defensive reaction among some white people, many of whom don't see themselves as being "racist" and may not have any intention to create harm. Robin DiAngelo has coined the term *white fragility* to describe this reaction: "White Fragility is a state in which even a minimum amount of racial stress becomes intolerable, triggering a range of defensive moves. These moves include the outward display of emotions such as anger, fear, and guilt, and behaviors such as argumentation, silence, and leaving the stress-inducing situation. These behaviors, in turn, function to reinstate white racial equilibrium. Racial stress results from an interruption to what is racially familiar."[14]

These challenges to familiarity might come from challenging a white person's objectivity by suggesting that his or her viewpoint is affected by race, or when people of color speak directly to a white person about their concerns in a way that upsets the white person. It may happen when a white person is given feedback that his or her behavior, intended or not, had a race-based impact, or when being told that his or her accomplishments were aided by whiteness. It might even be triggered by a person of color playing a previously white iconic role in a movie, on TV, or on the stage.[15]

On August 15, 2017, Fox News host Melissa Francis shared her own experience of white fragility while commenting on the reaction to Trump's statement that people "on both sides" had contributed to the event in Charlottesville, Virginia, three days earlier that had left a young woman dead and dozens more injured: " 'I am so uncomfortable having this conversation. I know what's in my heart and I know that I don't think anyone is different, better or worse based on the color of their skin,' Francis said, wiping away tears. 'But I feel like there is nothing any of us can say right now without being judged.' "[16]

The combination of white privilege and white fragility is a powerful one. Often when we acknowledge the system of race and the way it benefits white people, a white person may interpret that as an accusation—a response that often is fueled by guilt and/or shame. Because racial communications often do occur as angry indictments, white people frequently feel the very discussion of race is a threat to their sense of self and standing in the world. The reaction to this perceived threat often occurs as simple avoidance, yet many times people actually see the discussion of race as somehow violating the very principles the country stands for. People will often cite Martin Luther King Jr.'s "I Have a Dream" speech, in which he said that people "will not be judged by the color of their skin, but by the content of their character," and are confused by what seems like a contradiction between Dr. King's admonition and affirmative action programs which seem to be based on the "color of their skin." In fact, while his statement was aspirational, affirmative action programs are designed to correct past inequities and help us create the future that Dr. King was envisioning.

We can see how these kinds of reactions can create a serious impediment to healthy bridging in relationships. It is difficult to bridge in a healthy way when we are unable to be vulnerable, and fear of condemnation will inhibit most people from revealing their vulnerability.

We are all a part of this system. Traditional diversity advocates and programs, as well as many people advocating for marginalized groups, have often either used shame or guilt as tools to motivate change or communicated negative judgments about people who don't agree with them. Social shaming and potential exclusion almost always create some sense of defensiveness and all of its concomitant responses (anger, disengagement, self-justification, backlash, etc.), and such techniques tend to back-fire when dealing with the far larger percentage of the population who are unaware of how biased their position is. This is one of the reasons Hillary Clinton's admonishment of half of Trump supporters as "what I call the basket of deplorables . . . the racist, sexist, homophobic, xenophobic, Islamophobic—you name it" was so alienating to so many people. It came across as "I (and we) are better than you." Communications like this may be emotionally satisfying at the moment, but in the case of Clinton's comment they created a deep break in belonging between the candidate and the people who might have moved her way. One Trump voter, a university professor with whom I spoke, put it this way: "I grew up in Arkansas and my parents were, literally, cotton pickers who never finished elementary school. I didn't like Trump and still don't, but when she said that she was talking about my family, my friends, my community. She lost me that night on the news."

A similar conflict has emerged around the notion of political correctness. Political correctness is generally seen as an attempt to avoid or suppress forms of communication or self-expression that are seen as insulting, exclusive, or marginalizing toward groups of nondominant people. It is often well-meaning, with the intention being to create a "safe space" for people in these groups so that the language that is used around them does not leave them feeling marginalized or excluded. It makes perfect sense that people should have the right to choose how they are referred to. The problem is that the behavior, which in its original form was intended to be a way of communicating with others when language was offensive, has often been used excessively, and sometimes even as a way to isolate people, or even fire them from jobs, or to suppress people's expression. This has created a backlash, and now the term is being used as a calling card for opponents of diversity and inclusion. It is very difficult to have authentic and vulnerable conversations, the foundational glue for belonging, when you have to watch every word you say.

Acknowledging fragility and privilege doesn't mean embracing shame and guilt. It simply means being aware of how your identity might aid you in ways that you didn't realize, and that some other people who do not experience the same privilege might have to work harder than you. This may not be obvious, because often this kind of privilege occurs in the form of micro-behaviors (micro-inequities or micro-advantages) that are subtle and even unconscious.[17]

How Is This Manifesting?

Given our perpetual dilemma about race, what do we do now? It is not hard to see that our society has become more polarized over the past decades. We can see these differences most dramatically between whites and blacks. A huge majority of blacks (88 percent) believe that the country needs to keep making changes toward equal rights; 43 percent are skeptical that those changes will occur, 42 percent believe that the country will eventually make those changes, and only 8 percent believe that we already have. The white response is dramatically different. Only 53 percent of whites believe that the country needs to keep making changes toward equal rights; only 11 percent doubt that the changes will occur, with approximately 40 percent believing that the country will eventually make those changes and 38 percent believing that we already have.[18]

When asked whether they think race relations in this country are good, whites split almost down the middle, 46 percent to 45 percent. Blacks overwhelmingly feel negative, 34 percent to 61 percent. Not surprisingly, blacks are more than twice as likely as whites (58 percent to 27 percent) to think that too little attention is paid to race relations, whereas whites are almost twice as likely (41 percent to 22 percent) to believe there is too much attention focused on race relations.

Similar patterns exist among other identities as well. The presence in the United States of Mexican immigrants is used to explain joblessness among whites, even though study after study has shown that immigrants are not the reason those jobs are being lost.[19] And bias against other Hispanic populations, Asians, Native Americans, and other nonwhite groups has been proliferating.

We are living in different realities, each of us being pulled toward belonging to our own groups. And this can drive us further and further away from understanding and identifying with the other.

On the right, this has produced the rise of hate groups, white supremacy and neo-Nazi movements, political opposition to affirmative action, and attempts at voter suppression. All of this has been fed by media that provides "data" (some real and some "alternative facts") to support those positions. On the left, it has led to overreaches in political correctness, "trigger warnings" being used to restrict conversations on college campuses, and left-leaning militancy, fueled by similarly biased data streams. On both sides the politics of ideas has been replaced by the politics of personal vendetta.

It also occurs as strong differences in reactions to specific real and symbolic circumstances. For example, there are two different views of Civil War–related statues, memorials, and symbols. Many white people, and especially white southerners, see these as symbols of their heritage. They were raised in a region that was defeated and humiliated in a war that left them at the mercy of their opponents who, in their perception, were trying to force them to change their way of life. The erection of Civil War statues was a way to recapture, in their minds, some of that faded glory and to reestablish their sense of pride.

The problem is, that is a revisionist view of history. The reality is that the "way of life" that they were fighting for was slavery. As Confederate vice president Alexander Stephens said,

> The prevailing ideas entertained by [Thomas Jefferson] and most of the leading statesmen at the time of the formation of the old Constitution were, that the enslavement of the African was in violation of the laws of nature; that it was wrong in principle, socially, morally and politically. It was an evil they knew not well how to deal with. . . . Our new government is founded upon exactly the opposite ideas; its foundations are laid, its cornerstone rests, upon the great truth that the negro is not equal to the white man; that slavery, subordination to the superior race, is his natural and normal condition. This, our new government, is the first, in the history of the world, based upon this great physical, philosophical, and moral truth.[20]

A huge majority of these statues were actually erected within two major periods of American history. The first was after the 1896 Supreme Court ruling in *Plessy v. Ferguson*, which enshrined in law the concept of "separate but equal" and ushered in the development of Jim Crow practices throughout the South. This period saw a significant rise in the Ku Klux Klan and other racist organizations. The second period began after the 1954 *Brown v. Board of Education* ruling that led to the legal desegregation of schools. Both seemed to be times when terror became a valuable political tool.[21]

These statues, monuments, and related symbols have certain associations to people who grew up hearing about the "heroes" of the Confederacy. Within a segment of the white dominant culture, these symbols represent not pain but heritage. The truth—that they are symbols of a war that was fought to maintain slavery, as the Articles of Secession that were drawn up by the Confederate states clearly show—is replaced by a revisionist explanation of the Civil War that focuses on the issue of states' rights, even as that especially meant the right to keep slaves.[22] Whites in general, southern or not, can have the privilege of not worrying about this distinction. While some whites adapt to changes in historiography that illuminate the historical reality around the Civil War, for others the challenge to these symbols triggers concerns about "being replaced" by immigrants, Jews, people of color, women (for some men), and others who would "erase our history and culture." The data showing that we are moving toward a "majority-minority" country exacerbates this fear.[23] Their powerlessness to stop the demographic shifts that began in the past and are continuing today shows up in angry resistance, which can develop into the rise of the white supremacy movement. Underneath the hate, there is almost always pain and fear and, ironically, a sense of powerlessness, even though whites clearly have the upper hand in our social order.

For African Americans, there is no confusion. Every one of these symbols represents the celebration of people who fought a war to keep them enslaved and who mounted years of campaigns of terror to keep them as second-class citizens. The same Confederate flag that flies over statehouses in the South, in front of people's homes, on streets, in schools, and in front of courthouses was the flag carried by the Klan in their terrorizing night raids. The same heroes who are commemorated in statues paid for with black people's tax money and located in public parks, or who live on in the names given to roads, schools, and other institutions, were the people who fought for their exclusion and enslavement. The pain is real.

The past is never dead. It's not even past.

Building Bridges across Race

As Swedish Nobel laureate Gunnar Myrdal wrote more than seventy years ago, race is still the American dilemma. It is, of course, very difficult to build a bridge when the sides we are attempting to join are not level. Continuing to work toward societal equity is essential if we are to be able to create more bridging across racial differences. It is also, perhaps, a consummate act of patriotism, given the ethos of our country being built on "liberty and justice for all." It is understandable that we approach something as emotionally charged as race relations from the standpoint of how we can be successful in forwarding our own agenda. I can easily fall victim to that same line of thinking. There is nothing wrong with being a strong advocate for a point of view about the subject, *as long as you recognize it as a point of view.* How likely is it that we can open up a dialogue between two sides when both are convinced that they are right and that the other side is evil?

One of the greatest barriers we have to moving forward in the conversation is that many people, especially whites, are afraid to talk about it. The fear is that they will be put on the defensive, called a racist, say the wrong thing, offend people, or harm relationships that are at least peaceful, if not even closer. Sometimes people even pretend that they are "colorblind" and don't see race at all. Unless we can talk about something that is so central to people's existence and worldview, we will never create true intimacy. We will never move from association to true intimacy.

Not discussing race has its cost. Three researchers, Evan Apfelbaum from MIT, Michael Norton at Harvard, and Sam Sommers of Tufts University, gathered thirty white people and asked them to play the role of questioner in the children's game Guess Who. Each of the questioners was paired with a partner, some of whom were white and some black. The partner was assigned a target face on a sheet that included thirty-two faces. The questioners were told they could ask their partners yes-or-no questions to determine which face on the page was the target. Half of the faces on the sheet were white, the other half black.

Anybody who has played a game like this knows that the best strategy is to eliminate as many possibilities with as few questions as possible, so an obvious question would be to ask about the race of the target. That would have eliminated half of the faces immediately. However, very few people followed the logical strategy, especially when they had black partners. Only 57 percent of people who played with a white partner and only 21 percent whose partner was black asked the obvious question. When they did pose that question, the researchers said, they "looked uncomfortable and anxious."[24]

Not talking about race deepens the divisions between us. The pain of talking about race is nothing compared with the day-to-day pain of living with it every day that most people of color face.

There are a number of strategies that can help us to talk about it, both with people of our own race and with people of races different from our own:

Identify your own privilege(s). Almost everyone has some privilege. Identifying our privilege is the first step to seeing into the experiences of others, particularly those who do not have the same privilege. Explore how you can use your privilege to serve and benefit others or at least to avoid it hindering or harming others. It is also critical to realize that generations of white supremacy as well as existing patterns of white privilege and power make it much riskier for people of color to broach the subject of race. Trust needs to be built through a willingness of people, especially those in the dominant group, to expose their vulnerability.

Be willing to experience discomfort when talking about race. This is a subject that has caused immense pain and dissonance between people . . . even a civil war. It will be uncomfortable, especially when people expose that pain and the hurt it has caused. The separation is there; it's through dialogue that we can heal it. In order to be able to have these kinds of dialogues, we have to be willing to expose ourselves. That requires vulnerability and trust, and especially courage.

Set up an appropriate time and set of agreements to have the conversation. Conversations about race can be more effective if you're able to "talk about how you feel about talking about it" before jumping in. Acknowledging the discomfort can make it easier to proceed. Having the conversation in smaller groups or even one-on-one can manage image concerns about we show up to each other. It is also helpful to connect personally before jumping into the topic.

Begin by doing your own work. What is behind your interpretation of the situation? Try to trace how your views of race in America have developed. What is it triggering in you? This is true even if you see yourself as having progressive attitudes about people of other races than your own. People who advocate for diversity all too often haven't done their own work and are coming from their own wounds, which can cloud our ability to be open. Make sure that you are grounded in your own values.

Avoid assumptions about people and try to learn about them instead. You may think you *know* what people are thinking and feeling and why, but very few of us assess each other accurately. Be curious. The more you know about what others feel and why they feel it, even if you don't agree, the more likely it is that you will able to have a respectful conversation, increasing the chances that you will be heard. Try to connect with their humanity, and avoid the assumption that the person you are talking to represents the extremes. Recognize that when talking about difficult subjects, people rarely share exactly what they are feeling; they may not even be fully aware of those feelings themselves. And recognize that part of the task is to give people the freedom to share what they are ready to share, when they are ready to share it.

Study the issue of race from all sides. Read books or research that pertains to the subject. Watch and read different news and information sources. Expose yourself to literature that can help you see other cultures from a new perspective. Be open to learning, but be careful to avoid confirmation bias. Your echo chamber won't help you develop a better understanding of the other. Understanding somebody else does not necessarily mean that you agree with that person, but it may help you maintain a connection that can lead to finding some common ground.

Be willing to speak your truth. In the New Testament, John 8:32, Jesus tells his disciples, "You will know the truth, and the truth will set you free." What he didn't say is that it might cause upset first. Being open about your thoughts and feelings can make you feel vulnerable and may sometimes lead to a confrontation, but that vulnerability is an essential part of creating belonging.

Ultimately the greatest challenge that we have in understanding each other is that we would rather be *right* than be connected. Remember that the separation that we have created may feel like it keeps us safer, but ultimately it is tearing us apart. We would all do well to remember what Martin Luther King Jr. said in his "Letter from the Birmingham Jail": "In a real sense all life is inter-related. All men are caught in an inescapable network of mutuality, tied in a single garment of destiny. Whatever affects one directly, affects all indirectly. I can never be what I ought to be until you are what you ought to be, and you can never be what you ought to be until I am what I ought to be. . . . This is the inter-related structure of reality."[25]

We are, as King indicates, inherently social. Let's now look at how our brains are designed to be that way.

Chapter 5

The Social Brain

Much of the same machinery, the same brain regions and computational processing that are used in a social context to attribute awareness to someone else, are also used on a continuous basis to construct your own awareness and attribute it to yourself.

—MICHAEL S. A.
GRAZIANO

Have you ever found yourself talking to an inanimate object? Perhaps getting angry at your car, or encouraging it through snow, almost like the Little Engine that Could? Anybody who has children has likely seen them treat their stuffed animals as if they were alive, or, even more dramatically, create an imaginary friend out of thin air. Why would we talk to inanimate objects or imaginary ones as if they were alive?

In the 2000 movie *Cast Away*, Tom Hanks plays Chuck Noland, a FedEx employee who ends up stranded on an uninhabited island in the South Pacific after a plane crash. The film gained widespread critical acclaim and was heralded as a gripping survival story, a tribute to the resourcefulness and resilience of the human spirit. Perhaps most important, however, was that it also provided a poignant glimpse into the depths of our desire to connect.

Hanks's character attempts to regain his bearings following the dramatic crash by trying to start a fire. We watch as he rubs a stick back and forth against a flat piece of wood, building heat through the constant friction, until his hand suddenly slips and is gashed wide open. Noland lets out a primal scream as he grasps his injured hand, and in the moments of intense frustration that follow, he angrily throws several objects, including a volleyball from one of the FedEx packages that has washed ashore. The white ball ends up with a large bloody handprint on it. When Noland happens upon the ball several scenes later, viewers watch as he gently picks it up and silently examines it. After several moments of intense contemplation, he carefully dampens his makeshift cloth bandage with the sweat from his brow and uses it to rub two eyes, a nose, and a slightly smirking mouth in the bloody print. And thus Wilson (named after the brand of volleyball) is created.

Throughout the remainder of the film we watch as the relationship between Hanks's character and Wilson grows. He eats with him, confides in him, and even argues with him; he protects him from the physical elements, while Wilson protects Noland from the otherwise ubiquitous loneliness that now defines his existence. As we watch, we slowly grow to recognize the importance of Wilson to Noland. What seems at first to be nothing more than a device used to provide the audience with comedic relief slowly evolves into something far more meaningful. Though many initially laugh at the absurdity of this grown man interacting with an inanimate object, most of us also find ourselves inexplicably sad when, during his attempt to sail off the island four years after his crash, Noland dozes off and awakens to realize Wilson has fallen off their escape raft. He spots him slowly bobbing on the horizon, but as he desperately tries to rescue him he comes to the solemn realization that the ball has floated too far to be recovered. Noland weeps as he screams his now famous line: "I'm sorry, Wilson!" Noland had lost more than just an object—he had lost his only source of connection. Our experience may be an empathetic response to Hanks's character's loss, but, as irrational as it may seem, some of us may also have joined in the anthropomorphizing of Wilson ourselves.

This need to connect is more than just material. Wilson, in this case, provides no material benefits to Hanks's character—no food, water, or shelter. The need comes from a deeper imperative. Psychologist Harry Harlow famously established this with his experiments with monkeys in the 1950s and 1960s. Harlow separated infant monkeys from their real mothers and gave them two artificial mothers, one made of wire and the other made of cloth. The wire model was constructed with a bottle to feed the baby monkey. But the babies rarely stayed with the wire model longer than it took to get the necessary food. They clearly preferred cuddling with the softer cloth model, especially if they were frightened or stressed. When the cloth mother had the bottle, they ignored the wire mother entirely![1]

Harlow also conducted studies on social isolation in monkeys. After leaving monkeys alone for extended periods, he found that

> no monkey has died during isolation. When initially removed from total social isolation, however, they usually go into a state of emotional shock, characterized by ... autistic self-clutching and rocking. One of six monkeys isolated for 3 months refused to eat after release and died 5 days later. The autopsy report attributed death to emotional anorexia.
>
> ... The effects of 6 months of total social isolation were so devastating and debilitating that we had assumed initially that 12 months of isolation would not produce any additional decrement. This assumption proved to be false; 12 months of isolation almost obliterated the animals socially.[2]

Harlow had discovered the need that drove Hanks's character to anthropomorphize Wilson. It was the need for connection—the need to belong.

Science shows us that the behavior displayed by Hanks's character was less a product of the extremity of his circumstances and more a result of our brains functioning as designed when faced with the prospect of limited social connection. We are, above all else, social creatures, and when our social bonds are compromised, our brains adapt by desperately seeking *something* with which to connect.

This desperation can manifest itself in a variety of ways, but each serves a similar purpose: to regain some feeling of connection. Many of us have had a similar experience. Has there ever been a time when you were traveling somewhere alone, on vacation or on a business trip, and ran into somebody whom you barely knew, and yet even that little recognition was enough to make you inclined to hang out with them because at least there was somebody with whom you were connected?

Studies show that social isolation increases our tendency to *anthropomorphize*, or project human attributes onto nonhuman agents such as the previously mentioned stuffed animals, robots, and pets.[3] Think about how many people you know who relate to their pets as their "babies," and even dress them in clothing or take pictures of them in human-like poses. More interesting still is that this anthropomorphization is often highly specific to filling the void created by the absence of social support. Not only do chronically lonely individuals show a greater tendency to anthropomorphize their pets, but the traits they use to describe these anthropomorphic qualities overwhelmingly revolve around social support (e.g., describing pets as "thoughtful," "considerate," or "sympathetic").[4] When we feel lonely—either because we suffer from chronic loneliness *or* because we are manipulated to experience temporary loneliness in a laboratory setting—we try to compensate by enhancing the human-like traits of nonhuman entities.[5]

Our brains can also respond to loneliness by seeking refuge in *parasocial relationships*, in which we substitute alternative types of connection for human contact, like Hanks's character with Wilson. Parasocial relationships typically involve perceived connections between imaginary, supernatural, or otherwise fictional agents where reciprocity is impossible. For instance, individuals may form bonds with television characters or action figures. This tendency may also explain why people's personal relationship with a deity can be so fulfilling and sustaining. These entities become social surrogates, allowing an individual to experience connection even when no genuine human connection may be available. When genuine social connection is unavailable, imagined or vicarious social connection may suffice to fill our need. It is not only a function of having somebody to keep us company; it also appears to be foundational to how we define ourselves.

Our intense desire to connect is a by-product of our inherently social nature. Those who misunderstand evolution are often perplexed by the seemingly contradictory existence of "selfish genes" and cooperative action, but such a puzzle is actually quite simple to resolve. As humans progressed through stages of evolution, solitary living became untenable. An individual who either refused, avoided, or otherwise proved him- or herself unfit for cooperation found themselves at a competitive disadvantage, often unable to survive for long. In the harsh reality of our ancestral environments, individuals who stuck together benefitted from the protection afforded by group membership, the enhanced success of group hunting, and increased exposure to potential mates via group living. In short, being a cooperative person came with competitive advantages. Thus, individuals born with genes that predisposed them to preserve their good standing within a group—perhaps, for instance, by making them feel uncomfortable at the prospect of social rejection, leading them to avoid acting in ways that could trigger such rejection—would be more likely to pass on such genes, until they predominated in a population. If such tendencies conferred a survival advantage, they were likely to spread. Ever wondered why you get a knot in the pit of your stomach before stating an unpopular opinion in a group setting? It may well be because genes that generated such a feeling gave your ancestors a survival advantage. In fact, a 2010 meta-analysis demonstrated that people with stronger social relationships had a significantly lower risk of death than people with weaker social relationships![6]

This effect can be short-term as well as long-term. How many times, for example, have you felt better having somebody with you when you were dealing with an uncomfortable situation, rather than having to deal with it yourself? In the office party scenario, for example, Barry may have been at a social advantage because he had Sam with him, while Joan and Fatima had no other adult support.

Wired for Belonging

The brain seems to be designed to produce this very result. The circuitry of the reward system of our brain is anchored by a structure called the ventral striatum. Whenever we engage in an activity that elicits positive feelings, chances are the root of such feelings can be found in the activation of our ventral striatum. When asked to imagine what types of experiences might light up the reward centers of our brains, most people respond with one of two alliterative answers: sugary sweets or sexual satisfaction. While these assumptions are undoubtedly correct, science is showing that they also only represent a portion of the stimuli capable of activating our reward networks. It's not just tangible, physical experiences that send our ventral striatum into high gear, but intangible social signs of acceptance as well.

Research has shown, for instance, that reading emotionally meaningful statements from our families and closest friends can elicit the effect.[7] Because our brains crave social approval with as much enthusiasm as they crave a bar of chocolate, presumably trivial or inauthentic feedback can trigger striatum activity as well. The mental reward networks of research participants come humming to life when they receive feedback that complete strangers would be interested in interacting with them.[8] Similarly, the striatum comes online when participants receive praise from strangers who have never even met them, despite the fact that, having never have met one another in the first place, genuine praise would be impossible.[9] (So in that regard, any positive feedback from readers about this will be welcomed by my striatum.)

With social acceptance engendering reward circuit activity similar to what we'd expect to see were we to give someone a bar of chocolate or a large raise in salary, is it any wonder that people will go to such lengths to capture that feeling? Belonging literally feels good.

UCLA social neuroscientist Matthew Lieberman maintains that humans not only are predisposed to social behavior but are actually *social by default*. His claims are derived primarily from research undertaken by Washington University neuroscientist Gordon Shulman and his colleagues to determine which areas of the brain remain active when the brain is at rest (that is, not performing cognitive, motor, or visual tasks). They employed positron emission tomography (PET scanning) to monitor the blood flow of participants brains when they were engaged in an activity and when they were instructed to rest. It became clear that a very specific suite of neural regions, which has since been dubbed the *default network*, became active during these rest periods.[10]

The default network overlaps with what is known as the social cognition network. When we are thinking about our friends, family, co-workers, and ourselves, or trying to make sense of social ecosystems and the roles of different actors within them, we are engaging in social cognition.[11] Thus, the findings of Shulman and colleagues essentially mean that when our brains are at rest or not otherwise engaged in a task, they are thinking about people and about us relative to others. Such a finding may seem relatively trivial, especially considering the obviousness of such a conclusion in a world consumed by social media and immersed in reality television. But what's fascinating, Lieberman contends, is the *relationship* between the default network and our penchant for social cognition. Rather than turning on the default network because we're interested in our social world, we're actually interested in our social world *because* of the chronic activation of our default network.[12] In other words, when not engaging in a particular task, our brains are designed to stimulate an interest in thinking about, responding to, and ultimately connecting with others. Such a social nature is present from the moment we are born. Babies as young as two weeks old have shown evidence of default network activity.[13]

Even those of us who don't have a PET scanner hanging around the house can perform a simple test to demonstrate how our brains are social by default. More than sixty years ago, a pair of researchers concocted a test involving moving geometric shapes. Austrian psychologist Fritz Heider and American cognitive psychologist Marianne Simmel created a simple animation that displays geometric shapes moving about a screen for a short period of time (Figure 5.1).[14] The purpose of the test was simple: to investigate how individuals would describe what they were witnessing.

Why would such descriptions be of interest to a team of psychologists? Primarily because the manner in which we describe an ambiguous situation with minimal context gives us an insight into how we think about, perceive, and ultimately interpret our surroundings. Let's say, hypothetically, they had a group of participants from a distant planet—let's

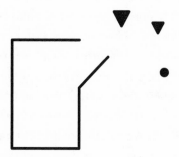

Figure 5.1 Heider and Simmel Animation

call it Planet Solitario—serve as subjects in the study. Inhabitants of Planet Solitario live solitary, nonsocial lives. When asked to describe the animation, they'd probably respond with some variation of the following: "The small triangle and circle are present on the screen. The small triangle and circle move toward each other. They make contact. The large triangle enters the top of the screen. The small circle and triangle move toward the bottom of the screen. The large triangle moves toward the small triangle. The circle moves upward toward a box on the left side of the screen. The circle enters the box."

Notice that these nonsocial subjects describe the scene in a very objective manner; they identify the shape and assess the directionality of movement. The descriptions are cold, mechanical, and almost robotic. Fascinatingly, the humans who participated in the original study showed a much different pattern of description. A typical response went something like this: "The small triangle and circle are playing together on the screen; they must be friends. They keep walking around together, enjoying each other's company. But then the big triangle comes in and the other two are scared. They run to the bottom of the screen but the big, mean triangle follows them. The big triangle starts bullying the smaller triangle, but the circle is able to escape—he goes and hides in the box, where he feels safe."

As social creatures, we can't help but describe the scene in terms of what we imagine to be the social intentions of each shape. Unlike the participants from Planet Solitario, who would have described the scene purely in terms of physical characteristic and movements, humans immediately make attributions about the social characteristics of the inanimate geometric shapes. They imbue the characters with personalities, emotions, and goals. This projection is what philosopher Daniel Dennett calls the *intentional stance.*[15] Humans are social actors, and in order to traverse a complex world full of other social actors, test our belonging, and determine if someone is in the tribe, we must learn to make assumptions about people's beliefs, desires, and motivations.

This can also lead us to make assumptions about the social intent of other humans. We cannot help but project our own assumptions into watching another's behavior. In the workplace, for example, when somebody doesn't include you in a communication, how easy is it to assume intentions without having any idea whether it was intentional or an innocent oversight? When somebody makes a comment that seems biased based on race or gender, how easy is it to assume intention, even after you know that they were unaware of the impact of what they were saying?

We receive clues about people that can be conscious and obvious, or unconscious and subtle, but without projecting intentional mental states onto others, we are rendered incapable of making predictions about behavior, and in the absence of behavioral expectations we leave ourselves unprepared and vulnerable to social rejection and physical harm. However, while such an intentional stance is a useful mechanism when interacting with those who actually *have* intentions (humans and certain nonhuman animals), we tend to deploy it indiscriminately, thus generating assumptions about things like the motives and personalities of geometric shapes on a screen. It doesn't always make sense, but as Canadian neuroscientist Sukhvinder Obhi, director of the Brain, Body and Action Laboratory at McMaster University, says, "Our brains seem to have evolved to be good enough, most of the time."

Mirror Neurons and Theory of Mind

The ability to sense what is going on with others is critically important to our belongingness and ultimately to our survival. Just think how many clues you pick up about others' emotions. While we may not always be right, we have a remarkable ability to sense what others are feeling. This ability lives in the premotor cortex of the brain. Discovered in macaque monkeys by a group of Italian researchers,[16] mirror neurons specifically evolved to help us "mirror" what is going on with others we encounter. The discovery of these mirror neurons, later identified in humans by UCLA neuroscientist Marco Iacoboni, are a window into how our brains have been "designed" by evolution to survive by sensing what's going on with people around us. Virtually everybody has had a mirror neuron experience. Think about a time when you were watching a movie or television show and something happens to a character that especially impacts you—a fall, for example. Remember the physical reaction in your body and how it mirrored what was happening to the character on screen?

This ability to "sense" what is happening with others has also been referred to as *theory of mind* (ToM), the ability to recognize mental states—thoughts, perceptions, desires, intentions, feelings—and to attribute them to oneself and to others and to understand how these mental states might affect behavior.[17]

To consider what it might be like without these capabilities, watch a child with Asperger's syndrome or another form of autism at a birthday party. Various studies have shown that autism has been linked to lower production of mirror neurons.[18] Without the ability to "read" other people's intentions, moods, and actions, children with this condition can often be found huddled in a corner, terrified by all of the activity. Belonging is very challenging without this capacity.

These "tools" help our social natures lead us to seek out people and groups to which we can belong. Contrary to popular belief, our desire to be part of the group—to feel included—is more than just a shallow mechanism with which to gain popularity or status; it's not as much about scaling the social hierarchy as about simply being woven into the social fabric. This urge to belong taps something far more fundamental in our nature. Science is beginning to show that our yearning for inclusion is strong, but our fear of the pain that is caused by exclusion may be what really drives our quest for connection. How easy is it to be the one person who breaks with the crowd and disagrees in a business environment? Most people have done it at one time or another, but it often feels rife with danger and the threat of being minimized.

Few people question the legitimacy of physical pain. It would be foolish to dismiss the seriousness of a deep cut, a pulled muscle, or a broken leg. When individuals suffer physical injuries, they are immediately concerned, and others are well aware that such misfortunes will inevitably affect how they are able to perform and concentrate throughout the day. We have the understanding that a broken bone or other physical injuries need time to heal. But what about social pain? Should the pain we experience when we are excluded, isolated, or otherwise made to feel as if we don't belong command the same type of respect? Most would be hesitant to put the two types of pain on the same level of seriousness, but researchers Matthew Lieberman, Naomi Eisenberger, and Kipling

Williams sought to challenge this view by creating an experiment they called Cyberball.[19]

The researchers recruited subjects to participate in a psychological experiment in which participants were asked to complete a simple task while in a functional magnetic resonance imaging (fMRI) machine so their neural activity could be monitored throughout the duration of the task. Subjects were told they would be playing a virtual ball-tossing game with two other subjects (who were in separate rooms). Each subject would be looking at a screen with three avatars on it, one representing each participant. On the screen also would be a ball that subjects would be tossing to one another. When a subject was tossed the ball, he or she simply selected which subject to throw it to next, and when that individual caught it, he or she made the same decision. This simple ball-tossing game lasted several minutes.

Unbeknownst to the actual participants, the two additional participants ostensibly in other rooms didn't actually exist. Study subjects would instead be playing this ball-tossing game with a computer program that was designed to share the ball amicably for the first few rounds and then isolate the actual participant, ensuring he or she would not be tossed the ball for the remainder of the game.

Big deal, right? Why would a person care if he or she was excluded from a silly ball-tossing game, especially since the person didn't even know the others he or she was allegedly playing with?

What emerged from this study were some of the most jarring results researchers had uncovered in years. The researchers found that when participants were excluded, the neural regions activated in response to the social pain of being left out overlapped almost perfectly with those activated in response to physical pain. In other words, social and physical pain are represented in a remarkably similar fashion in the brain—so similar that subsequent studies have shown that social pain may be reduced in the same manner as physical pain: by taking painkillers such as Tylenol, which address the physical manifestation of the stress in the dorsal anterior cingulate cortex and anterior insula, two of the brain centers associated with physical pain.[20] What's more, aversion to social exclusion is so innate that people continued to exhibit the neural signatures of pain even when they were explicitly told that the other "participants" didn't exist and that they were interacting with a computer program specifically designed to exclude them.[21]

The downside is that our brain appears to be designed to treat threats to social belonging in a similar manner as threats to physical well-being. The upside is that social rewards can catalyze neural responses similar to those that occur with physical rewards, as we'll now see.

Effects of Social Support on Pain and Visual Perception

Scientists have uncovered a multitude of negative impacts on the physical health of those experiencing social isolation. Could a reverse relationship be true for a reinforced sense of belongingness? Could the experience of social support alter our physical realities? The short answer is yes.

In a collaborative effort undertaken by a team of researchers from the University of Florida, Staffordshire University, and Wake Forest University, an experiment was developed that sought to investigate whether the mere presence of an individual can moderate levels of experienced pain in a patient. The researchers had participants first sit in a waiting room for three minutes prior to the pain task and then immerse their hands in uncomfortably cold water for a maximum of three minutes (or for as long as they could tolerate). During these two periods, participants were either completely alone, with an individual providing passive support (present in the waiting room and during the pain task but instructed not to speak or make eye contact with the participant), or with an individual providing active support (engaging and supporting the participant as much as possible). The results were unequivocal: participants receiving both active and passive support reported experiencing dramatically less pain than the participants required to undergo the procedure alone.[22] It seems that simply the presence of another can make us less susceptible to experiencing pain and discomfort. Many of us intuitively know this because we experience feeling better when somebody sits at our bedside when we are sick or in pain, even if they are doing nothing at all to alleviate the illness or pain. Anybody who has participated in some kind of physical or athletic challenge has probably noted that your performance can increase when there is somebody cheering you on, whether a teammate, fans, a coach, or a trainer. That's one of the reasons sports teams playing on their own turf are said to have a home field advantage.

Could it be that social support could *literally* change the way we see the world? In one of the most remarkable demonstrations of the power of social connectedness, researchers brought participants to the base of a large, steep hill. They were asked either to come alone or to be accompanied by a friend. The task was simple: estimate the slope of the hill. Such a task should be an objective measurement, unaffected by a psychosocial resource such as social support, but this turned out to be untrue. Participants who were accompanied by a friend estimated the hill to be significantly less steep than those who were asked to make an estimation without the presence of another. This same relationship was found when participants were simply asked to *imagine* the presence of another. Participants who imagined standing at the base of the hill with a friend perceived the hill as less steep than those who were asked to imagine standing with an enemy or a neutral individual.[23]

Results from these as well as dozens of other experiments speak to the profound importance of social connection. We can easily see why we want to "go along with the crowd" and why people act in some of the social ways I described in earlier chapters. It appears that social support— whether real or imagined—can affect how we view our social worlds, ostensibly making daunting tasks appear more manageable. It influences the way we see the world, the way we see ourselves, and the way we make decisions about how to survive.

So if we are this attached to our role in our own social world, what happens when people from different social worlds encounter each other, especially when those social worlds involve something as fundamental as religion?

Chapter 6

Divinity, Division, and Belonging

Once I saw this guy on a bridge about to jump. I said, "Don't do it!" He said,
"Nobody loves me." I said, "God loves you. Do you believe in God?"

He said, "Yes." I said, "Are you a Christian or a Jew?" He said, "A Christian."
I said, "Me, too! Protestant or Catholic?" He said, "Protestant." I said, "Me, too!
What franchise?" He said, "Baptist." I said, "Me, too! Northern Baptist or
Southern Baptist?" He said, "Northern Baptist." I said, "Me, too! Northern
Conservative Baptist or Northern Liberal Baptist?"

He said, "Northern Conservative Baptist." I said, "Me, too! Northern
Conservative Baptist Great Lakes Region, or Northern Conservative Baptist
Eastern Region?"
He said, "Northern Conservative Baptist Great Lakes Region." I said, "Me, too!

Northern Conservative Baptist Great Lakes Region Council of 1879, or
Northern Conservative Baptist Great Lakes Region Council of 1912?" He said,
"Northern Conservative Baptist Great Lakes Region Council of 1912." I said,
"Die, heretic!" And I pushed him over.

—EMO PHILIPS

This joke has been voted the funniest religious joke of all time.[1] It is undoubtedly funny, but more than that, it points to a great dichotomy: religion, perhaps as much as any other ideological or organizational structure, has the capacity to create and threaten belonging, sometimes even at the same time.

Before I get into this topic, I want to acknowledge the difficulty of dealing with a topic as complex as religion in such a limited way. Because for most people religion is so deeply ingrained in our upbringing, it has an enormous effect on our sense of self and, therefore, can be an area of our lives susceptible to pain and vulnerability. Many of our self-judgments are sourced in our religious upbringing, and our ability to feel open and connected can be affected by them. The break in belonging regarding religion can occur in multiple ways. On one level it can simply be the difference between our religious affiliations, both between denominations and within them. For example, Orthodox and Reform Jews may feel connected by their religious identity and, at the same time, feel separated by their different practices and beliefs.

In addition to that is people's vulnerability about sharing their beliefs. Fearing that they will be judged, people might be hesitant to share that they are a nonbeliever in a group of believers, or the opposite. I do not intend to definitively explore the impact of religion on people's lives in a few pages. As somebody with a strong spiritual practice myself, I understand how integral it can be. I do, however, believe it is a worthwhile exercise to look at how religion impacts our sense of belonging.

Religion and the United States

It is impossible to discuss the impact of religion on belonging in the United States without understanding the concept of religious freedom and the role it has played in the formation and development of our culture from the beginning. Many European immigrants who came to North America during the formative years of the United States came to escape religious persecution or attempts by state-affiliated churches to force belief. It was because of that resistance to government-supported religion, and because of a desire for the freedom to worship as they chose without fear of prosecution, that freedom of religion was enshrined in the First Amendment of the Constitution, which reads in part: "Congress shall make no law respecting an establishment of religion, or prohibiting the free exercise thereof."

The phrase "separation of church and state," which is viewed by many to be a constitutional assurance, was actually penned by Thomas Jefferson in a letter he wrote to the Danbury Baptist Association in Connecticut, in which he stated: "I contemplate with sovereign reverence that act of the whole American people which declared that their legislature should 'make no law respecting an establishment of religion, or prohibiting the free exercise thereof,' thus building a wall of separation between Church & State."[2]

Jefferson, as well as several other Founding Fathers, expressed uncertainty and even serious reservations about religion. In a letter to his nephew Peter Carr in 1787, Jefferson wrote: "Question with boldness even the existence of a god; because, if there be one, he must more approve the homage of reason, than that of blindfolded fear."[3] In a letter to the Prussian philosopher Alexander von Humboldt in 1813 he said, "History, I believe, furnishes no example of a priest-ridden people maintaining a free civil government."[4]

Benjamin Franklin has been quoted as saying: "Religion I found to be without any tendency to inspire, promote, or confirm morality, serves principally to divide us and make us unfriendly to one another."[5]

George Washington wrote: "If they are good workmen, they may be of Asia, Africa, or Europe. They may be Mahometans [Muslims], Jews or Christians of any Sect, or they may be Atheists."[6]

And in the treaty between the United States and Tripoli, signed in 1796, John Adams unequivocally stated: "As the Government of the United States of America is not in any sense founded on the Christian religion . . ."[7]

The United States was founded as a secular country. And yet a *USA Today* poll showed that 55 percent believe, erroneously, that the Constitution established the United States as a Christian nation.[8] This dissonance between the historical reality of the founding of the nation and the beliefs of many people in it serves as a perfect jumping-off point for a discussion about religion and belonging in the United States today.

As much as people of any other country, and more than many, we in the United States are overwhelmingly religious. In fact, the average American is more religious than the average Iranian.[9] According to a Pew Research study, 83 percent of Americans identify with some religious tradition, and about 40 percent go to a place of worship at least weekly, 59 percent pray at least once a week, and about a third read scripture at least weekly.[10]

Religion tends to be generational. Older people tend to be more religious, both because of the era that they grew up in and because people tend to become more religious as they age. For a significant percentage of people who grew up in the 1950s, attending religious services was as much a social activity as a religious one.

This pattern began to change in the 1960s. The social upheaval and questioning of all political, educational, and religious institutions, as well as the breaking down of barriers of racial and gender discrimination, all resulted in a tectonic shift in the way religion was seen in public life.

The counterreaction to the questioning of traditional values in the 1960s led to the rise of evangelicals and the religious right in the 1970s and 1980s. That, ironically, caused a similar backlash against conservative values from liberals, who began to see religion linked to conservatism and felt uncomfortable with the connection between religion and politics. For many people, the thinking became, "If being religious means being conservative and Republican, then it's not for me!"[11]

It is easy to see how this expanded into the polarity we live in today. People began to find themselves in a conundrum. Which side do you belong to? Where do you fit in?

This is the question that many Americans have found themselves answering over the past several decades, and it has led to several important trends. Christianity is still by far the largest faith group found within the United States. The religiously unaffiliated, sometimes referred to as the "nones," represent the second-largest group, following the subgroup of evangelical Christians. Additionally, Pew Research predicts that by 2050, Muslims will surpass Jews as the second-largest organized religious group after Christians.[12] The number of Hindus is also projected to almost double by 2050. "Other religions" (a category that includes Sikhs, Wiccans, and Unitarian Universalists) are also expected to continue growing in membership. The demographics, though widely disproportionate, are changing. If we were to look at the breakdown as if we were a population of 100 people, we would have 25 evangelical Protestants, 23 people who would declare themselves as "unaffiliated," 21 Catholics, 15 "mainline" Protestants, 6 historically black Protestants, 2 Mormons, 2 other Christians, 2 Jews, 1 Muslim, 1 Hindu, 1 Buddhist, and 2 people of various other faiths.[13]

There have been major changes in the religious landscape. Even as the evangelical movement has proliferated, belief in God in general has wavered. The number of those who identify as religiously unaffiliated has increased, and more Americans claim to be "spiritual" rather than "religious." The importance of religion in most Americans' daily lives has decreased. Church attendance has declined, and at the same time as the religious right has become more mobilized, interfaith practices have increased. The membership of non-Christian faiths has grown, even as Islamophobia has drastically increased. Religious scandals, such as accusations of and convictions for pedophilia among some Catholic priests, have increased cynicism. Religion as a market has grown tremendously as various different leaders and groups have used mass media to build megachurches and congregations. There are more women among the clergy. Religious and spiritual teachings and communities have become available online, and Neopaganism has emerged. At the same time, a new, more assertive form of atheism, or anti-theism, has expanded.

Many of these trends can be expected to continue. Additionally, predictions regarding the increase in both ethnic and religious diversity within the United States over the next fifty years lead us to also predict a heightened desire for clear-cut groups and, more specifically, a need to understand which one each of us belongs to.

Along with these changing demographics have come changing patterns of behavior. Fewer Americans are sticking to the religion in which they were raised. Mixed marriages and blended families have increased in number. More people than ever are switching their religious affiliations or combining them. Millions of Jews and Christians, for example, include the practices of Buddhism, Hinduism, or other mystical paths.

The shift in political/religious affiliation has had an impact as well. Because of the aforementioned patterns, religious people in the United States have moved more toward the right politically. In the past, labor organizing, civil rights, child welfare, "ban the bomb," antiwar, and other liberal social movements were often led by religious leaders. That has shifted as the conservative Christian movement has grown and liberals have moved toward weaker religious affiliation. Opinions on issues such as abortion rights and LGBTQ rights have fallen along religious lines and conflicted with patterns of generational beliefs, since younger people tend to disproportionately support these issues but people with strong religious affiliations generally do not.

Many of these demographic patterns are surprising. Most people have no idea how many people there are in particular religious communities, and many make false assumptions that there are, for example, far more Jews and Muslims than actually exist in the United States.[14] Yet as I have tried to make clear, we are not fully rational about how we make decisions about anything. What I want to look at here is how this divide is affecting our need to belong, and how that need is contributing to the polarization in our culture today.

Why Religion?

I deeply respect that for many people, their belief in God and their religion are sacrosanct. My intention here is not to question any of those beliefs, but rather to explore how religion affects our sense of societal belonging. Emile Durkheim defined religion as "a unified system of beliefs and practices relative to sacred things, that is to say, things set apart and surrounded by . . . beliefs and practices that unite its adherents in a single moral community."[15] Religion undoubtedly emerged to help establish and sustain a sense of belonging. We evolved from tribal communities that were largely based on kinship. Being related to people meant there was, by and large, a good reason to find harmony in living together. Our cooperation with each other allowed us to survive against other tribes. Infighting threatened that survival. As kinship-based tribes grew, being related began to be replaced by the need for rules and agreed-upon normative patterns of behavior that could ensure similar levels of harmony and cooperation.

On a personal level, religion helped explain the mysteries of life. On a social level, as it became advantageous to form communities that expanded beyond our kin, these rules became essential to establish ways that people from different clans could live together. Religion became a way to preserve and build a sense of community. Religion created the boundaries that kept people in concert with each other. At the same time, those rules gave people in power a way to maintain that power, even beyond whatever economic or military strength they had. By convincing people that there would be rewards in the afterlife for following the rules or punishments for challenging the social order, power was reinforced. This tactic was consciously used, for example, during slavery and by missionaries who used their faith to dominate indigenous peoples around the world under the guise of "saving their souls."

One way to reinforce power is by dividing social life into two domains, the sacred and the profane. There is nothing intrinsic about one particular object or behavior that makes it sacred or about another that makes it profane. Eating pork is profane in the Jewish culture of my birth, and in Islam, but perfectly normal in many others. Eating beef is fine for most Christians, but profane to a religious Hindu. An object or behavior becomes sacred only when the community imbues it with that meaning, sometimes because they believe in the scripture that defines it that way.

At some point it is not only the beliefs and artifacts of the community that become sacred but the power of the community itself. The community begins to establish power that transcends the existence of the individual. When that happens, the institution and its needs can transcend the actual connection to spirit. By venerating a deity or deities, many people are also acknowledging the power of the community over themselves. They yield their own sense of right and wrong, for example, to the greater sense of the group. They are, in effect, revering their society, and so belonging to that society can become tantamount to survival. This doesn't diminish the personal relationship people may have with their deities, but rather is the social component.

The word *religion* is most likely derived from the Latin root *religare*, "to retie or reconnect." This feeling of collective strength is what most people look for in the groups to which they belong. Ritualistic behavior, allegories of powerful characters who demonstrate the appropriate values, and the reward for participation all encourage worshippers to fall in line. That could then be combined with the cost of not conforming, both socially in terms of banishment and physically in terms of punishment. Together, they reinforce the need to belong. As people feel bound to each other's destiny, their shared sense of community begins to take over: *If you get hurt by the outsider, I might too; therefore, I will stand by you.* We might say that a sense of enlightened self-interest takes over. It makes sense, then, that religion provides a sense of knowing where one stands with others. Inside of the "us versus them" mind-set, religion makes it clear where I belong, and also what is expected of me in terms of my duties and obligations.

For some, religion dispels existential and material loneliness. If somebody is part of something bigger, and if they are connected always to a deity, then they are not alone. The community is there for them when they are hungry. People help take care of them when they are sick. People help take care of their children so that they can work. People help construct their house, or provide resources they may need.

The structure and communion of religious life provide a consistent sense of belonging, which can also lead to excessive conformity and increased isolation of "outsiders." In that sense, religious institutions have defined people socially, created social hierarchies, and determined who can stay and who needs to leave—sometimes by death.

All of this works pretty well, one could argue, as long as you are an intact community living separately from others with different beliefs. But what happens when different religious groups interact with each other? In that situation all that seems supportive, cooperative, and healthy begins to change. Encountering other tribes with different beliefs can easily become a perceived threat. The dominant religion provides a way to control those other tribes. If I absorb some of them into my community, the children who are born have to be "raised right," in order to grow into full members of my culture. My beliefs must then be organized in a way that allows behavior that may not have seemed justified before to be justified now. Power can begin to replace spirituality as a reason for belief, and, as we have seen earlier, the power of the mind to use confirmation bias to justify begins to take over. Alternative belief systems cannot be allowed to exist because they threaten the ability of leaders to maintain control. The out-group homogeneity effect leads to the stereotyping of the other as "heathen" or some similar characterization.

When one group has a profoundly dominant position in a social order, their view of the sacred and profane can become law. The campaigns against marriage equality and abortion rights are good examples of how a dominant majority believes that *their* sacred is *the* sacred. That scripture is used to justify marriage exclusively between men and women is conceivable only if the dominant majority believes that to be sacred. On the other hand, even though in my tradition we were forbidden to eat the flesh of pigs, there are not enough Jews in the United States to even consider forcing that prohibition into law for everybody else.

Hence the dilemma. Religion can provide incredible belonging and solace, but it can also be used as a powerful way to separate, divide, control, and conquer others. It morphs from simply being a set of beliefs and a code of living into a form of identity.

Religion as Identity

Identity is formed both socially and historically. We learn about ourselves through social comparison ("We are not *them*") and through interactions with our family, our friends, and the various organizations and institutions that we are part of. Our social and cultural identities are intricately linked to our interpretations of the experiences we have, the people we engage with, and the things we are exposed to, as well as dynamics of power, ideology, and values. They give us our internal "book of rules" to operate from, and they create expectations among others as to who we are. They include a language that we use, and as Lera Boroditsky, an associate professor of cognitive science at the University of California, San Diego, has found, our language actually *creates* the way we think.[16]

How do we sense ourselves? We do so through an internal language that allows us to conceptualize who were are, and also how we are feeling in relationship to others. Because we think in language, we can only conceptualize ourselves in the context of what that language allows. Boroditsky offers this example:

> Most questions of whether and how language shapes thought start with the simple observation that languages differ from one another. And a lot! Let's take a (very) hypothetical example. Suppose you want to say, "Bush read Chomsky's latest book." Let's focus on just the verb, "read." To say this sentence in English, we have to mark the verb for tense; in this case, we have to pro-

nounce it like "red" and not like "reed." In Indonesian you need not (in fact, you can't) alter the verb to mark tense. In Russian you would have to alter the verb to indicate tense and gender. So if it was Laura Bush who did the reading, you'd use a different form of the verb than if it was George. In Russian you'd also have to include in the verb information about completion. If George read only part of the book, you'd use a different form of the verb than if he'd diligently plowed through the whole thing. In Turkish you'd have to include in the verb how you acquired this information: if you had witnessed this unlikely event with your own two eyes, you'd use one verb form, but if you had simply read or heard about it, or inferred it from something Bush said, you'd use a different verb form.[17]

The experience of seeing ourselves and the world is entirely different, depending upon the language we are interpreting it through.

If we look at the United States today, we would have to say that for many people, religion, or being anti-religious, has become more of a matter of identity than it is a matter of sacred beliefs and practices. When I tell somebody that I am Jewish, that doesn't mean I keep kosher like my mother did, or that I go to synagogue. It is more a statement of how I identify myself. It defines to some degree how I fit into the world around me. In that sense it is no different from any other aspects of my self: my race, nationality, gender, culture, or sexual orientation, for example. In the sense of my actual lived experience, I may be far more similar to a secular Muslim or Christian than I am to an observant Hasidic Jew. I am far more likely to be defined by my social, political, and cultural mores than by my religion. And yet I am still Jewish.

The notion that most people draw their understanding of their religion from that religion's teachings is largely not true. It is more reasonable to suggest that most people choose the religious beliefs that align with their cultural or political perspectives. We can look at marriage equality as an example.

Most people who use biblical reasons for opposing equal rights for LGBTQ Americans cite two passages, Leviticus 18:22 and 20:13, that suggest a man "lying with" another man is "detestable," and another,

Romans 1:26–27, which castigates men for doing "shameful acts" with other men. However, at the same time, most don't strongly adhere to other passages such as

- Leviticus 20:10, which suggests that if a man commits adultery with another man's wife, both must be "immediately dispatched"
- Deuteronomy 22:20–21, which says that if a woman has sex before marriage, she must be stoned to death at her father's doorstep
- Leviticus 20:9, which says that talking back to a parent warrants the death penalty (don't even think about it—they'll probably grow out of it)
- Ephesians 5:22, which commands a wife to obey her husband, as he is the law in the household
- Samuel 15:3, which says to kill every man and woman, child and infant, ox and sheep, camel and donkey who worship any other god (though determining what god oxen, sheep, camels, and donkeys worship is tricky)

We are far more likely to modify our beliefs to meet our needs than to modify our needs to match our beliefs. Once again, this involves motivated reasoning and confirmation bias. Our own desires, biases, and interpretations justify these belief systems. That is how the same Jesus that is used by some to justify holding "welfare cheats" accountable is seen by others as motivation for serving one's fellow human being. It all depends on the mind-set of the follower.

As our religious affiliations polarize us, not unlike the political ones described in Chapter 2, we tend to move toward a greater sense of orthodoxy in our beliefs, and our sense of the "other" also becomes more uniform and stereotyped. The more different someone else is from us, the easier it is to stereotype and demonize that person as an "other" and protect ourselves from him or her. The more our beliefs are sacred to us, the more that "other" becomes the infidel, the profane. And the more we may feel the need to hide any differences we may have with the orthodoxy of the group we identify with, so as to avoid rejection.

We see this happening in the rise of Islamophobia. There is no question that there are segments of the Muslim population who hate the

United States and have committed terrorist acts against us. Yet rather than attempt to determine exactly who those people are, it is much easier to categorize the entire religion as a threat, because its roots are different from our Judeo-Christian ones. The roughly 1.6 billion Muslims in the world come from varied cultures, with many different values. Despite this, we tend to group them as a whole because they are a nondominant group in our context. We don't, for example, see Dylann Roof, Timothy McVeigh, or any of the thousands of white supremacists in our country as "Christian terrorists," even though many have espoused "Christian values" as a justification for their terrorism. Some people don't even speak about them as terrorists. There are many who justify acts of violence and terrorism because it is in the name of their religion. Christian settlers in the United States committed genocide against the indigenous Native American population and created a biblical justification for slavery. Did that represent all of Christianity? American-born Jewish doctor Baruch Goldstein, a member of the radical Kach movement, murdered 29 people and wounded 125 at the Ibrahimi Mosque in Hebron, in the West Bank. Did he represent all Jews? Are the Buddhist terrorists who persecute the Rohingya Muslim minority in Myanmar the same as the Dalai Lama? Do they represent all Buddhists, or are they seen as an aberration?

The more we begin to identify with a particular religious stream, the more it becomes sacralized, and the more likely we are to move to a more fundamentalist position. It is no longer a belief system; it is now representative of who I am. The Taliban becomes a political movement as much as a religious one, as does the fundamentalist Christian movement. Even atheism can embrace this kind of "fundamentalist" mind-set toward its religion: reason. We are once again being lawyers, gathering evidence to support our case.

As religious scholar and author Reza Aslan has said:

> Members of the Islamic State are Muslims for the simple fact that they declare themselves to be so. Dismissing their profession of belief prevents us from dealing honestly with the inherent problems of reconciling religious doctrine with the realities of the modern world. But considering that most of its victims are also Muslims—as are most of the forces fighting and condemning

the Islamic State—the group's self-ascribed Islamic identity cannot be used to make any logical statement about Islam as a global religion.

At the same time, critics of religion must refrain from simplistic generalizations about people of faith. It is true that in many Muslim countries, women do not have the same rights as men. But that fact alone is not enough to declare Islam a religion that is intrinsically more patriarchal than Christianity or Judaism. (It's worth noting that Muslim-majority nations have elected women leaders on several occasions, while some Americans still debate whether the United States is ready for a female president.)[18]

When our religious group is dominant, we may miss the impact that the systems and structures built around it might exclude people. This is where our search for belonging can get triggered. As a young Jewish boy, the time I felt the most "different" was during the Christmas holidays. In those days everything was Christmas, with very little mention of any other holidays. (Kwanzaa wasn't even invented yet.) As a result, I often felt like there was this big party that I wasn't invited to. The same feelings can be triggered by holiday decorations at an office, or the holidays that close a company versus the ones you have to take your personal leave for.

Saying "Merry Christmas" is fine, and it may also fall short if the person you are talking to is Jewish, Muslim, Hindu, etc. That doesn't mean you can't say it. Just be aware that it does not represent everybody. Saying "happy holidays" is not a "war on Christmas"; it is simply an attempt to be inclusive. However, if people are concerned that their Christianity is being denied, then they may perceive others' attempts to be inclusive as exclusive of *them*. Moving toward the inclusion of other religions might be perceived as favoring those religions over Christianity in the same way as affirmative action practices are seen by some whites as favoring people of color, even though they are a response to hundreds of years of practices that favored whites over people of color.

Dogma and the Sacred

Religion is, by its very nature and purpose, prone to dogma. It is difficult to have a structure designed to control a culture without there being some basic values or behaviors that we agree are absolutely true. This can be said for organizations, countries, or even families, but it is especially true about religion. This also makes it easier to evangelize and expand the scope of a religion by convincing others to accept the dogma as a new truth for themselves.

Unfortunately, that runs counter to one of the most valuable abilities that human beings possess: the ability to inquire with an open mind. This is the power of curiosity. Albert Einstein famously said, "I have no special talent. I am only passionately curious."[19] We could make the case that being open-minded is one of our most important virtues because it leads to investigation and understanding; dogma is its antithesis.

Religion has contributed enormously to culture through art, inspiration, the development of moral codes, and the development of science. It's only in the relatively recent past that science and religion have been positioned as counter to each other. The list of scientific geniuses who believed in God is almost endless: Einstein, Pascal, Mendel, Schrödinger, Bacon, Galileo, Leibniz, Marconi, Newton, Kepler, Pasteur, Planck, Faraday, Copernicus . . . the list goes on and on.

Religion has created a source of deep connection and belonging for people in communities around the world for millennia. It has inspired social justice movements and charity around the globe. It has also led to the Crusades, terrorism, and too many examples of horror and oppression to name. It has been the source of war, bigotry, and genocide.

Religious scholar Karen Armstrong argues that until the modern period, most major religions focused on practice, not belief. People were judged by how they practiced the tenets of the religion. If you were Jewish, did you observe the Sabbath and keep kosher? If you were Muslim, did you pray five times daily and make the hajj (pilgrimage to Mecca)? If you were Christian, did you support your church and help the needy?[20]

Religion becomes a problem when the social conditioning or personal psychology of an individual allows that person to use it to justify particular behaviors, or when it forbids any worldview other than the one it espouses. When dogma replaces inquiry and belief replaces reality, religion becomes a divider. Belonging begins to mean "the other is an infidel." Holding on to dogma can also cause self-destruction.

A classic example of this is the fate of the Norse Viking population in Greenland. A relatively small number of Norse settlers landed on Greenland in the tenth century and were able to transplant their lifestyle because it was a time of climatic warming. They built homes, brought livestock, and grew food as they needed it. Four hundred years later they were gone. All of them had starved to death, not because of a lack of food but because of dogma. When the weather turned back toward its normal cold pattern, European methods of farming and livestock could no longer support the settlers. However, the indigenous Inuit population survived by hunting whales and fish with spears. The Norse saw the Inuit as filthy savages and would not adopt their "heathen" practices. Their need to be "right" killed them.[21]

Even in abandoning religion, radical atheists or anti-theists can be just as dogmatic as the dogma they are condemning, claiming reason as a religion, even when neuroscientists around the world challenge the notion that we are as rational as we think we are. It is one thing to choose to believe or not believe something; it is another thing entirely to condemn, belittle, or label as "delusional" people who believe something that you do not.[22]

When we treat our beliefs as if they are sacred, and anybody else's as stupid, ignorant, dangerous, or wrong just because they are not ours, we are being closed-minded. Being closed-minded is not a necessary component of any religion. The problem is not which dogma you buy into. The problem is dogma itself.

Building Bridges across Religion

Many of the suggestions made earlier apply here as well. In terms of the dogmatic way we approach it, politics is a new religion for us. Some of these suggestions are obvious, yet just because something is simple does not make it easy.

Learn about the tenets of the religion from its source, not based on individuals' behavior. Every religion has been used to justify behavior that challenges its fundamental tenets. Try to look at the religion in balance. Both Martin Luther King Jr. and the Ku Klux Klan claimed to represent Christianity. Inquire into why people believe what they do, rather than just simply responding to their beliefs.

Spend time with people in their practice rather than judging it. If you are really interested in learning about a religion, visit a church, mosque, synagogue, meeting, temple, or other place of worship. Read their texts for yourself. Get a real feel for its tenets and actions.

Speak up and address discriminatory behavior whenever and wherever you see it. Calling out discriminatory or closed-minded behavior, especially in the public forum or in the workplace, helps create a safe space for everybody.

Ask for feedback. Encourage others to let you know when your behavior indicates potential bias, and be willing to consider whether it might be happening outside your consciousness.

Be aware of how structures, systems, and practices may be inadvertently exclusive. Many of the behaviors we consider normal may actually be exclusive. For example, be willing to put yourself in another's shoes and think how it feels to have someone else's holiday celebrated but not yours.

Explore organizations that encourage interfaith understanding. There are many organizations that actively promote interfaith understanding and provide information, education, and skills development. Some that come to mind are the Tanenbaum Center for Combating Religious Prejudice, based in New York City (tanenbaum.org), the International Association for Religious

Freedom (iarf.net), and the National Council for Community Justice (nccj.org). Dozens more are listed on the website of Religious Tolerance (religioustolerance.org). There are also many local congregations of all faiths that present programs to encourage understanding. Belong to places that encourage belonging.

If there is anything that the history of religion teaches us, it is that everybody is entitled to believe what they want, but when we start using others' beliefs as a way to judge and condemn them, we create a break in belonging. If, for example, Joan and Fatima were to try to dialogue with each other to understand each other's religious practices, they might find that they have much more in common than they realize. Stereotypes and bias can stop that from happening. That "us versus them" dynamic can have catastrophic results. We'll explore that more in Chapter 7.

Chapter 7

When Worlds Collide

People inside of belonging systems are very threatened by those who are not within that group. They are threatened by anyone who has found their citizenship in places they cannot control.

—RICHARD ROHR

Let's return for a moment to the opening scenario in Chapter 1. Joan, Barry, and Fatima each had their "home" community in which they felt very comfortable: Joan, among other political conservatives as well as her religious community, Barry among other folks who were either gay or felt completely comfortable with his sexual orientation, and Fatima, her religious community. Within each of those communities there is a certain sense of normative values and behavior, "rules" if you will, that all make sense, within the construct of that community. There is a sense of belonging. And yet, when the individuals from these different communities come together, something else happens. All of a sudden, their "otherness" seems to predominate. We live in a world of "us versus them."

Us versus Them

In Chapter 1, I discussed the work of Henri Tajfel and his revolutionary studies on minimal group paradigms. Tajfel's studies provide us with compelling evidence that we are wired to form groups. Even with benign differentiators, we seem to have an inherent preoccupation of defining and separating "us" from "them," regardless of how trivial such group designations might be.

William Graham Sumner, called by some the "father of modern sociology," classified these as in-group and out-group affiliations. Each of us belongs to a number of in-groups with which we define our identities. Members of in-groups tend to have feelings of attachment, sympathy, and affection toward other members of the same groups. In addition, members of in-groups can share a group consciousness, identifying with "we" in relationship to the others in the group. The sense of belonging within these groups is strong. In-groups can be somewhat fixed in terms of a shared identity (e.g., "women" or "African Americans") or can be based on a set of particular social circumstances (e.g., "gun control activists" or "anti-gun-control activists").

Sumner asserted that these groups are marked by a feeling of "ethnocentrism," in that the members of an in-group generally consider their group superior, or at least preferable, to other groups. One's family, clan, race, college, or hometown can all be in-groups. The members of an in-group often feel that their personal welfare is somehow connected with other members of their group. As a result, they are more likely to have a sense of belonging, be cooperative, and focus on maintaining love, goodwill, and respect, as well as seeking to help each other. They usually share some common normative behaviors and often demonstrate a sense of solidarity, as if "we are all in this together." There may even be a willingness to sacrifice themselves for the group.

Sumner classified groups into in-groups and out-groups on the basis of that "we" feeling. Out-groups are almost always defined in reference to the in-groups of which we are a part. Just as we cannot define "hot" without the concept of "cold," we cannot have out-groups or in-groups without establishing the other. Out-groups are often seen as "different" and threatening in some way, whether this is cautiously acknowledged or not. We may express disinterest in, overtly dislike, not understand, or even compete with an out-group.

Being part of an in-group doesn't mean that there isn't discord within the group; that discord, however, can disappear when an out-group member confronts or challenges another member of their in-group. Most of us can look at our families and see this phenomenon. My father and I loved each other, but back in the late 1960s we were on opposite sides of the issues regarding the Vietnam War. I was a protester against the war, whereas he was much more ambiguous, although he had no ambiguity about my long hair, which he unambiguously hated and criticized me for. One day we were in Baltimore at a family event and my uncle, who had served in the 82nd Airborne during World War II, began to criticize my appearance. All of a sudden, my father jumped to my defense, even telling my uncle, "His freedom to wear his hair the way he wants is what we fought for in the war!" My sisters and I looked at each other with shock. He and I could fight, it seemed, but when I was under attack, his in-group feelings toward his son trumped almost anything else.

We can also find ourselves torn between the competing needs of two groups that we relate to as in-groups. One of my law firm clients once had an issue that created tension between the lawyers, who were mostly white, and the administrative staff, who were mostly women of color. One of the partners in the firm, an African American woman, described how the conflict occurred for her: "It was challenging. On one hand, I could relate to the needs of my partners and what they were expecting from the administrative staff, because they were my needs as well. On the other hand, I couldn't help but relate to the mostly black women who were on the admin team and the way they were being treated by the mostly white partners. I remember thinking to myself, 'Who am I here?'"

Despite these conflicts, this "us versus them" paradigm is universal, and it's also arguably innate. Studies emerging from infant development labs provide compelling evidence that even as babies we are drawn to make assessments based on in-group favoritism and out-group condemnation.

In one experiment, nine- and fourteen-month-old infants were presented with two food options: green beans or graham crackers.[1] Once a preference had been established, the babies then watched as two rabbit puppets were presented with the same selection of food. The researchers manipulated the rabbit puppets in a way that looked like one would always prefer the graham crackers while disliking the green beans, and the other would do the opposite. In this way, a rudimentary form of in-group and out-group could be established, with babies ostensibly seeing the rabbit puppet who shared their food preference as a member of their own group.

The most fascinating aspect of the study was how infants would react to the second phase of the puppet show. Either the rabbit puppets who

shared the infant's food preference or the other rabbit puppets would re-
peatedly bounce and catch a ball. Every few bounces, they would acci-
dentally drop the ball, causing it to roll toward one of two dog puppets
positioned toward the back of the stage. One dog puppet was helpful,
always bringing the ball back to the rabbit puppet when it was dropped,
while the other was harmful, always taking the ball and running away.
After observing several rounds of ball-dropping followed by helpful and
harmful behavior, the babies were then given the chance to play with
either the helpful or harmful dogs. Which would they choose?

The results were not only conclusive but even alarming. Infants overwhelmingly preferred the helpful dog when the rabbit puppet that
dropped the ball shared their food preference and preferred the harmful
dog when the rabbit puppet dropping the ball had preferred the other food.
Eighty-three percent of the infants tested liked the dog who helped the
similar rabbit, and nearly 88 percent of all infants preferred the dog who
was mean to the dissimilar rabbit. Such evidence suggests that even at
an early age, tribalism permeates our worldview. We seek to interact with
those who are nice to people we like and mean to people we dislike. Even
for infants, the old adage rings true: the enemy of our enemy is our friend.
We've been exploring how this impacts politics, religion, and race in other
chapters.

Empathy

These infants eventually grow into adults whose preference for, indiffer-
ence toward, or hatred of other humans can have more dramatic consequences than not being chosen as a play partner. A prime determinant
of how positively we're likely to treat others is the degree to which we
empathize with them. Unfortunately, research is revealing that not all
empathic targets are created equal.

Recently, neuroscientists have begun to find that our brains are not
wired to deploy empathy indiscriminately, but rather to allocate our empathic resources preferentially toward those in our in-groups. Lack of
healthy responses to out-groups provides evidence for what scientists call
"empathic failures" or "dampened empathic responses." These diluted

responses to out-group targets can most accurately be defined by the reduced level of *empathic resonance* an onlooker displays relative to observing an in-group target. For instance, when white and black participants watched as a hand was pricked with a pin, the sight of such an act triggered what I referred to earlier as a mirror neuron response, evoking similar pain-related sensorimotor responses in the onlookers' own hand—they were, in a way, *feeling* that other person's pain. Unfortunately, there was a catch: such empathic resonance was far more pronounced when a white person watched a white hand get pricked, and similarly when a black person watched a black hand get pricked.[2]

Though disheartening, these findings do make sense from an evolutionary perspective. Many empathy researchers argue that the primary by-product of empathy should be an intention to respond in a socially beneficial manner to the benefit of all.[3] In this way, empathy is more than just a nice way to understand the state of another; it's also a pathway to improving the circumstances of the group. Such altruistic impulses would have conferred survival benefits to members of groups where other members were inclined to display them as well.[4] Within the ancestral environment, however, such groups were generally small in number and homogeneous in makeup. Consequently, though empathy evolved, it evolved in a tribal manner. Those with whom we share a sense of belonging more readily trigger our empathic impulses.

Tribal empathy becomes evident when we look at the people to whom we're most likely to extend help. A team of psychologists at Lancaster University in the United Kingdom set up a simple yet illustrative experiment to investigate how one's tribal identity can impact emergency intervention.[5] The researchers recruited participants who identified as Manchester United fans, a popular English soccer team. The Manchester fans were told they would be participating in a two-part experiment, where the second portion would require them to walk to a different building on campus. Unbeknownst to them, it was during this building transition that the actual experiment would take place. As participants walked to the second location, a seemingly uninvolved individual working with the researchers (called a confederate) would pretend to trip and fall in their line of sight, feigning an injury after hitting the ground. The only variable was the clothing of the individual: some wore Manchester United jerseys, others wore jerseys of a rival club, Liverpool FC, while a control group wore neutral clothing.

We would like to believe that something as seemingly trivial as the jersey of a rival sports team wouldn't impact the likelihood of receiving attention in the event of an accident, but it appears that we would be incorrect. Thirteen of the Manchester fans saw a fellow Manchester fan fall and hurt himself, and of that group only one didn't stop to offer help. For the ten who saw a Liverpool supporter unexpectedly injure himself, however, a full seven continued to their destination without offering assistance.

Such a result may confuse and anger those who see such rivalries as silly, but these days an allegiance to a sports team might be the closest many of us can come to the feeling of genuine, ancestral tribal membership. Such modern tribes may not be quite as ruthless as tribes of old, but the emotions they evoke are often similarly primal. It may even be in our collective best interests for people to have something as inconsequential as a sporting match to argue about, rather than "real-life" issues. This outlet for our competitive juices can satisfy something inside of us.

This dynamic is even more disturbing when it impacts something as critical as the media coverage given to missing women and girls, which can contribute significantly to whether the person is found. Research shows that both the frequency and intensity of news coverage is greater when the missing person is white.[6] It seems as though these girls and women draw more empathy and concern because of their race. And, in fact, our patriarchal protectiveness toward women may also make a missing female draw more attention and concern than a missing male.

Fear and Bias

Fear accentuates all of these dynamics. The amygdala is the most sensitive and reactive part of our brain. It is highly sensitized to threat, which helps keep us safe. When we are gripped by fear, especially prolonged periods of fear or post-traumatic stress, our amygdala goes into overdrive. The fear center of the brain creates a survival response that, quite literally, takes over the system. Daniel Goleman, who popularized the concept of "emotional intelligence," has referred to this as an "amygdala hijack."[7] The threat, either real or perceived, causes a survival reaction that can occur in three major ways. The first is reactive and well known to most of us: fight, flight, or freeze. Our brains are taken back to ancestral times when we had to decide instantly, "Do we fight this threat, run from it, or freeze in place?" Different personalities might react in different ways, and most of us have a clear sense of our default reactive responses. Think about it: when you feel attacked, do you attack back, do you retreat, or do you find yourself frozen?

The second response is more control oriented. When we are afraid, we want to feel like we can exercise control over the situation at hand. For some, this is characterized by becoming "control freaks." They want everything in their environment to be exactly as they would like it to be because the ability to control the environment creates a sense of safety. People who are generally fearful can often live with a perpetual need to be in control.

When we can't control the situation ourselves, we often find ourselves drawn to strong (and often male) authority figures who we perceive will provide that safety for us, almost as if we were turning to a parent for safety. Consider what happened in the United States in the period immediately following the 9/11 attacks. President George W. Bush, less than a year into his first term after one of the most contentious elections in American history, had a 51 percent approval rating before the attack, but afterward it rose to a 92 percent approval rating almost overnight, particularly after he stated, using a bullhorn at Ground Zero, that we would get revenge for the acts.[8] This tendency to look for a strong "protector" has historically led entire cultures to turn toward totalitarian leaders at times when a collective stress environment is present. It is no accident that most times in history when a dictator or dictatorial government has taken over, particularly in what had previously been a democracy, that it has been proceeded by rampant social unrest and instability (think of Hitler and Mussolini in the 1930s, or the Taliban in Afghanistan).

The third impact of the amygdala hijack is that we begin to see the situation at hand as permanent, pervasive, and personal ("It is always going to be this way!" "It's everywhere!" "It's going to get me!"). Rationality has little to do with this phenomenon. One of the reasons that

Donald Trump was able to win the presidential election in 2016 was because of his strong support in rural communities among people who felt terrorism was one of the most significant issues they were facing, even though the history of terrorism shows that people in rural communities are safer than those in larger city centers. The Montana state legislature passed a measure in March 2017 making Islamic law (sharia) illegal in the state, even though Montana has fewer Muslims than almost any other state in the country. The bill was eventually vetoed by the governor.[9]

Similarly, racial bias is sometimes strongest in places where there are fewer people of color, because people rely more on stereotypes than on their lived experience of people in these groups. This led to the development of the *contact hypothesis,* first proposed by Gordon Allport in 1954 in his landmark work *The Nature of Prejudice,* which theorizes that exposure to people different from us leads to humanization and lessens prejudice.[10]

Blind bias is not unusual when fear is present. In my previous book, *Everyday Bias,* I wrote about the ubiquitous nature of bias in our lives.[11] Human beings use bias to establish safety, and so we are far more likely to have negative biases against those we consider to be "others" and more positive ones toward those we consider to be in our own group. Hundreds of studies have demonstrated that this phenomenon is as natural to human beings as breathing, and it is undoubtedly the result of an evolutionary drive to find ways to be and feel safe. We tend to stereotype people more easily when they are outside of our bonded group than when they are "one of us." This can be as basic as assessments of appearance: people rarely say, "All of us look the same," but they often say, "All of them look the same to me." We know that empathy decreases when the potential target of that empathy is somebody of a different racial group, or even is wearing a different team jersey!

This same pattern is evident in study after study of how bias plays out. Looking just at racial bias as it impacts African Americans (and the same case could easily be made about other nondominant group members), it can be seen in the fact that doctors are more likely to send white patients for medical procedures than black patients, even when they have identical medical files, or in white people receiving more responses to inquiries about available housing than blacks and being shown more apartments to rent or buy.[12] It impacts political affiliations when white state legislators, of both parties, respond less to constituents with African American–sounding names.[13] It affects the way faculty members at major universities choose students for research opportunities.[14] Studies have even found that people pay 21 percent more in eBay auctions when an iPod being auctioned is being held by a white hand rather than a black hand.[15]

I could list hundreds of other examples relative to the impact of bias on people of many different identity groups, which all point to the same truth: human beings are consistently and pervasively biased.

This tendency to have strong reactions to those in out-groups can boggle the rational mind. I remember interviewing employees at a client site in Minneapolis a number of years ago. The company had undertaken an affirmative attempt to hire more people of color, and while interviewing employees, we asked a simple question: "How many people of color do you think work here now, of the approximately six hundred total employees who work in the office?" The results were telling. The average response among white employees was about eighty. The response among employees of color was almost exactly accurate: twenty-nine. It was almost as if a voice in the minds of the white employees was screaming, "They're everywhere!" White employees simply have less of a need to notice people like themselves in order to be safe in the environment, because they are actually the ones who are "everywhere."

Stigmatization and Dehumanization

This tendency to have one's view of things altered by bias can contribute to the stigmatization of out-group members. Stigmatization occurs when a facet of an individual's identity or culture becomes the object of contempt. Columbia University's Bruce Link and Jo Phelan argue that for stigmatization to occur, several components must be present.[16] The first three components involve separating "us" from "them," identifying factors that highlight these differences, and then labeling the differences that characterize out-groups as "undesirable." The final component concerns power dynamics. According to Link and Phelan, for stigmatization to be possible, the stigmatized group must lack the ability to exercise meaningful social power relative to the dominant group. This allows for the accumulation of tangible social consequences for stigmatized groups. Conversely, low-power groups attempting to stigmatize groups possessing disproportionate social power are typically unable to exert meaningful negative repercussions.

As stigmatization grows more insidious and vitriolic, dehumanization can occur. Dehumanization involves stripping individuals of their uniquely human qualities, rendering them less than human in domains such as intellectual capability, emotional depth, pain tolerance, or essence.

We can certainly find plenty of evidence to support this notion. In Chapter 3, Vital Akimana described how the Tutsis in Rwanda were characterized as "cockroaches who are invading from the mountains." The Nazis referred to Jews as "an alien race" or "vermin." American soldiers called the Japanese "Japs" and the Vietnamese "gooks." Even within our own country we have seen the use of terms such as *fag*, *wetback*, the *n*-word, *bitches*, and worse. Language is often one of the main tools of stigmatization and dehumanization.

Though generally referenced in discussions concerning overt and egregious instances of the phenomenon, findings suggest that dehumanization can be deployed with far greater subtlety—allowing it to serve not only as a psychological lubricant for battlefield atrocities but also as a mechanism to traverse everyday social environments.[17] As discussed earlier, this dehumanization can in the extreme even lead to genocide.

For example, when people pass a homeless individual on the street on a particularly cold night, they typically try to reduce the psychological discomfort engendered by seeing a human being in such a condition in one of two ways: attributing deservingness or employing dehumanization. The former allows one to feel less guilty by convincing oneself that such a person has somehow done something to deserve such a frigid fate. In psychological literature, this line of reasoning—where people "get what they deserve and deserve what they get"—is referred to as a *belief in a just world* and is a form of social Darwinism.[18] The latter, dehumanization, alleviates distress by painting the individual as someone who doesn't experience the pain of sitting in the cold in the same manner as you might. "Yeah, I'm freezing out here, but he's probably fine! He's used to it, right?" In this way, we effectively deny an individual's humanity by denying the likelihood that he or she experiences pain in the same way that we do. Even when something as egregious as human slavery was the norm, people were able to justify it by suggesting that the slaves were "happier that way."[19] I have long believed that we would not tolerate homelessness in this country if every person who had a home was required to introduce him- or herself to every homeless person he or she encountered. It is easy to discard someone when they are nameless, but much more difficult when we see them as human. The more we know people as *who* they are, the less we treat them like *what* they are.

In a striking set of findings, social neuroscientist Lasana Harris and social psychologist Susan Fiske found that dehumanization can dramatically impact the way our brains process people.[20] As was previously discussed, our default network overlaps tremendously with our social cognition network. The hub of each network is the medial prefrontal cortex (mPFC). When we think about other people, our mPFC is humming away. However, when Harris and Fiske asked participants to look at pictures while their neural activity was being monitored by a fMRI machine, they discovered something troubling. When participants viewed pictures of chronically dehumanized groups—such as the homeless or drug addicts—their mPFC failed to generate the typical signs of activity. Instead, the insula and amygdala were recruited—an activation pattern typical of disgust. The absence of normal mPFC activity suggests that such targets were being processed not as humans but rather as objects (perhaps quite literally) of disgust. In this way, dehumanization gives us license to remove certain individuals from the circle of caring.[21]

One of the saddest and most insidious qualities of prolonged stigmatization and dehumanization like this can be that it can result in *learned helplessness*, a behavior pattern that occurs when people, especially those in an out-group, have endured consistent and repeated painful or otherwise circumstances which they were unable to escape or avoid. In the late 1960s, J. Bruce Overmier and Martin Seligman conducted a series of experiments designed to test animal responses to aversive conditions.[22] The researchers first exposed dogs to a series of electric shocks. However, there were two conditions: dogs who could learn to control the duration of their shocks (by pressing a lever to stop them) and dogs who were given no control (whose lever had no bearing on shock duration). Next, researchers moved the dogs into what is known as a "shuttle box," or an enclosed pen with a barrier bisecting it, creating two sides. The procedure here was simple: the researchers would administer the shocks until the dogs leapt over the barrier to the other side of the pen, at which point the shocks would cease.

The dogs in the first condition had no issue learning the trick to get the shocks to stop in the shuttle box. They quickly mastered jumping the barrier upon the onset of shock, thus shuttling to the adjacent area and stopping the painful sensation. Something peculiar happened with the dogs in the second condition, however. Those dogs who had been forced to simply endure the shocks with no way to control or stop them in the first portion of the experiment continued to endure the shocks while in the shuttle box. Rather than jumping the barrier, or even searching for any way whatsoever to escape the pain, most simply lay down and accepted their fate. They had, in essence, learned to be helpless.

The researchers conjecture that this idea of learned helplessness stemmed from perceived locus of control. If an individual believes they are in full control of their lives, and that the events that befall them are theirs to adapt to and ultimately dictate, they are said to have an internal locus of control. If, however, it is believed that one has very little say in the events that transpire around them and their role within such an environment, they are said to believe in an external locus of control. The dogs from condition two learned that they could not control the shocks they received, creating a perceived external locus of control that persisted even when their circumstances shifted.

Many social scientists have speculated that learned helplessness is a pervasive challenge in the African American community. Centuries of discrimination on behalf of the dominant white American culture have resulted in a form of learned helplessness that Dr. Joy DeGruy, an African American social work researcher, refers to as *post-traumatic slave syndrome*, or PTSS: "P.T.S.S. is a theory that explains the etiology of many of the adaptive survival behaviors in African American communities throughout the United States and the Diaspora. It is a condition that exists as a consequence of multigenerational oppression of Africans and their descendants resulting from centuries of chattel slavery. A form of slavery which was predicated on the belief that African Americans were inherently/genetically inferior to whites. This was then followed by institutionalized racism which continues to perpetuate injury."[23]

DeGruy asserts that PTSS is characterized by a sense of "vacant esteem," which increases the risk of depression, hopelessness, and illness; by increased anger and violence toward oneself, property, and others, triggered by extreme feelings of suspicion and others' perceived negative motivation; and by racist socialization, including internalized racism, distorted self-concept, and antipathy or aversion to members of one's own group, cultural symbols, and physical characteristics of the group. All of this is reinforced by systemic examples of racism that occur on a daily basis. Our sense of belonging to the group, it seems, conflicts with the learned belief that there is something wrong with the group.

This is not to say that learned helplessness cannot be overcome, nor that all African Americans experience it. Even considering the circumstances that have led to experiences of learned helplessness within the African American community, how has this community managed such resilience? How does the African American community endure the atrocities of the past and present, and manage to stand and find success today despite all that has been placed against them? It has taken enormous courage, persistence and collective effort to overcome, using energy and effort that people in other communities have not had to spend, and through this privilege, often overlook. What it does mean, however, is that the need to overcome learned helplessness is an inequitable burden that other groups do not have to bear.

The experience of African Americans in this regard is different from those of black Americans born in predominantly black countries. This can sometimes cause tensions even between groups of black people born and raised in the United States and those born and raised in Africa and the Caribbean, for example, who have been raised in a completely different environment in which political and business leaders were overwhelmingly black and the major differentiator was socioeconomic or tribal status rather than race. People may be bonding by race, but only bridging by culture and background.

In many ways, learned helplessness is a coping mechanism. Hope can sometimes create immense frustration. Continually putting forth great effort with the hope of improvement yet perpetually failing to harvest positive results is time-consuming, physically exhausting, and emotionally draining. Thus, as depressing as it may seem, it can often be easier to simply abandon hope and resolve to accept the realities of one's current situation. Just as the dogs had done, many humans also find that giving up is often less distressing than continuing to try when failure seems to be inevitable.

This is one of the great challenges that people in dominant groups often have in understanding the challenges that people in nondominant groups face, which keeps the "us versus them" dynamic firmly locked in place. To the dominant group member, having never had to bear the yoke of systemic powerlessness, the answer to the problem is, "That's all in the past. Just get up and do something about it!" There is no recognition that the physical, economic, and psychological scars of the past still exist in the current reality. We have difficulty understanding the lived experiences of the "other" and can be fixated on our own version of the truth, which, as we have seen, we are wired to ensure stays aligned with our belief systems. Let's explore more of what gets in the way of an objective reality.

The Halo/Horns Effect

Imagine that your friend has just started her own nonprofit. One evening she asks you to accompany her to a networking event being held at a local restaurant. You realize that you won't know anyone there, but in the spirit of friendship you agree to attend. At one point during the evening, your friend gets pulled away to meet someone, leaving you to mingle by yourself. After a few moments of wandering, you find yourself striking up a conversation with a woman whom you instantly like; she's quick-witted, funny, and intelligent—a delightful conversation partner. Though the topics of conversation are kept light and innocuous, straying carefully away from anything too meaningful and potentially polarizing, you share an enjoyable dialogue and, as the night draws to a close, you go your separate ways.

On the car ride home, your friend mentions that the person she saw you speaking with is named Ms. Parker, and she is considering asking her to donate to her new charitable venture. "Do you think she'd make a donation?" Without a second thought, you reflexively answer, "Oh, absolutely!" But despite your confidence, your assumption has no empirical basis to it. You've fallen victim to the *halo effect*.

The halo effect is a cognitive bias wherein our liking for someone in one domain ends up producing unwarranted positive generalizations for other, unknown domains as well. It's a specific type of confirmation bias, where our affinity toward an individual permeates our evaluation of unrelated characteristics, causing us to interpret neutral, incomplete, or ambiguous information in a favorable manner. In essence, we give those we like, and often those with whom we share a sense of belonging, the benefit of the doubt when it comes to aspects of them we may know nothing about. Our minds take a leap of faith that the positive experience we associate with that person in one domain will translate into predictably positive behavior in a completely different domain.

In the case of Ms. Parker, your pleasant interaction has led you to assume she'd necessarily possess other positive traits (such as generosity) as well. This is heuristic-style thinking: "I like this person in one domain, and therefore she will probably possess other similarly likable traits in other domains." However, despite your confidence, the fact of the matter is that a brief, casual conversation has provided you with very little information regarding Ms. Parker's likelihood of donation.

The most reliable predictor of the halo effect is physical attractiveness. Physically beautiful people are often assumed to possess equally beautiful personalities. Research has shown that when given nothing but pictures of strangers, people overwhelmingly imbue physically attractive candidates with positive personality traits, creating the unwarranted extrapolation of physical beauty onto unrelated attributes such as altruism and trustworthiness.[24] The authors of one of the most famous halo-effect experiments summarized their findings succinctly in the title of their article: "What Is Beautiful Is Good." Similar studies have shown that physical appearance even impacts who we elect as our leaders.[25] It is important to remember, however, that since standards of physical beauty are often correspondingly associated with dynamics of power and influence in society, particularly race, what is considered "beautiful" may also be what is considered white.

Such an effect can also occur in the opposite direction, a phenomenon researchers have cleverly dubbed the *horns effect*. Whereas the halo effect produces a spreading of favorable judgments from a single liked aspect, the horns effect produces a similar spreading of unfavorable judgments. If an individual is hated enough for something he or she has done, that hatred can often spread like a virus, causing any semblance of positivity to evaporate from that person's legacy—think of how we view dictators and despots. The horns effect can occur at all levels of society. It can, for example, cause teachers to look for challenging behavior more in preschool children of color than in white children.[26] It can also result in police officers assuming that an unarmed African American man "looks like a bad dude too. Probably on something," and therefore taking aggressive action and shooting, as police officer Betty Shelby did when she shot and killed Terence Crutcher in Tulsa, Oklahoma.[27]

The horns effect can also be related to things other than appearance, and can occur at all socioeconomic levels. One of my clients is a large national law firm based in New York City. A young associate had started with their firm one fall a few years ago. He was, in the words of the partner who had been assigned as his mentor, "taking off like a rocket ship." The partner said he had never seen a new associate perform at this level in all of his years of experience. That spring the entire firm had their annual outing at a golf club in Westchester County. Many of the lawyers played golf, and the young associate did as well. However, it turned out his prowess as a lawyer did not translate to the golf course, on which he was abysmal.

The fascinating thing is what happened after they returned to the office. The partner said that all of a sudden the associate got fewer requests to work on cases. The partner realized what had happened when he heard several partners still joking about what a terrible golfer the associate was. The horns effect had taken over. Because he was a bad golfer, the partners had lost their respect for him as a lawyer.

Of course, the same thing can happen on a daily basis to white women, people of color, people with disabilities, LGBTQ people, or others in nondominant groups in all kinds of workplace environments. The bias that someone may have, consciously or unconsciously, can impact how much he or she values the input of another coworker. When we are bonded with a group, by contrast, we will tend to see their halo.

Confirmation Bias and the Backfire Effect

One of the reasons we have such a challenging time commiserating with those we perceive as ideological, identity, or political opponents is that our brains are not designed for objective evaluation but rather programmed to justify our own points of view. In short, as a product of our social natures, our brains have evolved to win arguments, not consider the respective merits of each piece of evidence.[28]

Much of the way we gather information can be classified as self-serving. Humans do not take in all data in a uniform manner, but rather process certain pieces of information preferentially if they serve to confirm our beliefs. This, as we have seen, is confirmation bias—the tendency to seek out and favor evidence that supports what one already believes.[29] Confirmation bias has been studied in a variety of contexts, and for those hoping for a promising view of our prospects of reaching compromises in domains such as social, political, and economic policy, the results thus far have been troubling.

Some of the first research done on confirmation bias was also some of the most striking. In 1954, Albert Hastorf and Hadley Cantril asked students from Dartmouth and Princeton to watch a recording of a football game played between the two schools and record how many penalties each team committed.[30] A stark division emerged between how members of each school evaluated the conduct of each team throughout the game; for example, Princeton students claimed Dartmouth had committed three times as many flagrant violations and twice as many regular penalties as their own team. This rigid divergence ultimately led the researchers to comment that the two groups of students effectively saw different games.

Newer studies have exposed opposing groups to identical clips of news coverage to analyze how perceptions are altered by group membership. When groups of Arab and Israeli students were exposed to identical news reports of the 1982 Beirut massacre, both sides emerged with a sense that their groups had been portrayed unfairly.[31] The phenomenon that emerged has been labeled the "hostile media effect." Because of our desire for confirmatory evidence, it appears even neutral coverage will be perceived as unflattering if it considers the opposing perspective fairly.

This particular effect may account for the wild successes of news outlets portraying issues in a manner designed to appeal to one side of the political aisle. Clearly this effect has been exacerbated in our current political environment, with various media outlets being accused of portraying "fake news" or "alternative facts." This will be discussed in more depth in Chapter 8.

While the prior studies demonstrate our biased interpretation of evidence, we are also biased in the manner in which we search for and subsequently assimilate evidence. In another classic study, people with strong opinions about capital punishment were presented with mixed evidence concerning capital punishment's efficacy in deterring crime.[32] One might think that mixed evidence would encourage more moderate views, but it appears to do the opposite. People rated the evidence supporting their original views more compelling than the contrary evidence, and as a result, both opponents and proponents of capital punishment became more confident in their views after exposure to a series of balanced evidence. This type of polarization resulting from the presentation of balanced coverage is disheartening, and speaks to why debates often fail to change minds and rather serve to further entrench people in their initial opinions.

Confirmation bias is bolstered by a peculiar phenomenon known as the "backfire effect." Essentially, rather than individuals changing their opinions when confronted with facts that contradict their position, they actually report believing in their original positions even more strongly than before.[33] Psychologists Brendan Nyhan and Jason Reifler believe this effect is catalyzed by how we respond to the presentation of contradictory information. As opposed to giving the new, incongruent evidence full consideration, humans tend to immediately go to work attempting to refute the facts with counterarguments. This vigorous internal exercise of producing counterarguments to fend off unwelcome information often helps us to generate more attitudinally congruent information than we had before, leading to even more extreme positions. It can also, as we easily see when looking at others (but less easily when looking at ourselves), create a propensity toward hypocrisy, as we cobble together the things we agree with and like, and somehow find justification for the contradictions they may create. As the great economist John Kenneth

Galbraith purportedly said, "Most human beings, given a strongly held point of view and evidence to the contrary, will quickly go about refuting the evidence."

Do Power and Privilege Make You Mean?

It is easy to see from this research why we get fixed in our points of view, and how deeply those points of view are influenced by our groups. It's worth raising the question of whether there are certain group identities that represent especially deep patterns of judgment. I've discussed earlier how our hypersensitivity to the judgmental gaze of others can activate an inclination to behave in socially desirable ways when we're reminded that we might be watched. There are, however, similarly subtle influences that can cause us to act in less desirable ways. A factor of particular importance is the possession of social power.

The possession of social power is a potent elixir that bolsters one's sense of confidence, certainty, and conviction. Those with power have a higher sense of self-esteem, increased pride, and greater feelings of control.

Social power affords individuals the privilege of dedicating less time and effort to understanding the concerns of low-power others. For instance, in primates, low-status members must remain constantly vigilant, paying keen attention to those of higher rank so as to win their favor and avoid incurring their wrath. High-status primates, conversely, need not concern themselves with the behavior of their social inferiors, allowing them to selectively allocate their attention instead only to primates of similar social status, of which there are relatively few.[34] Virtually identical results have been found in people, as Sukhvinder Obhi and his colleagues Jeremy Hogeveen and Michael Inzlicht found: "It turned out that when people were in a 'powerless' mindset, their mirror system was increased. . . . They became more sensitive to external stimulus, whereas when people were feeling powerful, the mirror neuron activation was lower. Power, it turns out, diminishes our sense of empathy.[35]

Most of us know Lord Acton's famous admonition, "Power corrupts, and absolute power corrupts absolutely." Power has become notorious and almost synonymous with corruption.[36] According to Susan Fiske, the corruptive nature of power has to do, in part, with power-holders' greater willingness to utilize stereotypes.[37] In an effort to establish control of their social environments, powerless individuals must make correct interpersonal predictions; this places a premium on accurate evaluations of others. The focus on accuracy as opposed to expediency promotes nonstereotypic thinking, as being precise in social judgments requires that we treat each individual separately. For power-holders, however, stereotyping can be an efficient and practical strategy, as they need not pay attention to each individual (because they face far fewer negative consequences for inaccuracy) or they choose not to do so (because those with power often consider the powerless to be irrelevant to the pursuit of their goals). So power and stereotyping become mutually reinforcing, with stereotyping bolstering the status quo, solidifying power hierarchies, and thus validating the use of continued stereotypic thinking.

Corroborating Fiske's work, psychologist Paul Piff and a team of scientists from UC Berkeley and the University of Toronto have shown that upper-class individuals—who would hypothetically possess correspondingly high degrees of social power—are more likely to engage in unethical behavior than their lower-class peers. Among their social transgressions, upper-class subjects were "more likely to break the law while driving, relative to lower-class individuals. In follow-up laboratory studies, upper-class individuals were more likely to exhibit unethical decision-making tendencies, take valued goods from others, lie in a negotiation, cheat to increase their chances of winning a prize, and endorse unethical behavior at work than were lower-class individuals."[38]

Though there is no shortcut to attaining social power, there are methods that can dramatically accelerate the process. The most efficient method? Money. Increases in power predictably accompany increases in wealth, and researchers have taken care to document the distinct behavioral changes that money can catalyze.

The research team of Kathleen Vohs, Nicole Mean, and Miranda Goode has found that even the idea of having more money increases the perceived self-sufficiency of participants.[39] Though self-sufficiency sounds like an admirable quality, in this case it leads to the deployment of selfish social strategizing. Such newfound self-sufficiency inclined participants to seek to reduce dependency and eschew dependents, leading them to ask for less help *from* others and offer less help *to* others, respectively.

Perhaps even more striking, Vohs, along with Sun Yat-Sen University psychologist Xinyue Zhou and Florida State University psychologist Roy Baumeister, have shown that subtle manipulations involving money can impact how we experience both physical and social pain.[40] Participants asked to handle money (as opposed to plain paper) exhibited less distress when confronted with social exclusion and reported reduced pain during a pain-inducement activity (immersing their hand in hot water). Interestingly, participants who were exposed to a manipulation designed to remind them of having *less* money (by asking them to itemize monthly expenses) showed more pronounced responses to both pain measures.

All of the dynamics in the past several chapters can only lead to the conclusion that our lives are run by our need to belong, the impact that belonging has on our group identity, and the perspective that identity gives us in the world. Given that we live at the intersection of multiple identities, any one of which can be "driving the bus," so to speak, at any given time, this is a complex system. This need to belong can bring us together or tear us apart. When bonding is healthy, it can lead to our feeling supported and strengthened by our in-group affiliations and therefore able to bridge in a healthy way to members of other groups. When bonding is unhealthy, however, it can breed a defensive "circle the wagons" mind-set, in which we have to protect our own at all costs and all members of outside groups become a threat; this makes bridging difficult if not impossible.

When I conducted the research for *Everyday Bias,* the most significant realization was that bias is part of the way we are designed to function as human beings. We all have biases, and they can be beneficial when they help us make quick, lifesaving decisions, or they can be harmful when they cause us to hurt others. This research has led me to a similar conclusion about our tendency toward "us versus them" thinking. It is the way we see the world, beginning from our infancy and throughout the rest of our lives. We cannot escape it. We can only learn to find ways to minimize its negative impact. In Chapter 8 we will look at how the information we get both creates and is impacted by the groups in which we belong.

Chapter 8

The Media Is the Message

The medium is the message. This is merely to say that the personal and social consequences of any medium—that is, of any extension of ourselves—result from the new scale that is introduced into our affairs by each extension of ourselves, or by any new technology.

—MARSHALL
McLUHAN

The media's the most powerful entity on Earth. They have the power to make the innocent guilty and to make the guilty innocent, and that's power. Because they can control the minds of the masses.

—EL-HAJJ MALIK
EL-SHABAZZ
(MALCOLM X)

In our opening scenario, Barry watches MSNBC to start his day, Joan watches Fox News, and Fatima watches the BBC. How are their attitudes and opinions being shaped by what they see every morning? How does that difference impact the "us versus them" dynamic among them?

How do you get *your* news?

On June 8, 2017, former FBI director James Comey testified before the United States Senate. Comey had been fired by President Donald Trump a month earlier. The firing created a media firestorm that, under examination, reveals a lot about our culture today. Over the course of the testimony, cable news programs not only covered Comey's testimony but also added to the viewer's experience by providing captions, usually in all capital letters, at the bottom of the screen (often called *chyrons* or *lower-thirds*). These chyrons are significant because they guide viewers' understanding of what key points are being made during the broadcast and how a viewer should perceive and react to such points, thus guiding them toward particular conclusions. A look at some of the differences in how three major news outlets, CNN, Fox News, and MSNBC, chose to highlight what was being said is an illustrative example of one of the major reasons we exist in a world of separation.[1]

- Director Comey mentioned twice during his testimony that President Trump had lied or might lie. CNN had thirty-four chyrons that were in some way related to "Trump admin lied about me & FBI," Fox had only nine such references, and MSNBC had forty-nine.
- Sen. Joe Manchin (D-WV) asked Comey, "Do you believe this rises to obstruction of justice?" to which Comey replied, "I don't know. That's Bob Mueller's job to sort that out." CNN had two chyrons regarding this comment, Fox had seventeen, and MSNBC had twenty-three.
- Comey said that he had taken the president's words asking to stop the probe on Flynn "as directive." CNN ran twenty-one chyrons regarding this statement, and MSNBC ran two; Fox did not mention it.
- Comey said that nobody explicitly asked him to stop the Russia probe. CNN did not run a chyron regarding this comment, Fox ran it in two variations ("Nobody asked me to stop Russia probe" and "Pres did not order me to let Flynn probe go") a total of thirty-six times, and MSNBC ran it twice.

What station were you watching? Perhaps even more important, what station(s) do you get your news from on a daily basis, and how does this choice impact what you believe about our world today?

It is virtually impossible to discuss the intense polarization in our society without looking at the sources of our information and how we process it. We are, by our very nature and also because of the limitations of our neurocognitive abilities, somewhat limited in the information we absorb. Some neuroscientists estimate that we are exposed to as many as 11 million pieces of data at any one time and can absorb less than fifty.[2] We're going to take a side trip to explore the phenomenon that scientists refer to as *selective attention* when it shapes what we see or as *inattentional blindness* when it causes us to miss something because we are focused on something else. Then we'll come back and look at the impact of social media on our decision-making.

We think that we see all of what is in front of us, but actually we see only a small amount. This can be demonstrated very easily using a cognitive illusion. Take a look at the design below (Figure 8.1) and see if you notice any black dots.

If you are like most people, you likely see dots randomly occurring at odd intervals. In actuality there are twelve black dots in the design: four on each of the first, third, and fifth vertical lines, beginning from the first column and alternating on the first, third, fifth, and seventh horizontally. Yet even when you know that you may be able to see two or three at a time, it is virtually impossible to see them all at once.

We absorb virtually all kinds of information in the same way. In Chapter 3, I spoke about the background through which we see the world, informed by our internalized book of rules and the way it shapes our schema, which gives us what we see, how we see it, and what we

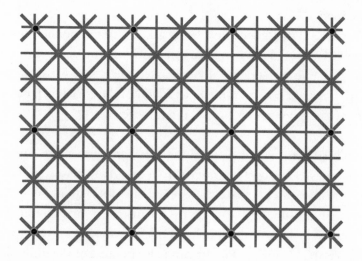

Figure 8.1 Selective Attention

don't see. Some of those rules are simple and obvious: the way we greet people, the clothing we are or are not supposed to wear, manners, various social behaviors. Many of the rules themselves are less obvious and even unconscious. They impact what we value and what we deem "important." In physics, the term *background* is used to refer to "the totality of effects that tend to obscure a phenomenon under investigation and above which the phenomenon must be detected."[3] Or, as John Searle said, this background "enables linguistic interpretation to take place . . . enables perceptual interpretation to take place . . . [and] structures consciousness."[4]

In simple terms, we see what we look for, and we look for what we know.[5] We also see what we expect to see, and expectations matter. Intuitively we all know this to be true, but few of us grasp how impactful expectations can be in shaping our world. While there are undoubtedly objective truths when it comes to reality, many of our experiences are actively constructed based on our interpretations of these external realities, and a major factor in this process hinges on our expectations. When it comes to our views about other people, this is reinforced by the out-group homogeneity paradigm that was discussed in Chapter 1. We all have a tendency to assume that those in the other group are the same or similar to each other. Statements on one cable channel about "liberals" or "the left" and on another about "conservatives" or "the right" reinforce this tendency. And the credibility of any points of view that are expressed is assessed through these lenses. We see what we look for, and we look for what we know.

The Pepsi Paradox

In the 1970s, Pepsi launched an innovative marketing campaign called the Pepsi Challenge. At the time, Coca-Cola held a massive portion of the market share of cola drinkers, but Pepsi believed this market dominance was based more on tradition and less on quality; the company was confident that its product could go toe-to-toe with the cola behemoth on pure taste. The premise of the campaign was simple: have people perform blind taste tests and decide which one they prefer. Fascinatingly, although consumers tended to enjoy the taste of Pepsi more than

Coca-Cola when the colas were unlabeled, the preference reversed when they knew the brand, causing people to report enjoying the taste of the latter more. What was causing such a reversal? In short, expectations.

Samuel McClure, director of the Decision Neuroscience Lab at Arizona State University, and his colleagues replicated the Pepsi Challenge in their lab while participants were hooked up to fMRI machines. They found that taste-testers exhibited nearly identical patterns of neural activation when blindly sampling each cola, but decidedly different patterns when brands were made available. When participants were cognizant of brand, distinct neural responses emerged. Crucially, the activity in the dorsolateral prefrontal cortex (DLPFC, an area implicated in higher-order cognition such as associations and ideas) was significantly more pronounced when participants were told they would be drinking Coke (but not Pepsi).[6] The researchers concluded that the superior brand recognition of Coke affected people's expectations of the experience they were about to have, which quite literally changed the experience itself: people expected Coke to be better, and so it tasted better. The same can be said for the way we consume political information: the brand that it is coming from impacts how palatable it is to us.

Examples with food and drink are illustrative but perhaps not especially provocative. Although how we respond to food is interesting, for most of us it is relatively inconsequential. But what about how we respond to people? In one of the most exceptional (yet unsettling) studies concerning the power of expectations, psychologist Robert Rosenthal teamed up with elementary school principal Lenore Jacobson to determine how expectations of intellectual potential can affect academic growth and performance.

Rosenthal and Jacobson told teachers in a San Francisco elementary school that they were working with a team from Harvard on developing tests that were designed to predict untapped academic potential in young students. They had the teachers administer an intelligence test to each of their classes, following which—they were told—the tests would be sent back to Harvard for evaluation. In May 1964, all students in kindergarten through fifth grade were tested prior to summer break.

The following September, during the first staff meeting of the new school year, the results of the tests were shared with the teachers. The revelations were handled in a deliberately flippant manner, so as to not unduly influence teachers to place disproportionate weight on the results. Teachers were told something to the effect of "Oh, and by the way, if you're interested in the results of the Harvard tests," at which point each teacher was told about five children in his or her class who were deemed to be "spurters," or students whose tests indicated they were primed for exceptional intellectual growth in the coming academic year.

The catch was that these supposed spurters were actually students who had been randomly selected. However, with such information now available to them, teachers' expectations of their five "gifted" children had undoubtedly changed. Children who were previously seen as dim, average, or otherwise unexceptional were suddenly presumed to be brimming with untapped potential.

How did such expectations impact student performance? Substantially, especially for younger children who may be more reliant on teacher instruction and interaction. The average gain in IQ points for the handful of second graders identified as spurters one year after the initial test was about 17 points, while the average gain for all others within that grade was only about 7 points. For first graders, the results were even more pronounced: an average increase of almost 28 points for spurters, compared to about 12 for their classmates. More impressively, over 20 percent of the randomly assigned spurters gained more than 30 points on their IQ, while only about 5 percent of all other students achieved such substantial gains. In the words of Rosenthal: "It would seem that the explanation we are seeking lies in a subtler feature in the interaction of the teacher and her pupils. [The teacher's] tone of voice, facial expression, touch and posture may be the means by which—probably quite unwittingly—she communicates her expectations to the pupils. Such communication might help the child by changing the conception of himself, his anticipation of his own behavior, his motivation or his cognitive skills."[7]

The findings can be summarized rather succinctly: expectations tend to create self-fulfilling prophecies. When we expect an individual to act in a certain way, we have a tendency to unconsciously, unintentionally, and subtly communicate our expectations as we interact with that person. From the tone of our voice to the postures we assume and the facial expressions we display, we reveal to someone how we see him or her.

So how does this phenomenon of the "self-fulfilling prophecy" take us back to the Comey testimony? Think about it from your own standpoint. What were you listening for? Whom were you listening to? And, for that matter, where do you get your information?

It is no secret that we get our news far differently than we used to. When I was growing up, we had three basic network television stations, each of which had, at most, a couple of hours of news on every day. The news was generally delivered in thirty-minute intervals and in a relatively homogenized way that was barely differentiated from one station to another. It was considered to be unprofessional or borderline unethical for news people (almost always white men) to voice their opinion about the events of the day. The interpretation of the news, except perhaps for the editorial in the daily newspaper, was left largely to the viewer.

Our current relationship with the news is vastly different. For most people in the modern world, keeping up with the news is an ongoing activity that occurs throughout their waking hours, on any number of platforms. According to a 2014 American Press Institute report, the largest percentage of Americans follow the news all day long (33 percent), while 24 percent report getting it in the morning and 26 percent in the evening.[8] A more recent study indicated that the percentage who seek out the news throughout the day may have risen to as high as 65 percent.[9] For many of us, the headlines are flashed across our smartphone screen throughout the day—but, of course, these are headlines from the particular news outlets that we authorize to do so.

Additionally, the sources for that news have expanded dramatically. According to the Pew Research Center, approximately 50 percent of Americans still get their news on television, 43 percent get their news online (news feeds, social media, etc.), 25 percent hear it on radio, and only 18 percent get news from print newspapers.[10] The younger the generation, the greater the importance of online sources. Most of us don't go and watch the news anymore; the news comes right to us.

The greater challenge is that the news each of us is getting now is very likely not the same news our neighbor gets. Comey's testimony is a prime example. Cable news has created a different structure and schema for sharing news. Because there were only limited news sources at earlier times in our history, news stations could not afford to alienate one whole segment of the population by taking too strong a position philosophically or politically. The advent of cable news changed all of that. Stations and websites can now go after their "demographic," providing programming that is specifically aligned with a particular point of view. The monetization of news sources has also added to the draw to get "our viewers" and provide "what they want to hear" so that advertising dollars are increased by larger viewership.

Depending upon what you watch, read, or listen to, you may be having your newsfeed pre-filtered for you. According to another Pew Research study, people who see themselves as "consistent liberals" got 15 percent of their news from CNN, 12 percent from MSNBC, 13 percent from NPR, and 10 percent from the *New York Times*.[11] Conservatives are more likely to be centered around a common news source, Fox News (47 percent).

Yet another critical factor is the realization that we actually rarely watch the news at all anymore; instead, we watch other people watching the news. Most of what we see is filtered through the vast array of pundits, bloggers, or other similar "journalists" who interpret the news for us. One incredibly unnerving example of this is how many people now say that they get their "news" from sources like Comedy Central's *The Daily Show* or similar satirical formats. *The Daily Show* and its ilk are amusing and entertaining, but they are not journalism.

We now have our own tailored news from the stations we trust, and we easily discount the others. And that doesn't even include what is perhaps the biggest factor in the equation, social media.

Social Media

Social media has greatly expanded the segmentation of our access to information because it allows that information to be shared with virtually no standard protocols or credibility.[12] As of 2016, 67 percent of people say they receive their news from social media.[13] Social media platforms such as Facebook, Twitter, Reddit, and LinkedIn theoretically can provide us with virtually limitless news from all sides, but they are very conducive to group separation, enabling people to find their niche and stay inside a bubble that becomes an echo chamber, providing us with the perfect mechanism for dividing into tribes and finding people "like us." The algorithms that many of the social networking sites are built around actually lead us toward people who like and believe the same things we do, and away from those we disagree with. It is increasingly atypical for people to have virtual friends who are different from them. For many it is a normal activity to "unfriend" people who disagree with them. In the best sense, this can create a safe space for people to share ideas without conflict. In its worst state, it can create a kind of cyber-Balkanization.

If you have any question about whether or not this is true, you might want to begin consciously connecting to sites on the other side of the political spectrum from yours, and watch how your feeds begin to change rapidly. All of a sudden you get headlines of different kinds of stories from different sources. Recommendations for connections start to change. For the past several years I have made a point of watching the news on different stations and expanding my news feed to include articles from all sides of the political spectrum. It is difficult to do, but incredibly illuminating regarding the different ways the same story is covered.

This is not to say that social media and the internet in general have been the only things contributing to political polarity in our country. I believe, and some research suggests, that it may be much more of a mixed bag.[14] However, it is clearly part of a social reorientation that is trending toward that polarization.

We used to rely on neighbors for essential aspects of our social and material needs: babysitting, medical emergencies, help getting things done, the proverbial cup of sugar. Now many, if not most, people barely know most of their neighbors. Social media has become the modern neighborhood. And while you couldn't always choose the politics of the people who lived next door, you can now decide who your cyber-neighbors with just a click on the keyboard. In addition, because social media fulfills some sense of need for human connection, people are less likely to seek in-person interactions with people who are different from them. As one man said to me: "I have lived alone for most of my adult life, and when I was lonely I used to go out to a local place and hang out. I would meet new people and engage with old friends. If there was an important event on TV, for example a political debate, I would either invite people over or go to someone else's house. Now I do all of that online. I tweet with friends during the debate, and interact with others on Facebook. It's just easier than going out."

It is easy to see how people who are suffering from social separation syndrome (Chapter 1) can easily fall into this pattern as a way to create some sense of bonding with others they encounter in online communities. However, it is also easy to see how this can reinforce the tendency toward social conformity, because one can pick and choose whom to build those relationships with, based on ideology.

The factors of group conformity that we discussed in earlier chapters are far stronger when you are face-to-face with somebody than when you are an amorphous name on the internet. We tend to moderate our behavior more when we are confronted with a real live person. In his research, Gleb Tsipursky, professor of history and decision sciences at Ohio State University, found that "engaging with people face-to-face elicits more favorable attitudes towards people who are different than virtual interactions do; alternatively, virtual interactions allow people to feel more comfortable acting unfavorably towards others."[15]

Most people in social media construct identities based on the way they want to see themselves portrayed in public. This is true for all human interactions to some degree, but the distance factor in social media amplifies the effect dramatically. Some post Photoshopped pictures from years ago, or only the happy experiences or good news in their lives. Others post only from one aspect of their identity. So the constructed identities we form may be in relationship with other constructed identities, creating relationships that are actually less authentic and more facile than the ones we form in face-to-face interaction.

As Tsipursky says, "Facebook tends to give us the information that we like, not the information that is true. Facebook as a medium goes against diversity and for tribalism. It goes against truth and for lies. It focuses the followers' attention on the divides and reinforces beliefs against groups of 'others'."[16]

Twitter, by historically limiting people to only 140 characters at a time and even now 280, forces the conversation to be reductionist. Excessive use of social media has even been linked in some studies to depression, because the more superficial relationships that people create through the medium don't sufficiently fill the need for human interaction and belonging.[17]

I am not trashing social media, and I am not anti-Facebook or any other medium. I regularly use social media as a form of communication and a way of sharing ideas. There are aspects of it that are incredibly valuable: the ability to communicate broadly; the ability to garner a vast array of ideas, if one is so inclined; the opportunity to have a voice, stay in touch with people, and keep up with events. However, I do think that we have to be careful to realize that when we reduce important communications to sound bites of 140 characters, we risk missing the complexity of the issues of our time. The very format leads to the proliferation of memes—oversimplified, often derogatory caricatures of political adversaries that reinforce a point of view through humor, sarcasm, or outright falsehoods.

We have to be conscious about how we gather information, or else we leave ourselves susceptible to being "programmed" by others. In addition, while many people have found that social media provides an extraordinarily effective method of getting many people involved in a movement very quickly, they can also coalesce groups of misanthropic individuals, who in the past were fairly isolated in mainstream society, and turn them into frightening organizations with vast reach and recruiting capability, whether they are domestic hate groups or foreign terrorist organizations.[18]

If we are willing to work at it, social media can give us an opportunity for healthy, rigorous debate. I often post articles or thoughts designed to express my point of view. As a result, I sometimes get hostile responses from random readers. Recently I have started to respond to these with a simple note: "I am willing to have a civil debate about this if you're interested." Most people respond by toning down their remarks and making their case. In some circumstances this has led to robust conversations. My personal experience bears out suggestions that people who actively work to curate voices from the "other side" can do so.

For some time now I have had an ongoing Twitter relationship with a man I will call Bob. Bob responded to one of my tweets with a hostile note about "libtards," and so, out of curiosity, I looked him up. He was shown with his family, holding a gun and wearing a "Make America Great Again" hat. He called himself a "Christian Conservative NRA member." Nonetheless we began a conversation that by now has continued for over a year. At some point he sent me a note telling me that he could see that I travel and if I was ever in the part of Florida he lives in, he would love to take me to dinner. When Hurricane Irma hit the Florida coast I reached out to him to be sure that he and his family were safe, and received a warm note from him thanking me for the respect I had shown him. I don't know that I have changed his point of view very much (although I was able to shift his point of view about Civil War memorials), but I am very clear that he has shifted his point of view about "liberals," and mine has undoubtedly similarly shifted.

A 2015 study carried out by a team of social scientists from the University of Michigan and the Pew Research Center sought to examine the relationship between social network composition and exposure to opposing viewpoints (which they refer to as "cross-cutting content").[19] Given how simple it is to inoculate ourselves against opposing viewpoints on social media, the researchers hoped to form a more in-depth understanding of the extent to which social networks have allowed us to separate ourselves from ideas that run counter to our own.

The team analyzed the Facebook news feed activity of more than 10.1 million users who self-reported their ideological affiliation. The first finding of note was the percentage of friendships that crossed party lines. Though there was a strong tendency to be friends with those who share and reinforce one's political views, on average more than 20 percent of an individual's network identified as an opposing party member. However, a 2017 study by the Pew Research Center indicates that these numbers are slipping and that people's media choices are getting more and more homogeneous on both sides.[20]

Though algorithms played a role in content exposure, the team maintains that the findings support the notion that individual choice (that is, whom one chooses to connect with and, perhaps more important, whom one chooses to *remain* connected with) plays the primary role in exposure to cross-cutting content on Facebook.

Beyond all of this, however, is the question, "How can you trust that what you see is real?"

Fake News

In today's world, if you have a computer and an opinion, you can be a journalist, a social critic, or a political pundit. Not necessarily a good one, mind you, but the opportunity to speak and be heard has never been more achievable. Advances in media accessibility, in terms of both development and distribution, have proven to be a double-edged sword. The positive of such advances is that they have allowed individuals to share their thoughts and experiences with whoever is inclined to listen, allowing for an unprecedented influx of diverse ideas and rich debate. The negative, unfortunately, happens to be the same thing: with so many people sharing an opinion, "true news" can get lost in the shuffle. When everyone claims to be an expert, actual expertise can become diluted and overlooked—especially if such experts are not saying what someone is wanting to hear. If someone wants to intentionally post a lie and make it seem like real news, it is a fairly easy thing to do.

Social media platforms such as Facebook and websites that have an intentional political or social point of view have proven to be fertile breeding ground for the emergence of what has been dubbed "fake news." While many savvy internet veterans can spot the telltale signs of a fake news story, many more are likely to fall prey and believe them, especially if the perceived legitimacy of the story is bolstered by its inclusion on some pseudo-professional or irreparably biased news outlets.[21]

The shifting landscape of news media, and specifically the rapid emergence of fake news, has prompted some pressing questions. With a full 62 percent of adults in the United States relying on social media for news, it's fair to explore the implications of such exposure for public opinion.[22] Could fake news stories be so pervasive that they could impact the results of a presidential election?

This is precisely the question that researchers Hunt Allcott and Matthew Gentzkow took on. With many commentators attributing the improbable victory of Donald Trump to the insidious influence of fake news stories championing him while deriding his opponent, Hillary Clinton, the researchers were intent on deducing the actual likelihood that such stories had a tangible impact on the election results.[23] To do so, they analyzed Web browsing data and reading habits of internet users, focusing specifically on a database of 156 election-related articles that had been classified as false by nonpartisan fact-checking websites. To supplement their research, they also distributed a post-election survey to 1,200 participants.

Their findings could be interpreted as either comforting or troubling. By extrapolating their data, they estimated that there were approximately 760 million instances of individuals clicking through and reading a fake news story, or an average of about three such stories read per each American adult. Perhaps unsurprisingly, they found social media to be a crucial incubator for fake news articles, with a disproportionate share of such stories being circulated on sites such as Facebook. There is no question that fake news is not the exclusive purview of one political side versus the other; however, the large majority of such stories decidedly favored Donald Trump, with pro-Trump fake news stories outnumbering pro-Clinton stories 115 to 41 in the database, resulting in 30 million versus 7.6 million article shares, respectively. The researchers were also able to identify several factors, including education, age, and total media consumption, that correlated with an accurate ability to discern true from fake news. Partisanship, on the other hand, appeared to skew judgment, with both Republicans and Democrats showing a 15 percent increase in the likelihood of accepting fake headlines as true if those headlines were ideologically aligned with their own beliefs. This type of motivated reasoning is certainly not without precedent.[24]

With minimal data regarding the actual influence of fake news on voting decisions, the researchers applied standards from television campaign ads to their study to calculate the overall effect.[25] Despite the unsettling ubiquity of fake news, the authors did ultimately conclude that it's doubtful fake news had the monumental impact on the election some experts had decried; however, many believe that the subtlety of these influences makes it hard to determine the actual effect.[26] With the revelations about Russia tampering with the 2016 election by posting millions of fake news stories on Facebook and Twitter, these findings may shift over time.

Either way, "fake news" is largely a function of confirmation bias. We tend to believe the fake stories that confirm our point of view, whether they are about Hillary Clinton supposedly running a child sex ring out of a Washington, D.C., pizza parlor or about President Trump suppos-edly telling *People* in 1998 that "Republican [voters are] . . . the dumbest group of voters in the country."[27] On top of the challenge posed by fake news, we now also have to deal with the pattern of real news stories be-ing labeled as fake when somebody simply doesn't like the message they are communicating. This can create an unhealthy form of bonding in which people are connecting mostly around their hate of the other, rather than for a constructive purpose.

The net impact of these media phenomena on our political system is that they have begun to shape the way people in politics make choices about what to advocate for, or even believe in. As Marshall McLuhan, the legendary communications philosopher, said in 1972, "Politics will even-tually be replaced by imagery. The politician will be only too happy to abdicate in favor of his image, because the image will be much more powerful than he could ever be."[28] The challenge this poses is deeply dis-turbing. If we can go on the internet and find information to confirm any point of view, no matter how outrageous, what do we use as a basis for credible confirmation of factualness?

The Paradox of Choice

An important aspect of the challenge we face in all of this is the sheer amount of information that is available to us today. One study estimated that 90 percent of the world's data was generated in just two years, between 2011 and 2013, and the pace has only continued to quicken since then.[29] It is estimated that one weekday edition of today's *New York Times* contains more information than the average person in seventeenth-century England was likely to come across in an entire lifetime. How do we possibly sort through all of it? How do we choose what to pay atten-tion to and what to ignore?

Freedom is good. Even a born-and-bred contrarian would be hard-pressed to argue with a statement as seemingly noncontroversial as that. But is there such a thing as too much freedom? Psychologist Barry Schwartz believes there is, and he believes that our incessant quest to in-crease our freedom may have inadvertently led to a decrease in our over-all happiness.

When most Americans are asked to expound upon the relationship between freedom and happiness, their answers are uniform and unwaveringly confident: the more freedom we have, the greater happiness we experience. In this way, there is believed to be a positive linear relationship between the two: as one increases, the other does as well. Schwartz believes that this idea—that the maximization of individual freedom unequivocally leads to a maximization of welfare—is tragically (but perhaps understandably) misguided.[30]

The most effective way to maximize freedom is to provide an individual with more choice. According to folk wisdom, then, more choice should produce greater happiness, but this doesn't seem to be the case. Schwartz argues that instead of happiness increasing infinitely as our range of choices expands, we actually reach a point of peak happiness, after which the addition of extra choices begins to erode our satisfaction.[31]

Let's use cell phones as an example. If you were to do an online search for cell phones, you would be inundated with hundreds of different models to choose from, each with a plethora of options in terms of features and specifications. From screen size to battery life to storage capacity, the number of unique possible combinations would be dizzying. So why is this a bad thing? Doesn't this mean we have a better opportunity to find just the right one for us? Theoretically, yes, but Schwartz has found that in practice such an expansive range of choices may ultimately make us feel worse.

There are several reasons for this. The first has to do with how we tend to respond to a virtually unbounded variety of choices. Rather than delight at the prospect of limitless options, many of us find ourselves frustrated and overwhelmed. The second reason for the adverse effect of abundant choice on happiness concerns alternatives. With more choices available, we also find ourselves with more opportunity for regret. Most options have some redeeming qualities, but few have all of them. The final reason Schwartz cites for the nonlinear relationship between choice and happiness has to do with the burden of responsibility. When our choices are limited, we can easily blame others for not having what we want. When the choices are virtually limitless, it is our own fault.

So the glut of information to choose from can tend to lead to a sense of resignation and powerlessness, as we wonder what we should actually be looking at. This ties directly to our sense of belonging, because when we are overwhelmed with choices, we will tend to fall back on what our group is supposed to like.

Is there any way to manage it all?

Building Bridges through Information

One message rings loud and clear from the research. We are not doomed to live in echo chambers and lose sight of the bigger picture. Each of us, individually and within families and organizations, can take responsibility for informing ourselves more broadly. There are several things that we can do:

Consciously watch several different news outlets, especially when there is a major news story occurring, being careful not to let your preconceived beliefs limit your listening. In our home we watch CNN, Fox News, MSNBC, the BBC, and Al Jazeera America (when it was available). It is remarkably illuminating to see the way each covers the same story. The more we understand each other's perspectives, the better chance we have to find common ground. Once again, I am not advocating for not having a point of view. I am suggesting that we treat our point of view *as a point of view*, and not as ultimate truth. In any case, by understanding better the reasoning behind other points of view, you will be better able to engage constructively with people from the other side.

Consciously engage in respectful dialogue (as opposed to debate) with people who represent a point of view different from yours. I know this can be difficult to do, but if you think that *everybody* who believes something other than what you believe is stupid or evil, you have become part of the problem. I will describe some strategies for conducting these kinds of conversations in Chapter 9.

Consider taking the Pro-Truth Pledge that has been created by Tsipursky and a group of scientists as a way of bridging the gap (protruthpledge.org). The pledge is intended to draw attention to the need for accurate information that can allow us to have a civil discourse based on shared values of respect and civility, even when we disagree. Will all people be able to put aside their differences to have those conversations? Of course not. But many are looking for ways to connect with reasonable people on the other side of the political divide.

Perhaps the greatest challenge we face today is that most people look at issues from the perspective of preparing to prove their point. We have moved from issue orientation, in which we interact with each other with an orientation to the particular issue we are discussing (such as gun control or foreign policy), to an identity orientation, in which we see the other as fundamentally different from us. We can bridge across issues, but it is much more difficult to bridge across opposing identities, especially during times of strife. Rather than bonding with each other in a healthy way, as human beings, we are creating coalitions of identity that tend to emphasize "us versus them" thinking and create unhealthy bonds.

Now that we've fully established the challenges we face, let's look at some of the things we can do about them.

Chapter 9

Bridges to Bonding

Eight Pathways for Building Belonging

Everyone can rise above their circumstances and achieve success if they
are dedicated to and passionate about what they do. It always seems
impossible until it's done.

—NELSON MANDELA

It is easy to feel resigned about the separation that we are experiencing. It seems like it continues to worsen every day. The reality is, as we discovered in looking at the neuroscience and social science behind our behavior, that we will always separate people into "us" and "them." But that doesn't mean we are doomed to have those differences cripple our ability to function as a collective. In fact, when we realize that it is our natural state to figure out who we are by realizing that we are not somebody else, it can liberate us from the folly of trying to have everybody act and feel the same. It can allow us to shift our focus from trying to convince or "fix" each other to trying to *understand* each other and find ways to coexist.

It begins with our own personal work. We each have something to say about our own attitudes and behaviors. However, we also have a remarkable ability to work together in our institutions: workplaces, schools, places of worship, and other places where we come together. Belonging is, by its very nature, more than just an individual process. The institutions we are a part of give us an opportunity to create healthy bridging that can build and sustain a sense of connection.

History is filled with remarkable examples of people coming together to solve long-standing conflicts in relationships, in organizations, and, as we'll now see, in countries.

Ending Lifetimes of Conflict

On August 10, 1998, Jamil Mahuad was inaugurated as the fifty-first president of Ecuador. It was a difficult time. The Ecuadorian economy was in shambles, having the highest rate of inflation in Latin America. Even more threatening was the continuing border conflict with Peru, the longest-running international armed conflict in the Western Hemisphere, lasting over 175 years. The country was still reeling from the effects of the last active war in 1995. Three days before his inauguration, Mahuad was told by the Joint Chiefs of the Ecuadorian Armed Forces that Peru was planning to invade Ecuador "next week."

"Windows of opportunity exist," Mahuad said. "They are often small, not always present, not always clear, changing all the time. Sometimes they just flicker, so when you find an opportunity, use it, because it may not be there later."[1]

Mahuad realized that the bully pulpit of the presidency was a great tool for focusing the attention of the country. In the first hours after taking office, Mahuad called a press conference to announce that he was going to Paraguay to meet with Peruvian president Alberto Fujimori. The meeting was the first in a series of ten that occurred on a weekly basis until they were able to sign a peace treaty, just seventy-seven days after Mahuad had assumed the presidency. How did he work to end 175 years of hostility in seventy-seven days?

"It is never an event," Mahuad said. "True reforms are processes, and we needed a process-oriented mentality."

The first decision was to respect the partial agreements both countries had reached in a three-year negotiation process. The second was to make a personal connection with Fujimori. Mahuad found him to be surprisingly open and also searching for a solution. He was ready to talk about alternatives.

Mahuad went on to say, "Once the atmosphere of cooperation had been created, we each had to work with our people to gain alignment. We had to change the mind-set. In Ecuador we wanted peace with dignity, a different situation than before when we had been forced by military occupation to sign the Rio Protocol in 1942. After Rio, Ecuadorians felt abused and humiliated. 'Even though our signature is there in the protocol,' they argued, 'we never had free will to decide. It was a treaty imposed by force.'" Ecuadorians were clear that any solution had to create an atmosphere of true agreement, not just going through the motions.

"Actually you have to listen actively, not just speak," Mahuad said. "The moment you feel that your words count and see that they have been included in the final document, you are relieved and open to cooperate. You need various tools: a systemic way of thinking, the capacity to understand that everything is related, a personal decision-making process, your definition of what leadership is about, your personal way to negotiate, your theory and style of communication. Some variables are more significant than others, and things that you don't expect may pop up. You have to share that news with your group so they know what you are facing, why you are proceeding, what information you need. You're helping your group help you."

Mahuad's method stresses that it is necessary to define the problem appropriately, create an action plan, and act accordingly. The essence of a person, a society, or a country has to be distilled down. "What are the values we cannot sacrifice? What are we willing to fight for? How are we going to rewrite our history books to reflect a new reality? The characterization of Peru as 'the enemy' had existed beyond the lifetime of anybody who was alive."

The treaty was signed on October 26, 1998. The *New York Times* reported that day,

> In an emotional ceremony that officially ends a bitter conflict that spanned generations, the Presidents of Peru and Ecuador signed a peace treaty here today to open their borders and create avenues for trade and development. . . .
>
> "We must continue to free ourselves of our prejudices, to overcome traumas that have been generated over more than half a century," President Alberto K. Fujimori of Peru said today.[2]

President Bill Clinton called the agreement "the end of the last and longest running source of armed international conflict in the Western Hemisphere."[3] In 1999, Fujimori and Mahuad were nominated for the Nobel Peace Prize.

There is a possibility of using processes and tools that can undo patterns of separation that have existed for generations and create a new sense of belonging. Let's look at some of the pathways.

Pathways to Belonging

I have described belonging and why it is essential to human survival, and have also talked about the break in belonging that exists in our culture today. The example at the beginning of this chapter demonstrates that there are pathways to belonging that we can use in families, companies, communities, and countries. It takes commitment and hard work, but it is possible to create breakthroughs in human understanding that can expand our circles of belonging.

We start by understanding that *things need to get real before they can get better*. We have to develop an honest understanding of human behavior if we are going to learn to work with it. In my years of studying bias, the biggest breakthrough I had was when I realized how normal bias was to the human mind and the human condition. I had grown up in the 1960s singing songs of peace and harmony, forcing myself to believe that people were inherently good. But we all have bias, and understanding and accepting that actually gives us the awareness to address the bias and learn to mitigate it.

Similarly, we would like to think that people inherently want to get along, but we know now that is anything but the case. Just as we inherently turn toward bias to understand and feel safe in our world, we also naturally turn toward a pattern of "us versus them" to make sense of where we stand in the world around us. That is human nature. If we accept it rather than resist it, we can work to find ways to bridge those gaps and create communities of belonging that might just be able to bring us closer together.

These pathways can provide a guideline for getting there.

Pathway One: A Clear Vision and Sense of Purpose

Developing a sense of belonging that extends beyond simple identity means that we have to know what we are belonging to and why we are together. This is true whether we are joining a political party, a church group, or a company. What separated Martin Luther King Jr., Nelson Mandela, and Mahatma Gandhi from other leaders? One big factor was that they had a vision for the future that was clearly articulated and repeated time after time. When King proclaimed, "I have a dream," it was more than a rhetorical flourish. He was creating a future for others to aspire to.

Great leaders almost always speak in this way. They are clear about what they are doing, describe what it will look like when they are successful, and communicate a deep understanding of why it is important to get there. They lead from that understanding. They lead from the inside out.

Think about the companies or leaders that inspire you. Usually we are inspired because some part of their message stimulates an emotional reaction. You can feel this in some advertisements. One company that does this particularly effectively is Subaru. Watch their ads. In one of them we see people with a puppy; the puppy playing with little children; a young dog playing with older children; an older dog running alongside his human; an old dog with gray muzzle in the backseat of the car.

The first time I saw it, I didn't even know what the ad was about until its final frame. That's because the ad is not selling cars; it is selling the company's mantra, "Live. Love. Subaru." The ad triggers an emotional connection to a feeling that is essential to all of us. It taps into *our* purpose. Understanding the sense of purpose gives us a "true north," a clear sense of direction.

Whether you are in a formal leadership position or not, set your vision clearly. What are you asking people to belong to and why? What purpose does the group, community, or company serve? When you are able to clarify and articulate your vision, you are more likely to enroll others.

Pathway Two: Creating the Container

Anytime we bring people together, there is a set of understandings and agreements that we are operating within. Sometimes these are articulated, and other times they are assumed. This container creates the culture of the group to which we belong. The more conscious we are about creating this container, the more likely we are to have alignment. The container should include a clear statement of values, beliefs, and purpose. Every person in the group should know why the group exists and what it is trying to accomplish, even in a family. It should also create a clear statement of the rules of engagement for the group. How are we supposed to act with each other? What are the norms? How do we deal with different circumstances? All of these create a greater sense of comfort for people because they know what is expected of them and how to function within the group. Cultures can be shifted to create more belonging in a group or community through intentionality, as evidenced by Elliot Aronson's ability to make the newly integrated school system in Austin, Texas, almost fifty years ago into a more cooperative system rather than a competitive one, to the benefit of all the students regardless of their identity.

Austin had recently desegregated, leaving school districts and administrations to cope with what was an unprecedented and highly volatile situation. Black, white, and Hispanic students were suddenly thrust into classrooms with one another, bringing with them their interracial distrust, anxiety, and stereotypical thinking. The natural competitiveness of the classroom suddenly took on another layer of complexity, one that Austin was desperate to navigate peacefully and productively. So Aronson and a team of graduate students devised a plan to reimagine the way students learn and interact, and the Jigsaw Classroom was born.[4]

The underlying concept of the Jigsaw Classroom was simple: design the route to success so that it relies on cooperation, while competition becomes counterproductive. Aronson and his team achieved this by ensuring that each student played an invaluable role in the education of all other students.

The beauty of the Jigsaw Classroom is that it not only encourages cooperation, it *necessitates* it! In order to do well, each student must rely on the others in his or her group to be competent. Aronson found that when Jigsaw Classrooms were first introduced in Austin, some of the students were slow to break old habits. When it was the turn of a student who was shy or struggling, crueler group members would mock and taunt the student. But when the test came and they realized they didn't know certain segments because they had been victimizing the individual responsible for teaching them, it quickly dawned on them that such behavior was counterproductive. Whether they liked it or not, their fates were intertwined: *If that student struggles, I'll struggle as well.* And so mockery quickly turned into helping behavior, encouragement, and positive reinforcement. Cruelty dissipated as symbiotic relationships began to form. Students who were once the victims of ridicule and exclusion saw their confidence grow as their peers began supporting them and cheering them on. And out of that, genuine friendships often sprang organically. One of Aronson's proudest achievements was an unintended byproduct of the Jigsaw Classroom. Working together cooperatively within the classroom inadvertently spilled over into the playground as well, and teachers started to notice greater interracial harmony and connectedness.[5]

This is not to suggest that any system will work in every circumstance. Yet what can we learn from this example? Aronson created a container in the classroom by developing a set of rules, norms, and agreements for the students that naturally evoked a certain kind of behavior—and it doesn't only work with little children. Stanford University professors conducted a similar experiment by developing a pattern of behaviors designed to encourage social belonging among a group of minority students at Stanford. The net result was that the students not only improved their grade point averages but also increased their self-reported sense of health and well-being. In addition, the students were less likely to see adversity on campus as an indictment of their personhood.[6]

Ritual can provide a "container" for people to operate within. Ritual is the use of certain activities that are designed to formally acknowledge the connection of the group. Sometimes they are built around life-changing moments such as weddings, funerals, births or naming ceremonies. Sometimes they occur around transitions, like the bar/bat mitzvah that teenagers go through in my religious culture, Judaism. Sometimes they are simply lines of demarcation that tell us, *Something important is happening here.* Ritual confirms our connection.

Pathway Three: Personal Connection, Vulnerability, and Consciousness

Belonging is ultimately personal; it comes from a sense of being known and welcomed for who we are. This was deeply evident in the testimony of the recovering alcoholics in Chapter 1. Each of them credited the fellowship of AA with aiding in their recovery and encouraging their sense of belonging. Being in an environment in which they could expose their vulnerability and fully be themselves is the breakthrough that has them stay connected and stay sober.

Part of creating a community of belonging is understanding who you are sharing the experience with, and that begins with understanding yourself. Developing a practice of mindfulness fully supports knowing yourself. Mindfulness is simply the practice of training one's mind to bring oneself fully into the present moment, without reacting from past projections and fears or concerns about the future. Being mindful does not mean that the past and future don't exist; it means that they don't dominate your thoughts, feelings, or decision-making. The practice of mindfulness has been proliferating in organizations over the past decade as more and more people find themselves searching for ways to reduce stress and tension in themselves and in their interactions with others. Self-knowledge can limit the impact of bias on our reactions to people, and it can also allow us to bring nonjudgmental awareness to ourselves, to those we are interacting with, and to the situation at hand. The more aware we are of how we are responding, the easier it is to see how others around us are responding. The combination diminishes reactivity and increases connection.

The other critical component is vulnerability. Connecting deeply with another person means we have to be willing to expose ourselves. Most of us find that to be challenging, but it is at the heart of feeling deeply connected with others and feeling a genuine sense of belonging. How can I truly belong anywhere if I don't even really know who "I" am? Setting up the ground rules and agreements in Pathway Two creates more safety for you to bring your fully authentic self—including your vulnerability. But ultimately vulnerability is an act of courage. As Audre Lorde so brilliantly said, "We are taught to respect fear more than ourselves. We've been taught that silence would save us, but it won't . . . and that visibility which makes us most vulnerable is that which also is the source of our greatest strength."[7]

Pathway Four: Inclusion and Enrollment

Years of research have shown that the most powerful groups are inclusive. Having a diverse group of people who can engage fully in the process of building that group opens possibilities that a limited or more homogeneous group may never achieve. A number of years ago our company was considering developing our first e-learning program. We had talked to several local companies about developing the platform and technology behind the design. One day while we were in a meeting, one of our interns, a twenty-year-old who was with us for the summer, excused himself and left the room. Twenty minutes later he returned with the names of three companies, two in India and one in the Philippines, who could do the work for a fraction of what the local companies were going to charge. None of us in the room, all considerably older, had even considered the virtual world that this younger person had grown up living in.

I have worked for more than thirty years supporting organizations in developing cultures of inclusion. It is a task that can be inspiring and leads people to a greater sense of understanding of the human condition and resources and opportunities far beyond what we have seen. Although our natural pattern is to live inside relatively homogeneous communities, we will have to be willing to consciously reach out to others outside our inner circle and invite them in. That means people of different races, cultures, ethnicities, genders, sexual orientations, ages, abilities, and disabilities—and, yes, even different political orientations. Belonging has to include the uncomfortable. We might say that if we limit ourselves only to those who we feel comfortable with, we will have a pretty limited life.

Creating inclusion always includes some combination of education that allows us to better understand ourselves and others, and clear systems and structures to ensure that everybody has a chance to participate fully and be successful within the system. It also requires an understanding that discomfort and resistance are all a part of the process of creating belonging.

A big part of a healthy, inclusive environment is conscious allyship. Allies work to understand and support people in groups outside of themselves. This is particularly important for the well-being of people who are in nondominant groups.

A number of years ago I was leading a training program with a colleague who was a woman of color. At some point while she was leading the group, one of the participants strongly challenged something she was saying. I jumped up and defended her, interacting strongly with the participant and making it "right." I felt like a hero. When we went on a break, my colleague was upset—but not with the participant. She was upset with me!

Despite my good intentions, I had been blind to the fact that by "rescuing" her I had communicated that she was not capable of handling the situation. I had taken over the room and made myself the focus. I thought I had handled the situation in the short term, but in the long term, I had undermined her position with the group; I was not serving as her ally.

It is no secret to anyone who has his or her eyes open that we are living and working in a time of increasing diversity. The expansion of that diversity in the workforce, the workplace, and the marketplace will only accelerate in the future. Members of dominant groups especially have an opportunity to constructively contribute to creating more successful workplaces by developing more inclusive environments, remember that this is not a "problem" of any one group, it is a challenge to the whole of our society that we all need to address.

Here's how:

- **Support and develop others**. You can do this through friendship, support, and mentoring. You can also do this by looking out for other people's best interests in a more behind-the-scenes way— frequently called sponsorship. Those in nondominant groups are often overlooked by the dominant culture. It's important to be aware of your influence and look broadly for these opportunities and to engage in them in partnership, not in paternalistic ways.

- **Be an active ally, even when nobody is looking.** It's not about looking good; it's about increasing belonging and positively affecting the life experience of others.
- **Challenge the normative patterns of behavior.** Make it clear, especially when you're in the dominant group, that these are your concerns as well.
- **Ask the courageous questions.** Speak truth to power and address exclusion when you see it.
- **Be conscious about equity in the decisions that you see being made.** If certain groups of people are being treated inequitably, then be the one who calls it out.
- **Leverage some of your personal capital to advance others.** We tend to see power as a zero-sum game, but that is only "power over." When we share power, we develop a much more potent form, "power with." This is the essence of bridging—to identify, access, and share resources across groups to the betterment of all.

On any winning sports team, players sacrifice their personal statistics for the good of the whole. Baseball players lay down bunts. Football players block. Soccer players pass the ball so that another player can take a shot. The reason is simply that when all team members are focused on winning, everybody wins. As the saying goes, a rising tide lifts all ships.

Pathway Five: Cultivate Open-Minded Thinking

Our observations of the world and our conclusions about others are not so much objective appraisals of a concrete reality as subjective interpretations of events—shaded by our backgrounds, colored by our cultures, and blinded by our biases.

Science is pretty clear that humans are not designed to be correct as much as to possess the ability to *convince others* that we are correct. As we've seen earlier, we are not very good scientists, but we are great lawyers! Rather than engaging in calculated, systematic evaluations of all possible explanations of evidence, we are better equipped to simply "feel" a certain way and to subsequently gather information to support that belief. It appears, then, that closed-minded thinking comes naturally to us, and so perhaps it's inevitable that, in order to truly think about things with an open mind, we need to do so consciously and deliberately.

Jonathan Baron is a professor of psychology at the University of Pennsylvania as well as the founding editor of the academic journal *Judgment and Decision Making*. Baron has long recognized the need for a set of guiding principles to help people overcome the inherent subjectivity of their thinking. In response, he has posited a set of rules to help others engage in what he has referred to as "actively open-minded thinking."

Actively open-minded thinking is fundamental to academic inquiry, is a foundation upon which the scientific method rests, and is the essence of intentionally challenging stereotypes, fixed worldviews, and limiting thinking about the "other." Baron has developed a series of guidelines designed to ensure his students are practicing actively open-minded thinking. I have amended those guidelines so they are applicable not only in a classroom setting but outside academia as well:

- Select an issue, determine why that issue is important, and understand your stance on that issue.
- Evaluate the evidence that supports your stance. Where has this evidence come from? Are the sources unbiased and trustworthy? Is the evidence rooted in empirical research or is it based on some combination of emotion, tradition, and anecdotal evidence?
- Consider the evidence and opinions that run counter to your stance. Since it is unlikely that everyone who does not share your opinion is foolish, misinformed, or confused, why would others think that way? What reasons could they have? How could their background differ from your own, and how could these disparate experiences have shaped their view?
- Determine how your original stance should be modified, whether in terms of overall confidence or in terms of accommodating legitimate alternative points of view.

Practicing actively open-minded thinking is essential to creating an inclusive sense of belonging because it allows us to open up to the possibilities of new ways of thinking.

Pathway Six: Develop Shared Structures and Forms of Communication

Human relationship is built on communication. The clarity of our language, what it means, and how it is communicated are all essential to belonging. Language, in this sense, is the connective tissue of belonging. This includes not just spoken language but any way that we communicate, *even with our silence.*

In a culture of belonging, language needs a sense of civility to guide it. It creates a state of being, and so it needs a sense of generosity and inclusion that communicates spirit as much as information. Language can be a source of belonging or a source of suffering. This is what people who reflexively rail against "political correctness" fail to understand. Language can, by its very nature, create pain by triggering memories of past trauma. Part of being in a civil community and encouraging a sense of belonging includes not actively causing pain to another by using language that you know elicits pain.

I'm not justifying an overreach in language control that, when left unchecked, can remind us of Newspeak, the language that George Orwell imagined in his novel *1984* and which in the book was used by the totalitarian leaders to control people's thinking and limit the development of concepts that threatened the regime. The problem with this overreach is that life does not naturally come with trigger warnings. It is fired at us point-blank. When we are overly consumed with language control, we actually are not present at the moment, because we are responding from a sense of control that is past-based. So while I'm not advocating excessive policing of people's language, I am suggesting that each of us has a responsibility to understand how our language can exacerbate old wounds and cause pain.

There is a place for free expression and a place for civil discourse. The inclusion of both enhances belonging. Either one in the extreme prevents it.

Pathway Seven: Honoring Narrative

The English polymath Gregory Bateson told a story that captures humanity as well as any: "A man wanted to know about mind, not in nature, but in his private, large computer. He asked it, 'Did you compute that you will ever think like a human being?' The machine then set to work to analyze its own computational habits. Finally, the machine printed its answer on a piece of paper . . . : 'That reminds me of a story.' Surely the computer was right. This is indeed how people think."[8]

We are the narrative within which each of our lives unfold. Anybody reading this has had an example of a time when realizing that something had a different story associated with it changed its entire meaning and impact. Stephen Covey told such a story. He was sitting on a subway when a man got on with his children. The children were noisy, rambunctious, and obnoxious. Everybody was affected, yet the man sat silent. Finally Covey turned to the man and, expressing the feelings of most in the car, said, "Sir, your children are really disturbing a lot of people. I wonder if you couldn't control them a little more?" The man looked up and said softly, "Oh, you're right. I guess I should do something about it. We just came from the hospital where their mother died about an hour ago. I don't know what to think, and I guess they don't know how to handle it either."[9]

Our stories dictate how we see the world. Part of belonging is the art of sharing stories. In a community that invites the sharing of stories, people feel known, and also know each other. This requires time, attention, and active listening. It requires presence so that we can hear people's stories *in terms of how they are affected,* without our interpretation. Understanding our own stories can also change our lives.

Understanding and honoring the narrative behind the formation of an organization, community, or country is essential in people's understanding of the core purpose of the group. This is why our historical narratives about the American experience are so important, and why having them be accurate and inclusive is so critical.

Exciting new research is teaching us that these stories can be rewritten. University of Virginia psychologist Timothy Wilson makes a compelling case that some of our most insurmountable obstacles may be products not of culture but rather of cognition. He has found that we have the capacity to reframe our experiences in a way that creates new possibilities for the future.[10]

Without a doubt many of our barriers are external: the relative power (or lack thereof) our skin color affords us, our socioeconomic circumstances, whether systems and policies were structured in a manner designed to benefit us or confine us to a perpetual struggle. Wilson forwards the argument that the narrative that we have developed about these experiences sometimes creates our own internalized shackles—shackles that we can free ourselves from if we can learn to reshape our own narratives.

Borrowing from practices such as cognitive behavioral therapy (CBT), a type of therapeutic technique focusing on challenging and realigning negative thought patterns, Wilson argues that our experiences are profoundly affected by our interpretations. While this freedom to decide your narrative can be liberating for some, many of us seem to have a tendency to distort our stories in a destructive and unhealthy way. The purpose of this exercise is not to rewrite the truth of what happened. It is to rewrite the way you are dealing with that reality.

Let's say you were unlucky enough to find yourself in a situation similar to the one I was subjected to a number of years ago. As I sat in my car with my eleven-year-old son, we were suddenly attacked by two men who emptied a can of pepper spray in my face and rifled through my pockets for money. Disabled by the spray, I implored them to take whatever they wanted but to please not harm my son. I was fortunate in that all they stole were material possessions.

Over the next several weeks I grappled with the unenviable task of sifting through a complicated assortment of feelings as they arose. Many of us have imagined how a scene like this would play out in our own heads. I certainly pictured myself fearlessly standing up to such a threat and talking my way out of trouble or doling out justice with my own bare hands. In our thoughts, we always play the unquestioned role of hero. It's always so simple: good triumphs over evil.

But reality is not always so simple, and I was left wondering if I had done the right thing. Was I a coward for not acting as valiantly as I had always imagined I would? Would I really have been able to protect my son had they tried to hurt him or abduct him? Using this approach, over a period of time I was able to reinterpret the situation, to write my own narrative. It took some time, but I was able to find a perspective for myself that was healthy and constructive.

Wilson has noticed that many people chronically interpret their stories in an unproductive manner. They paint themselves as the coward, the quitter, and the victim when they could have just as easily chosen to construe these roles as the risk-avoider, the seeker of better opportunities, and the survivor.

So how can we start to rewrite our own narratives in a way that will lead to more productive behavior? Wilson suggests three techniques, derived from the work of famed psychologist Kurt Lewin:

- **Story editing.** Comb through your personal narratives and look for opportunities where you can reshape your story—and ultimately your self-image and consequent behaviors—in healthier ways.
- **Story prompting.** Help others—and even yourself—to follow particular narrative paths by using various cues and nudges that lead the story to the interpretation you are trying to elicit.
- **Do good, be good.** This is based on the premise that the most effective way to alter people's self-concept is to allow them to see themselves behaving in admirable ways. If you can alter their behavior, you can alter their attitudes. Said another way: fake it till you make it!

My own experience is that communities of people can work together to reframe their experience. Sometimes having the support of others makes this process even more powerful.

Pathway Eight: Tools for Negotiation and Conflict Resolution

The final critical pathway to belonging is to have a system of tools in place to help manage the inevitable conflicts that arise in any group. We often set ourselves up for disappointment and failure because life does not occur without breakdowns, and yet most of us live as if it should.

Mediation and Conflict Resolution

There is a wide array of ways that we can learn to deal with breakdowns with people around us. Some simply involve listening to each other with empathy and compassion. Others are processes that have been found to be incredibly valuable over time. I have adapted my own approach from a very effective and simple model that was developed by Roger Fischer and William Ury of the Harvard Negotiation Project.[11] Over the last thirty years, I have personally used this model countless times in business negotiations and personal disputes, some of which I never could have imagined could have been peacefully resolved. It is brilliant in its simplicity. The model can be used by two people or groups on their own, but usually works best with a neutral facilitator. In that case, the facilitator would:

1. Begin by gathering information by talking independently to the two parties involved. This allows for both voices to be heard without interruption, and form their own point of view.
2. Set up a time for both parties to meet, preferably in a neutral place.
3. Declare a breakdown. This may seem obvious, simple, or even unnecessary, but it is an important step because most people want to blame the other rather than looking at the circumstance as one that is not working. A breakdown is not the same as a problem. A problem is something that needs to be fixed. It naturally calls for complaints. A breakdown is an interruption in our intention to accomplish something. It naturally calls for a solution. Imagine, for example, that your car breaks down on the way home. It is unlikely that you ever consider the possibility of not getting home, because you are clear that you are committed to that. You immediately begin looking at options. Get under the hood and fix the problem? Call roadside assistance? Call a friend or loved one? Call a Lyft or Uber? You will find some way to get home. When we declare a breakdown, it occurs in the context of the commitment to get to where you want to be. It requires clarity about what that goal is.
4. At this point, it is time for the first person (or side) to speak and share his or her perception of the breakdown in its entirety. This is not a dialogue. The second person just listens.
5. Then the second person (or side) echoes back what he or she heard, without commentary. In other words, the second person simply affirms having heard the first person's point of view, so

that the first person knows he or she got the point across. The second person can also ask clarifying questions (e.g., "Can you say a little bit more about what you mean by . . . ?").

6. The second person (or side) now has a turn to speak.

7. The first person then echoes back what he or she heard the second person say.

8. Next, both sides list areas of agreement that they hear in the two points of view. This is a critical step, because we usually start by focusing on difference. By emphasizing areas of agreement, we establish a pattern of being able to agree that shifts the mind-set and creates more possibility that we can come to agreement about different things. I have been asked at times to facilitate separation agreements between couples. People always want to start with the hardest and most contentious issues, perhaps the kids or the house. But when they start by listing all of the things they agree about (for example, who gets the dishes, the CDs, pieces of furniture, and so on), at some point they realize that they actually are not as far apart as they thought. They become more reasonable and willing to compromise on the things they disagree about.

9. The next step is to list the areas of disagreement.

10. For each item on the disagreement list, starting with the easiest and then moving to the most difficult, start by asking each person if he or she has any requests for the other. Requests unhinge complaints because they call people to look for solutions. See if you can get them to come to agreement on each point, through give-and-take. Identify any promises and commitments that people make to each other.

11. Determine if there is anything that needs to be said to clean up hurtful things from the past, such as apologies or promises of new behavior. This is an important step because it allows the past to be complete so that a new future can be created.

12. Finally, set a follow-up date to ensure that there is accountability for the promises that people made to each other. Knowing that they will have to sit down with you again in a week, a couple of weeks, or a month will encourage people to stick to their commitments with each other.

Decision-Making

There are also some very valuable tools for decision-making. One that I find most helpful was created by Edward de Bono, the Maltese educational philosopher. De Bono's approach is based on the notion that we all are born with a brain but that thinking is a separate skill that we can cultivate. As he says, "Intelligence is the engine, thinking is the driver." He identified six ways of thinking that people usually engage in: *process, objectives, intuitive/emotional, skeptical, visionary*, and *creative*. Generally, each of us comes into a conversation with one of these more dominant than the others. For example, I might be coming from the visionary perspective and encounter somebody who is skeptical, leading us to drive each other crazy and getting little done. De Bono uses the metaphor of six hats and recommends that the group "put on" each hat one at a time, going through all six.[12] I have used this tool often in group process, both in business and in personal situations, and have found it helpful for the quality of thinking and for the inclusiveness that it creates.

Once again, the key to this pathway is not which model you choose, but that you establish an agreed-upon method for decision-making and dispute resolution. Without it, every disagreement or decision can be a threat to belonging.

As most people live pretty segregated lives, the people we encounter in our neighborhoods, schools, and places of worship are, more often than not, very similar to us. There is one place where we have little control over the diversity we are exposed to, and that is the workplace. In Chapter 10, we will look at the workplace as a domain where a new hope for belonging is germinating and can be manifest.

Chapter 10

Institutions Can Build Bridges to Belonging

There is immense power when a group of people with similar interests gets together to work toward the same goals.

—IDOWU KOYENIKAN

A community is the mental and spiritual condition of knowing that the place is shared, and that the people who share the place define and limit the possibilities of each other's lives. It is the knowledge that people have of each other, their concern for each other, their trust in each other, the freedom with which they come and go among themselves.

—WENDELL BERRY

I started this book with the story of three people, Joan Smith, Barry Jones, and Fatima Mohammed, and their meeting at the Munchester Industries holiday party. The coincidental meeting of these characters at the party points to the reality and the promise of organizations as a source of belonging in our world today. At that moment, the three are confronted with their differences. Yet at the same time they are confronted with the reality that despite those dissimilarities, they have to come together on a daily basis and work together toward the common goals of their company.

One of the few places where people from different backgrounds come together and have to live and operate side by side is in the workplace. We don't always get to choose who sits in the office or the cubicle next to us. We generally don't get to choose the people we have to work with, the people we team up with on projects, and the people we see every day in the hallways. In that sense the workplace has, for many people replaced other social institutions as our main place of belonging. We identify ourselves, at least to some degree, by what we do and where we do it. We often form relationships with the people we work with that extend past the end of the workday. The workplace has the potential to build bridges to belonging by bringing together bonded groups and helping them bridge with each other, providing people with a sense of belonging that cuts across the areas of difference that we've examined.

That is not to say that workplaces are inherently great places. Many are still very difficult and have their own tribalism, race and gender biases, and many other issues that make them anything but ideal. Yet my own experience, after having spent the better part of the past thirty-five years working as a consultant with businesses in forty-eight of the fifty states and more than forty other countries, has been that workplace environments have the potential to orient people toward working across differences more than anyplace else we have available.

Building the Organizational Community

It is not unusual for a healthy workplace culture to be described as a "family-like environment," generally meaning that employees actually know and care about each other. I'd like to offer an alternative to that because I don't believe that "family" is the best metaphor to use in describing a healthy workplace. Families, for the most part, do not choose to be together. They are put together by the accident of birth, or because one of our relatives created a relationship. Many families have a great deal of dysfunction to them. I'm not sure that "like a family" is always the highest state of being for a workplace environment.

Additionally, families are generally, although not exclusively, homogeneous. The greater diversity of the workforce is a factor that has proven to improve business performance, as well as to provide a place for people who are very different to have to find a way to work together. This is why embracing diversity at work is important. The challenge is that greater diversity, in a structure or system that is not prepared to support it, can yield increased tension among employees. All of this supports the notion that it is in an organization's best interest to learn how to structurally and systemically embrace belonging within an increasingly diverse workforce.

I believe that a more appropriate metaphor for the workplace is that of a community. One dictionary defines *community* as "(1) a group of people living in the same place or having a particular characteristic in common; (2) a feeling of fellowship with others, as a result of sharing common attitudes, interests, and goals; (3) a group of interdependent organisms of different species growing or living together in a specified habitat."[1]

I see community very much the way Scott Peck defines it: "If we are going to use the word meaningfully we must restrict it to a group of individuals who have learned how to communicate honestly with each other, whose relationships go deeper than their masks of composure, and who have developed some significant commitment to 'rejoice together, mourn together,' and to 'delight in each other, make others' conditions our own.'"[2] I am not being a Pollyanna and suggesting that all workplaces are like that. My own experience has shown that even with the best of intentions, maintaining a healthy work environment requires constant hard work. But the workplace offers a modern hope for creating places of belonging for people in which they can come together and fulfill a mission. Our work relationships, on the whole, cut across race, gender, sexual orientation, and religion. They force us to collaborate with people who have more or less education than we do and who earn more or less money. We work next to people who are of different ages and who have different family situations and different politics. In all of it, we have to find a way to be successful in pursuing our goals and objectives. In that sense, the workplace offers the impetus and the opportunity for community and belonging to exist.

Major corporations are recognizing the reality that a healthier organizational culture creates a healthier work environment, which creates healthier, happier, more productive employees. Organizations such as Aetna, Google, Target, Goldman Sachs, General Mills, and Intel, among dozens of others, are offering mindfulness training to help their employees learn to deal with stress and be able to be more focused at work. Twenty-two percent of companies currently offer some kind of meditation training at work, and another 21 percent plan to add it in the immediate future.[3] More than 90 percent of Fortune 500 companies have some kind of diversity and inclusion effort, designed to help employees understand their differences and work together more effectively. Some have begun to add the word *belonging* to their goals in this area.

Organizations are creating more flexible work environments to help improve work-life juggling (I've seen very few people who actually *balance* work and their lives outside work!), and employees with flexible schedules have a higher level of job satisfaction, less absenteeism, and less turnover. Similarly, companies have been instituting telework arrangements or variable schedules that allow people to better manage family obligations while meeting their work objectives.

Ways to Cultivate a Culture of Belonging

The eight pathways to belonging outlined in the last chapter all apply to developing organizational community. Now I want to focus on some of the more specific behaviors that people in organizations can embrace in order to help make that happen.

Actively Promote the Core Narrative of the Organization and Invite Employees to Share Theirs

Our consciousness lives in story. It shapes how we respond to people and circumstances around us. It gives us our perception of the world. Our organizations are no different. The narrative that we weave about who we are, why we are here, and what we stand for sets both our internal community and the external community on a path to understanding us. It gives people something to belong to. Having a powerful and positive organizational narrative around belonging and the value of diversity and dissenting views, and frequently communicating and reinforcing that narrative, produces a story that employees can repeat, reflect on, and internalize.

That being said, it is also important to encourage employees to share their own stories with each other and to support them in doing so, because sharing personal stories is a way of belonging, of being heard and seen. Sharing stories can happen in meetings, in employee resource groups, in diversity education, or anyplace else it fits into the daily lived employee experience. Sharing stories is one way to learn not only about each other personally but also about our distinctive worldviews.

Chimanda Ngozi Adichie shares a story that shines a light on how important it is that we learn each other's worldviews:

> I thought about this when I left Nigeria to go to university in the United States. I was 19. My American roommate was shocked by me. She asked where I had learned to speak English so well, and was confused when I said that Nigeria happened to have English as its official language. She asked if she could listen to what she called my "tribal music," and was consequently very disappointed when I produced my tape of Mariah Carey.
>
> She assumed that I did not know how to use a stove.
>
> What struck me was this: she had felt sorry for me even before she saw me. Her default position toward me, as an African, was a kind of patronizing, well-meaning pity. My roommate had a single story of Africa: a single story of catastrophe. In this single story, there was no possibility of Africans being similar to her in any way, no possibility of feelings more complex than pity, no possibility of a connection as human equals.[4]

By surfacing stories, we can understand people's conceptions and misconceptions. And by clarifying these, we can help people connect and deeply understand each other, and also help them understand why they relate and react the way they do.

Recognize That the Affective Side of the Business Is as Important as the Material Side

Businesses often have operated as if the only thing that matters is from the neck up. The more technical the business, the stronger the belief that this is true. But that notion couldn't be further from the truth. Decision-making is overwhelmingly intuitive and deeply affected by how people are feeling. Creating an open environment to discuss how people are feeling is critical to leadership in an organizational community. Be sensitive to times when there is stress, whether it is inside the organization or societal. People need to talk about it, or at least be offered the opportunity to do so. We often avoid this kind of encounter because we are uncomfortable dealing with people's feelings, but that doesn't make it any less critical to success.

Educate People and Provide Them with the Tools to Be Successful

Education is critical to making sure that all employees have a common understanding and a consistent framework and skills for operating within the organizational community. While many organizations provide skills training, it is just as important to provide training in more interpersonal areas such as communication, diversity, inclusion, and unconscious bias.

Much has been written about diversity and/or unconscious bias training, especially regarding the question of whether such training has the ability to affect organizational performance. This is a vital inquiry because the time and costs associated with training programs are great enough to warrant a close examination of the results they produce.

As with many initiatives, there are a variety of ways in which diversity and unconscious bias training can be conducted, and results often depend on the approach taken. I have been studying the research about unconscious bias for more than fifteen years and actively working with clients in hundreds of companies all over the world, and have found ways to help our clients create significant, measurable success. This framework, which has four areas of focus, is an intervention strategy that uses education to impact the entire organization.

Education

Traditional diversity training often emphasizes differences, which can increase tension between groups. This tension can result in backlash once participants complete the training, and so people sometimes claim that "diversity training doesn't work." There are eight factors that contribute to an *effective* training:

- Emphasize that bias is fundamental to the way human beings process the world.

- Be evidence-based.
- Speak to common ground rather than to differences.
- Provide an understanding of the human mind and how people think.[5]
- Create experiential learning.
- Make the training relevant and applicable to people's worlds.
- Shift awareness and behavior.
- Focus both individually and collectively.

Training about unconscious bias can be an important part of a culture-based, systemic process of developing more inclusive workplaces, and beyond the workplace a more inclusive society, because it helps people understand how they make decisions that go far beyond the question of diversity or even individuals' talents.

There is no simple way to resolve the challenge of unconscious bias. In many cases it is not possible to eliminate it. However, we can often mitigate the impact of bias by employing a thoughtful, systemic approach that focuses on four interventions: introducing the right kind of education, installing priming techniques, modifying structures and systems, and building the appropriate accountability measures. In this way, we can create organizational systems that support people in being more aware of their decision-making and more inclusive in their behavior. Ultimately, this produces an organization in which people's biases don't get in the way of their need for belonging and allows organizational community to thrive.

Priming

Completing a training is like joining a gym: it's great to sign up for a gym membership, but if you don't go work out regularly, you won't see any results. In the same way, training starts the process of changing the organization's culture, but without a commitment to a regular pattern of behavior, nothing will fundamentally change. Priming is a critical part of the process of behavioral sustainability because it can be used to remind people to apply their learning at the appropriate time, as well as to be prepared to take in new understandings. *Priming* refers to activating particular representations or associations in memory just before carrying out an action or task. For example, if I were to ask you to say the word *silk* ten times, and then ask you what cows drink, you would likely answer "milk," even though the correct answer is "water." You have been primed.

We have identified several ways to use priming techniques to trigger more mindful behaviors, including performance support tools, nudging, and physical environment cues.[6]

Structures and Systems

It is important to understand how to build organizational structures and systems that create inclusive communities. When we build alternative ways to structure some of our basic systems, we can dramatically affect the level of conscious decision-making. Focus on the primary talent management systems: recruitment, sourcing, interviewing, hiring, onboarding, mentoring and sponsorship, performance review, calibration, recognizing talent, and developing and promoting talent. Remember, organizational structures can create both positive and negative results.

For example, many people have started to use "blind resumes" (resumes that have some information excised) in order to remove bias, along the lines of having musicians audition for orchestras behind a screen so they cannot be seen. This does, in fact, remove some opportunity for bias. However, it also makes it more difficult to identify a potentially valuable employee who may have a compelling story but because of that story has a resume that does not compare as well to someone else's on paper. It promotes, unwittingly, the notion that what's on paper is always the best way to make the choice. I'm not suggesting that we don't use blinded strategies, just that we be careful to watch for unintended consequences and patterns.

Accountability

The fourth intervention strategy is to use carefully constructed analytics to track organization performance around diversity, inclusion, and belonging. An effective way to accomplish this is by using batches of metrics instead of a single metric. Often, diversity and inclusion metrics are reduced to a question like "How many X's are there"? But if we combine a batch of metrics, including measuring levels of engagement, inclusion, and belonging, we get a much deeper understanding of where breakdowns exist in our system. Work with a team internally and identify the milestones that you will be watching, *and then watch them and communicate how you are doing.* And be sure that feedback from employees to their leaders is always welcome.

Create Opportunities for People to Dialogue with Each Other on Challenging Topics

My premise has been that we live in a world in which challenging differences confront us on a daily basis. We often live in the illusion that we can keep these challenges at home and just "come to work to do work." As we saw in the discomfort between Joan, Barry, and Fatima at the company party in Chapter 1, people bring their concerns with them wherever they go, whether it is reaction to the political circumstances of the day, breakdowns in religious or moral beliefs, or emotional responses to a racially charged incident in our community. It is not easy to bring up topics like these. As Michael Norton has said, "It's so appealing on the surface to think that the best way to approach race is to pretend that it doesn't exist. But research shows that it simply doesn't work. We do notice race, and there's no way of getting around that fact."[7]

Create a space where people have an opportunity to participate in dialogue using some of the ideas below. It is incredibly valuable to engage with different points of view, but it's essential that this be done as a dialogue rather than a debate—we want to be more like scientists than like lawyers. We can validate the humanity of people on the other side of an issue, even if we disagree completely with their point of view. There is no problem with arguing for a point of view, even in strenuous terms, *as long as you remember it's a point of view, not the definitive truth.* One of the great challenges we have in our interactions is that we work harder at trying to convince each other, to win the argument, or to be right than we do at trying to understand each other's point of view.

Caroline Wanga, the chief diversity officer at Target, has conducted many "courageous conversation" sessions for Target employees that represent many dimensions of difference including various religious perspectives; political perspectives; across the spectrum of gender identity, race, sexual orientation and age; military active duty and veterans; work experiences and geographic regions; learning and communication styles; and physical and mental abilities and socioeconomic backgrounds. She has found that

> We don't automatically listen the same when we agree, versus when we disagree, to what we are hearing. The value of listening to a point of view different from yours is that you learn how additional perspectives can help you craft your personal narrative. In my experience, courageous conversations are really more about courageous listening. The most important part of courageous listening is that we allow all perspectives to exist equitably, so we learn how to be one group and the one in a group. When I talk to our team members about how to listen courageously to a point of view they disagree with, I encourage them to resist what they normally do: debate, cut it off, drive agreement, try to convince the other person and win the argument.

Caroline goes on to say that the conversations have had a broader impact then she imagined.

> At Target, we know we're most successful when we listen to what our guests (customers) want. By listening courageously to each other, we are sharpening the discipline of listening to what our guests need and want, agnostic of if they are saying something comfortable or uncomfortable for us to hear. This behavior increases the likelihood that you we hear the entirety of what the guest (customer) wants, which accelerates our success toward accomplishing our business objectives. It also equips our team members to impact an inclusive society by modeling how to co-exist amongst the dimensions of difference their communities represent, which ultimately enables them to play a role in helping their communities thrive. It has a multiplier effect that's pretty powerful.

> Fear is always a factor in these kinds of interactions. Going back to the social science and neuroscience findings described in earlier chapters, we know that people want to be accepted and need to be validated in order to

feel safe. Sharing differences of opinions about emotional issues in the workplace can not only threaten our social standing but, in our mind's eye, maybe even threaten our jobs. Fearful times intensify "us versus them" thinking. Although much has been written about creating dialogue across groups in the workplace, here are a few ideas to help get you started:

- **Create a safe space for the conversation.** Be sure that there is enough time and that distractions are limited. It also helps to create a safe container and ground rules for the conversation.
- **Invite everybody to recognize their own biases.** It is helpful to do this at the beginning of the conversation, so that employees are aware of how those biases might affect their participation.
- **Encourage participants to be willing to be emotionally vulnerable as well as intellectually engaged.** That includes inviting them to share what they are afraid of.
- **Consider having participants reflect what they are hearing.** This will help others be sure they have been heard.
- **Distinguish between group perspective and personal perspective.** Keep doing this throughout the conversation.
- **Resist the temptation for perfectionism.** Focus on promoting the progress of the conversation. Just being able to listen to each other without being defensive can be a significant accomplishment.
- **Look for ways to move the conversation forward.** Collective action can be especially helpful in doing this, so seek out ways people can work together toward continuing the conversation.

Engage in Constant and Regular Communication

Leaders should be regularly communicating with employees. Where are we being successful? Where are we struggling? What are the challenges that we see coming down the road? Communication strengthens and updates the narrative, reinforces the values of the organization, and gives employees a sense of security and also belonging. Employees begin to feel that they are part of something, and that their being informed matters to their leaders. Even if there are times when a leader doesn't know the answer to something or certain information has to be kept private, you can still let people know what you know and what you don't. Being honest and acknowledging what you don't know is not a weakness!

I remember working with two utility organizations that were attempting a merger. When companies are merging, there is often information that cannot be legally shared because it may impact stock values. I was conducting a listening session with the designated human resources leader of the combined company, and people were expressing a general frustration at the lack of information. All of a sudden one of the people in the back stood up and said, "Our manager tells us everything!" The HR lead and I were surprised, and frankly a bit concerned that this manager might have been sharing too much, but later we found out from the man who had spoken up that his manager was not telling his team any more than any other manager but was just regularly pulling the team together to say, "Here's what I know and here's what I don't know." Just taking the time to do that left the team feeling like they could count on him to keep them informed. It reinforced their sense of connection to him and to the organization.

Recognize That Breakdowns Are a Part of Life

One of the great frustrations I have had as a business owner is the reality that organizational cultural challenges never seem to be fixed. One day everybody seems satisfied and happy; the next there's nothing but complaints. Sometimes both seem to occur at the same time. It is important to realize that these are the natural ups and downs of life. There is no way for any organization to be perfect all the time. Maintaining a healthy dose of reality about this can help us avoid feeling discouraged and resigned when we have to deal with "that issue, again?"

"Ain't Nothing Like the Real Thing": A Case Study in Organizational Belonging

Kaiser Permanente is the real thing in terms of creating a culture of belonging. Kaiser was founded in 1945 and is one of the largest not-for-profit health plans in the United States, serving almost 12 million members, over 8 million of them in California. Kaiser employs more than 200,000 people, including almost 22,000 physicians and more than 54,000 nurses.

By almost any measure imaginable, Kaiser would have to be considered a major business success story. In addition to being financially successful, Kaiser has been recognized as one of America's best employers and one of "America's happiest companies" by *Forbes*; has been recognized for excellence by *U.S. News and World Report*; has been selected by *ComputerWorld* as one of the best places to work in IT; has been chosen by *Diversity Inc.* magazine as a Top 50 company in diversity and inclusion; and has received a host of other health care leadership awards.

George Halvorson served as CEO and chairman of Kaiser from 2002 until retiring as CEO in 2013 and chairman in 2014. Halvorson had a very clear vision for the kind of culture of belonging that he wanted to create at Kaiser. Understanding the natural tendency of people to separate themselves into "us versus them," Halvorson set about creating a culture in which people could gain at least a significant component of their identity from their association with their employer.

Halvorson created a model that outlined all of the key elements of the culture development process that he and the leadership team of Kaiser employed (Figure 10.1).

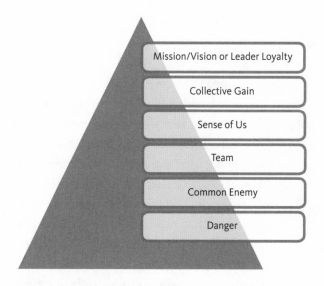

Figure 10.1 George Halvorson's Culture Model

Mission/Vision or Leader Loyalty

A company's mission or vision involves creating a clear goal for what the company is trying to accomplish, why that is important, and what kind of impact the company wants to have. Having a mission or vision is essential. Sometimes there is a singular, charismatic leader whose vision is so powerful and attractive that employees want to align with it. If that's the case, the leader's vision needs to evolve into an organizational vision if it is to become sustainable and persist after the leader's tenure is over. In most cases, however, the company is better served by a mission that is not tied to any individual.

Halvorson found that driving from mission was more powerful at Kaiser: "I never had leader loyalty as a motivator because I did not want people to think they were doing anything because of me. I wanted them doing it for the right reasons . . . for our mission and vision . . . and for our members. That was particularly valuable for labor unions, for example. They were much more inspired to be working for the members than to be working for a corporation."[8] This also made it much easier to transition leadership when Halvorson retired and was replaced by the company's chief operating officer, Bernard Tyson. Because the company was focused on mission more than on any one person, it has been able to continue to thrive.

It is easy to understand how powerful a mission can be. The tension between unions and management can be a great example of how two groups can be pulled apart by competing needs. Management's responsibility is the effective running of the organization, including maximizing the organization's financial health. Unions exist to protect their members. Yet when we slip into "us versus them" thinking, management can move toward trying to get any cost reductions they can, regardless of the impact on workers, and union leaders can move toward protecting the union as an institution without considering the long-term benefits to their members in having a stable organization with which to work.

One of my clients, a health care system in the Midwest, had this very thing happen. It resulted in four labor stoppages over a seven-year period, each of which closed the hospital for a time. The impact was devastating to the hospital's reputation in the community, to the largely low-income

African American population whom the hospital served, and to the employees, who found themselves out of work for extended periods of time.

We worked to bring all of the parties together to clean up the past. Each had an opportunity to take responsibility for what they had contributed to these breakdowns. As a result, we worked to create a committee comprising representatives of unions, management, patients, and the community alike. The committee members met regularly and established a sense of belonging among themselves in service of the goal of improving the community's overall well-being. They have not had another work stoppage in the past twenty years.

Collective Gain

Organizations function best as a unit when all associates have a stake in the organization's success. This often includes financial reward. This can be done by making sure people are paid a fair wage relative to their job classification, as well as by having a strong retirement program and benefits. We have also found that creating a profit-sharing program for all employees helps people feel that the success of the organization will tie directly into their own personal success. The message becomes "We do well by supporting each other."

In a less material sense, it is important that every employee understands how his or her role serves the greater good. Does the person at the front desk understand how welcoming people can affect the mood of what follows? Are the people who do administrative work and almost never actually see the customer acknowledged for how what they do contributes to the customer experience? The acknowledgment of everybody's contribution to the mission keeps people focused on the big picture and away from thinking that nobody cares how well they perform.

It's like an old story I heard years ago about a traveler who comes across three stonemasons in a quarry: the first one in a somber mood, the second one more focused, the third seemingly elated by what he is doing. The traveler asks each what they are doing. "Cutting this rock into a brick," says the first. "I am building a cathedral," says the second. And then came the third, who looked up, almost glowing, and said, "I am working to allow people to celebrate the greater glory of the Divine."

Everybody has to know that his or her contribution, regardless of how small or mundane it may seem on the surface, is contributing to the fulfillment of the mission.

Sense of Us

In an organization where belonging is practiced and generated, everybody sees him- or herself as part of a team. At Kaiser, Halvorson said, all employees were encouraged to see themselves as a caregiver for their members and patients. "Even the computer programmers felt like they were a part of the caregiving team," he told me. "Even if they never saw the members, they thought of themselves that way. Treating every patient like they were a member of our family was another way of treating the patients like an *us*."

As I've emphasized throughout this book, human beings naturally gravitate to an "us versus them" orientation. It is a core survival instinct. We protect those who are in our "us" group, providing support, defending them, and nurturing them. We are suspicious and territorial toward anyone in the *"them"* group. We have seen this in the dehumanizing language used toward other people in war, and in the ease many people feel in considering a Muslim ban today. *"They* are different and dangerous," we are told. "You can see that by the way *they* look, and the way *they* dress, and the way *they* pray. Keep *them* away so *we* will be safe." Even though we know statistically that only a tiny percentage of Muslims are actually a threat, which can really be said about almost any identity group, it becomes easier to keep all of *them* away from us than to figure out which ones are safe. When our organization fosters a culture of "us," we look out for each other in a different way. It can override our individual and societal belief systems.

A lot of the work of generating belonging occurs in language. The way we talk affects what we think, and what we think affects the way we act. Halvorson said it this way: "What we did in the corporate setting is to try to create a larger 'us.' We languaged the values in terms of 'we the people of Kaiser Permanente.' . . . I refused to let anybody refer to the labor groups or others as 'them.' It was all 'we' or 'us.' I even had to let go of a leader who just couldn't get himself to do this. People feel good about being an 'us' because when we are an 'us' you can rely on things, you can trust that you are supported."[9]

Halvorson went on to say: "If people have a sense that somebody in the organization or outside the organization is a 'them,' then you suspend conscience. It becomes okay to lie to them, to take things from them. As soon as somebody becomes a 'them' the basic rules of ethics drift away. As soon as they are an 'us' their well-being is our well-being. It's very dangerous when any part of the company is a 'them' because that part of the company doesn't feel the need to tell the truth or take the other's concerns in mind."[10] This applies to a company's customers too: organizations that countenance language like "the client from hell" or "those overly demanding customers" won't be able to provide consistently good customer service.

Halvorson also wrote a letter to his employees every week to celebrate "who we were and what we were doing." The letters were so positively received that they were used for recruiting new employees.

Team

Our need to belong often shows up in our relationship to teams. We have strong instincts to be in teams, to work in teams. If we go back just a relatively short time historically, that was overwhelmingly the way people lived. It was almost impossible to survive otherwise. It's only recently that we have bought into the worship of individual achievement over team performance.

Emphasize all of the behaviors that people engage in, but especially emphasize team behaviors. Halvorson and his leadership team taught leaders to be team leaders rather than bosses. There were hundreds of teams, and they were all based on the organization's values. Every team was given the task of trying to improve the organization's stated values, and then best practices were shared.

Common Enemies

Our "us" is defined when we have a visible "them." It helps strengthen our ability to coalesce around our vision, and it helps us see the connectedness between us in ways that are more important than our petty, internal "us versus them" dynamics. We have seen this in the way Americans came together in the immediate aftermath of 9/11. It has even been celebrated in movies such as *Independence Day,* when all of the world puts aside their differences to confront an alien invasion.

Competition can be healthy, and sometimes it can even be fun. As Jonathan Haidt has said, "Cooperation and competition are opposite sides of the same coin. And we've gotten this far because we cooperate to compete."[11] We sometimes get our need for it filled in watching sporting events. People will dress up in their team jerseys, paint their faces or bodies with team colors, and throw themselves into the energy of competition. It can be unhealthy as well. When beating the other becomes more important than our own values, the competition has pulled us away from our reason for being. This can occur when people get so fully identified with a team that they can't let go, possibly resulting in violence or depression after a game. The key is not to outlaw competition, as many New Age parents have tried to do with their children (to no avail), because competition is a great motivator. The key is to compete *consciously* and only within the construct of your stated values. This is true whether you are playing cards or golf with a friend, running a company, or running a country. When you leave your core values behind and focus only on "winning," nothing else holds up over time.

Halvorson used the names of the other health plans and their presidents to motivate his team. You can use the competition that you face as well. This doesn't mean that we can't work with our competitors at times when the challenge is coming from outside.

Danger

When you look at this lower level in Halvorson's model, it's easy to see the likeness to the lowest level of Maslow's hierarchy—the need for physical survival. The French writer Voltaire once penned, "Le mieux est l'ennemi du bien"—in English, "The perfect is the enemy of the good."[12] And it is often hardest to get people motivated to take on change when they are doing well. My own experience in consulting has definitely shown that. A client who is confronting a change but has a relatively well-functioning organization often has the attitude that "if it ain't broke, don't fix it." The problem is that what "ain't broke" today may be insufficient for tomorrow. Ask any of the hundreds of companies that have gone under or been rendered largely irrelevant by new advances that they could have seen coming but didn't because they didn't appreciate the threat. This is especially important when we are experiencing a paradigm shift, which seems to happen almost weekly in business these days. The rules suddenly change because of new technology, new needs, or new products, and, seemingly all of a sudden, what has worked before doesn't work as well anymore.

One classic example is Encyclopaedia Britannica, a historically successful business that got into real trouble a number of years ago because they continued to see themselves as a book publisher instead of realizing that their job was to get information out to people as easily as possible. Once Wikipedia and other similar formats were created, it made little sense for people to pay for sets of books that would become obsolete over time and had to be upgraded regularly, at a continued cost to the user. Older readers may remember a time when encyclopedias were sold door-to-door. Now Britannica's sales force has been dropped and staffing cut, and while print versions can still be bought in bookstores, the focus is on electronic products. But the company responded too late to preserve its financial standing.

The danger in a business environment might be forces that could undermine us. In the case of diversity and inclusion work, that might mean lawsuits or bad press, missing out on the incredible diversity of talent that's in the marketplace, or not getting a share of the multicultural marketplace. These pitfalls can be framed in terms of competition. Halvorson said he constantly reminded people at Kaiser that "the competition wants to steal our patients from us," and "if we don't do this we are going to go out of business" or "we won't have jobs and pensions." Keeping an eye on potential dangers helps motivate people to understand the risk in not creating a culture of belonging.

Belonging Breeds Success

What the Kaiser story shows us so powerfully is that belonging breeds success in organizations. There is a reason that so many great companies, including Panera Bread, Nordstrom, The Container Store, Tom's Shoes, and the giant Indian corporation Tata, among many others, have formed an organization called the Conscious Capitalism Institute to promote this kind of approach. Not only is it the right thing to do in terms of creating a healthier organization and community, but the members of the institute who are publicly traded companies outperformed the S&P 500 index by a factor of 10.5 over the years 1996–2011.[13]

What it finally comes down to is the reality that we can do well by doing good.

What are you waiting for?

Chapter 11

"Belonging Creates and Undoes Us Both"

Belonging creates and undoes us both. Agreement has rarely been the mandate for people who love each other. Maybe on some things, but actually, when you look at some people who are lovers and friends, actually they might disagree really deeply on things, but they're somehow—I like the phrase "the argument of being alive." Or in Irish, when you talk about trust, there's a beautiful phrase from West Kerry where you say, "Mo sheasamh ort lá na choise tinne," "You are the place where I stand on the day when my feet are sore." And that is soft and kind language, but it is so robust. That is what we can have with each other.

—PÁDRAIG Ó TUAMA

Corrymeela is the oldest peace and reconciliation organization in Northern Ireland. Located in the Northern Ireland village of Ballycastle, Corrymeela began before "the troubles" and continued on in Northern Ireland's changing postconflict society after the Good Friday Agreement was signed in 1998. The organization has grown and now has almost forty full-time staff and dozens of volunteers who work with the 11,000 people who attend programs at the center every year.

Theologian, poet, and group worker Pádraig Ó Tuama is one of the leaders of the community. He has conducted programs on mediation, group conflict, and dialogue for thousands of people. Ó Tuama quotes poet David Wagoner, who wrote, "Wherever you are is called Here, and you must treat it as a powerful stranger." Ó Tuama goes on to say, "And powerful strangers might be benevolent, but only might. Powerful strangers can also be unsettling and troubling. And powerful strangers can have their own hostilities, and have their own way within, [and] they cause you to question who you are and where you're from. And that is a way within which, for me, the notion of saying hello to 'here' requires a fairly robust capacity to tell the truth about what is really going on. And that can be very difficult."[1]

In a way, Ó Tuama captures the core message of this book. Belonging is indeed a "powerful stranger." Belonging can be the greatest of human gifts. It can give us comfort, identity, companionship, and material support. It can ease our fear and help us feel not so alone on this journey of life. It defines who we are as human beings.

Belonging also causes behavior that is deeply "unsettling and troubling." It leads to hostility, intransigence, tribalism, war, oppression, and even genocide.

This is the great conundrum. Which will we have?

I have tried to help provide a deeper understanding of this core aspect of our lives by looking at the pain in our world of separation, how we are wired to separate ourselves, and how that is impacting key areas of our lives. I've also tried to build the case that there are things we can do to heal that divide and create a stronger sense of belonging in our personal, organizational, and community lives.

We looked at ways to search for common ground, to cross the divide between each other and create a greater sense of collective belonging. Finally, we looked at how the workplace can serve as a source of belonging in the modern world.

The great Swiss psychologist Carl Jung purportedly said, "Until you make the unconscious conscious it will direct your life and you will call it fate. We cannot change anything until we accept it. Condemnation does not liberate, it oppresses!"

All that we have looked at tells us something very clearly: The tendency to divide ourselves between "us" and "them" is the way we are designed to function as human beings. I know we may not like that. We may wish it were different. But sometimes things are just the way they are.

When I was a young person doing civil rights work, I used to go volunteer at a black Baptist church about thirty minutes from where I lived. I was one of only a few white young people there, and a woman named

Maybelle Jones became our mentor. She would guide us, often through the use of aphorisms. One of the ones I remember best is, "Things ain't about what they're supposed to be . . . they're about what they is!"

The fact that we inherently divide ourselves into tribes may seem deflating, but it doesn't have to be. When we accept something for what it is, we actually have far more ability to impact it than when we are deluding ourselves into thinking it is something else. Learning to understand the dynamic is essential to addressing it.

As I hope you have seen, the tension between our need to belong and our tribalism can be addressed consciously and thoughtfully in ways that can help us bridge the divide and turn our competitiveness and our differences into assets. It will never happen if we avoid dealing with those differences, refuse to talk about them, or pretend they are not there. The process may be challenging, but as Jung also purportedly said, "Everything that irritates us about others can lead us to an understanding of ourselves."

Separation frightens us. We are afraid of breakdowns in our relationships with others, but breakdowns can be the source of breakthroughs. In many cases, unless we have a breakdown we don't look at what needs to be done. That is why so many people avoid changing their lives until they hit bottom.

There is no question that confronting the "dark night of the soul" can be painful. Sometimes it comes as a growing awareness; other times it arrives as the shock of a single event. However it shows up, it can threaten our sense of the fundamental meaning of life. It can feel depressing and hopeless. We might feel that nothing makes sense anymore. But if we decide to take on the new reality that has been presented to us, to turn away from denial and embrace reality, that awareness is the seed of breakthroughs. In the case of our search for belonging, those breakthroughs begin with communication.

Ó Tuama believes that language is a key to reconciliation:

Language needs courtesy to guide it, and an inclusion and a generosity that goes beyond precision and becomes something much more akin to sacrament, something much more akin to how is it you can be attentive to the implications of language for those in the room who may have suffered. . . . We infuse words with a sense of who we are. And so therefore, you're not just saying a word; you're communicating something that feels like your soul. And it might even be your soul. So the choice of a particular word is really, really important. And there is what is in the text, and whether that's a sacred text or the text of somebody's life. And then there is the lenses through which you read and interpret that. And those lenses I find to be extraordinarily practical.

. . . But there does need to be the stage then where we can go, "What can this mean for the wider civilization?" And I would like that public conversation can be a way within which we can talk about things with less fear. . . . We are failed by headlines that just demonize the other and are lazy. And where I might read a headline about myself and go, "I don't recognize myself in the language that's being spoken about there," we are failed by that. But we are upheld by something that has a quality of deep virtues of kindness, of goodness, of curiosity, and the jostle and enjoyment of saying, "Yeah, we disagree."[2]

That is at the heart of what is possible. We can see our disagreement as a beginning rather than as a threat. We can take on the challenge of transforming the dissonance of fear into the prospect of curiosity. We can build bridges to belonging.

I know it may seem overly optimistic to suggest that. I know it will be hard. The motivation may not be for ourselves, but for our children and their children. It has been done before.

There has been no greater example of that possibility in my lifetime than Nelson Mandela. After being imprisoned for twenty-seven years, much of it in solitary confinement, by a brutal, racist apartheid regime, Mandela emerged from prison on February 11, 1990. Very few people imagined that a ruthless government that had been at war with its black citizens for longer than any living person's lifetime would transition peacefully. Civil war was considered by most to be an inevitability. Yet it didn't happen.

Was it just that Mandela was extraordinary? Perhaps, but not according to him. "I do not want to be presented as some deity. I would like to be remembered as an ordinary human being with virtues and vices," he said.[3] Mandela actually saw that embracing forgiveness was a strategic necessity. Jelani Cobb, professor of journalism at Columbia University, said this:

> It's one thing to make forgiveness an element of a humanitarian movement; it's quite another to enact it as public policy. [Martin Luther] King sagely and sincerely presented racial reconciliation as a function of Christian love; Mandela knew that beyond his own spiritual inclinations racial reconciliation was an imperative of national survival.
>
> No figure could garner Mandela's moral standing by simply pantomiming forgiveness out of necessity. He believed in the redemptive power of forgiveness. But he also recognized that it was the only route that lay between civil war and the mass exodus of the moneyed, educated class of white people who were integral to the economy.
>
> Mandela emerged at that rare point in history where idealism and pragmatism were practically indistinguishable.[4]

Aren't we at that point in our history now, where the needs for idealism and pragmatism are practically indistinguishable? It is easy to fall into the lazy conclusion that we are doomed, that there is nothing we can do to stem the tide of tribalism that is tearing us apart.

Mandela said:

> There is no passion to be found playing small—in settling for a life that is less than the one you are capable of living. . . . There is no easy walk to freedom anywhere, and many of us will have to pass through the valley of the shadow of death again and again before we reach the mountaintop of our desires. . . . I learned that courage was not the absence of fear, but the triumph over it. The brave man is not he who does not feel afraid, but he who conquers that fear. . . . A good leader can engage in a debate

frankly and thoroughly, knowing that at the end he and the other side must be closer, and thus emerge stronger.[5]

The future is in our hands. We can continue on the pathway to separation, or we can take on the challenge of creating a future of belonging. It will require courage, determination, and a willingness to get off the path of self-righteousness. It is a personal task that leads to a collective future. And yet it is a future that is there for all of us if we are willing to take the steps to get there.

It begins with every conversation we have, every relationship we heal. Perhaps a fitting end to this inquiry is this story, which originated with the philosopher and science writer Loren Eiseley:

A man was walking on the beach one morning at dawn. In the distance he saw somebody who appeared to be dancing on the beach. As he got closer, he realized the woman was not dancing. In fact, she was reaching to the ground time and again and lifting things and throwing them into the ocean. As the man approached he shouted out, "What are you doing?"

"I'm throwing these starfish into the ocean," the woman responded. "The tide brings them in and leaves them on the beach, and when the sun comes up it will dry them out and kill them if they don't get back in the water." She reached down to lift and toss another.

The man looked down the beach and saw thousands of starfish similarly laid out in the morning sun. "Surely your efforts will be futile. How can you possibly make a difference with all of these starfish every morning?"

The woman reached down again without speaking and lifted another starfish, once again throwing it into the water. Then, turning toward the man, she shrugged and said, "It made a difference to that one."[6]

The task before us is daunting, and yet the path is clear. What starfish will you throw today?

Notes

Preface

1. Thomas Friedman, "Win, Lose, but No Compromise," *New York Times*, August 31, 2016.
2. Howard Ross, *ReInventing Diversity: Transforming Organizational Community to Strengthen People, Purpose and Performance* (Lanham, MD: Rowman & Littlefield, 2011), and Howard Ross, *Everyday Bias: Identifying and Navigating Unconscious Judgments in Our Daily Lives* (Lanham, MD: Rowman & Littlefield, 2014).

Introduction

1. "LGBTQ" is used to represent lesbian, gay, bisexual, transgender and "questioning" or "queer."
2. "Political Polarization in the American Public," Pew Research Center, June 12, 2014.
3. David Wasserman, "Senate Control Could Come Down to Whole Foods vs. Cracker Barrel," FiveThirtyEight, October 8, 2014, https://fivethirtyeight.com/features/senate-control-could-come-down-to-whole-foods-vs-cracker-barrel.
4. At the date of this writing, figures for the 2016 election were not available; however the general breakdown between red and blue states supports the pattern.
5. Bill Bishop and Robert G. Cushing, *The Big Sort: Why the Clustering of Like-Minded America Is Tearing Us Apart* (Boston: Houghton Mifflin, 2008).
6. Joy Huang, Samuel Jacoby, Michael Strickland, and Rebecca Lai, "Election 2016: Exit Polls," *New York Times*, November 8, 2016.
7. Emma Brown, "On the Anniversary of *Brown v. Board*, New Evidence That U.S. Schools Are Resegregating," *Washington Post*, May 17, 2016.
8. "Better Use of Information Could Help Agencies Identify Disparities and Address Racial Discrimination," U.S. Government Accountability Office, GAO-16-345, May 17, 2016.
9. David Neiwert, "Trump Condemns Attacks on Jews—After Earlier Suggesting They Are Meant to Make Him Look Bad," Southern Poverty Law Center, March 1, 2017.
10. Wikipedia, s.v. "Public Facilties Privacy & Security Act," https://en.wikipedia.org/wiki/Public_Facilities_Privacy_%26_Security_Act, accessed August 11, 2017.

11. Andrew Cohen, "It's Time to Investigate Voter Fraud," Brennan Center for Justice, New York University School of Law, January 24, 2017.

12. Sabrina Tavernise and Katharine Q. Seelye, "Political Divide Splits Relationships—and Thanksgiving, Too," *New York Times*, November 15, 2016.

13. Maimuna Majumder, "Election Got You Feeling Down? Good News: It Isn't Just You," *Wired*, November 8, 2016.

14. "Teacher Caught Telling Students Their Parents Would Be Deported," WorldNet-Daily.com, November 12, 2016.

Chapter 1: Wired for Belonging

1. The Human Rights Campaign's Corporate Equality Index is the national benchmarking tool on corporate policies and practices pertinent to lesbian, gay, bisexual, and transgender employees; see https://www.hrc.org/campaigns/corporate-equality-index.

2. Abraham H. Maslow, "A Theory of Human Motivation," *Psychological Review* 50, no. 4 (1943): 370–396.

3. Ibid., 370.

4. Patrick A. Gambrel and Rebecca Cianci, "Maslow's Hierarchy of Needs: Does It Apply in a Collectivist Culture?," *Journal of Applied Management and Entrepreneurship* 8, no. 2 (2003).

5. For the purpose of brevity, I will sometimes use the term "America" in this book to refer to the United States of America, and not the American continents.

6. Alexis de Tocqueville, *Democracy in America: Historical-Critical Edition of "De la démocratie en Amérique,"* vol. 3, ed. Eduardo Nolla, trans. James T. Schleifer (Indianapolis, IN: Liberty Fund, 2010) part 2, ch. 1.

7. Robert D. Putnam, *Bowling Alone: The Collapse and Revival of American Community* (New York: Touchstone Books, 2001).

8. Francis Fukuyama, "Social Capital and Development: The Coming Agenda," *SAIS Review* 22, no. 1 (2002): 23–37.

9. Ibid.

10. George N. Appell, "The Social Separation Syndrome," *Survival International Review* 5, no. 1 (1980): 13–15.

11. Alan I. Leshner, "Addiction Is a Brain Disease, and It Matters," *Science* 278, no. 5335 (1997): 45–47.

12. B. K. Alexander, R. B. Coambs, and P. F. Hadaway, "The Effect of Housing and Gender on Morphine Self-Administration in Rats," *National Center for Biotechnology Information Journal*, July 6, 1978, 175–179.

13. D. Morgan, K. A. Grant, H. D. Gage, R. H. Mach, J. R. Kaplan, O. Prioleau, S. H. Nader, R. Buchheimer, R. L. Ehrenkaufer, and M. A. Nader, "Social Dominance in Monkeys: Dopamine D2 Receptors and Cocaine Self-Administration," *National Center for Biotechnology Information Journal*, February 5, 2002, 169–174. In this study, macaque monkeys were placed into an environment similar to that of Rat Park and,

after they had established a social hierarchy, performed a series of tests. One such test involved giving each macaque an opportunity to self-administer cocaine. Did all macaques administer equivalent amounts of the highly addictive drug? No. It became apparent that the most aggressive users were the monkeys lowest on the social hierarchy. Similarly to Alexander's study, where the rats confined to a depressing cage were more likely to continue to consume the morphine, monkeys confined to a life on the lower end of the social hierarchy also sought drugs as a means to escape their less-than-ideal conditions.

14. B. O. Hagan, E. A. Wang, J. A. Aminawung, C. E. Albizu-Garcia, N. Zaller, S. Nyamu, S. Shavit, J. Deluca, and A. D. Fox, "History of Solitary Confinement Is Associated with Post-Traumatic Stress Disorder Symptoms among Individuals Recently Released from Prison," *Journal of Urban Health*, March 9, 2017, doi: 10.1007/s11524-017-0138-1.

15. Quoted from Ramin Skibba, "Solitary Confinement Screws Up the Brains of Prisoners," *Newsweek*, April 18, 2017.

16. Lee N. Robins, "Vietnam Veterans' Rapid Recovery from Heroin Addiction: A Fluke or Normal Expectation?," *Addiction Journal* 88 (1993): 1041–1054.

17. Caitlin Ryan, "Helping Families Support Their Lesbian, Gay, Bisexual, and Transgender (LGBT) Children," National Center for Cultural Competence, Georgetown University Center for Child and Human Development, 2009.

18. Scott E. Page, *The Difference: How the Power of Diversity Creates Better Groups, Firms, Schools, and Societies* (Princeton, NJ: Princeton University Press, 2007).

19. Robert D. Putnam, "E Pluribus Unum: Diversity and Community in the Twenty-First Century," Johan Skytte Prize Lecture, June 15, 2007, http://onlinelibrary.wiley.com/doi/10.1111/j.1467-9477.2007.00176.x/abstract.

20. Brené Brown, *Braving the Wilderness: The Quest for True Belonging and the Courage to Stand Alone* (New York: Random House, 2017).

21. Nelson Mandela, *Long Walk to Freedom: The Autobiography of Nelson Mandela* (Boston: Back Bay Books, 1995), 401–402.

22. Nelson Mandela, *Nelson Mandela by Himself: The Authorised Book of Quotations* (Johannesburg: Nelson Mandela Foundation, 2002).

23. L. F. Berkman and S. L. Syme, "Social Networks, Host Resistance, and Mortality: A Nine-Year Follow-Up Study of Alameda County Residents," *National Center for Biotechnology Information Journal*, February 1979, 186–204.

24. John Cacioppo and William Patrick, *Loneliness: Human Nature and the Need for Social Connection* (New York: W. W. Norton, 2009); J. Cacioppo, M. E. Hughes, L. J. Waite, L. C. Hawkley, and R. A. Thisted, "Loneliness as a Specific Risk Factor for Depressive Symptoms: Cross-Sectional and Longitudinal Analyses," *National Center for Biotechnology Information Journal*, March 21, 2006, 140–151.

25. James S. House, Karl R. Landis, and Debra Umberson, "Social Relationships and Health," *Science* 241, no. 4865 (1988): 540–545.

26. A. Lacey and D. G. Cornell, "Impact of Teasing and Bullying on Schoolwide Academic Performance," *Journal of Applied School Psychology*, August 13, 2013, 262–283.

27. R. F. Baumeister, J. M. Twenge, and C. K. Nuss, "Effects of Social Exclusion on Cognitive Processes: Anticipated Aloneness Reduces Intelligent Thought," *Journal of Personality and Social Psychology*, November 2002, 817–827.

28. J. T. Cacioppo, J. M. Ernst, M. H. Burleson, M. K. McClintock, W. B. Malarkey, L. C. Hawkley, R. B. Kowalewski, A. Paulsen, J. A. Hobson, K. Hugdahl, D. Spiegel, and G. G. Berntson, "Lonely Traits and Concomitant Physiological Processes: The MacArthur Social Neuroscience Studies," *National Center for Biotechnology Information Journal*, March 2000, 143–154.

29. Louise C. Hawkley and John T. Cacioppo, "Loneliness Matters: A Theoretical and Empirical Review of Consequences and Mechanisms," *Annals of Behavioral Medicine* 40 (October 2010): 218–227.

30. Xiaojing Xu, Xiangyu Zuo, Xiaoying Wang, and Shihui Han, "Do You Feel My Pain? Racial Group Membership Modulates Empathic Neural Responses," *Journal of Neurosciences* 29, no. 26 (2009): 8525–8529; M. Cikara, E. G. Bruneau, and R. R. Saxe, "Us and Them: Intergroup Failures of Empathy," *Current Directions in Psychological Science* 20, no. 3 (2011): 149–153; S. M. Aglioti, V. Santangelo, A. Avenanti, V. Cazzato, R. T. Azevedo, and E. Macaluso, "Their Pain Is Not Our Pain: Brain and Autonomic Correlates of Empathic Resonance with the Pain of Same and Different Race Individuals." *Human Brain Mapping* 34, no. 12 (2013): 3168–3181.

31. H. Tajfel, "Experiments in Intergroup Discrimination," *Scientific American* 223, no. 5 (1970): 96–103.

32. "Races Disagree on Impact of Simpson Trial," CNN-*Time* Poll, October 6, 1995, http://www.cnn.com/US/OJ/daily/9510/10-06/poll_race/oj_poll_txt.html.

33. G. A. Quattrone and E. E. Jones, "The Perception of Variability within In-Groups and Out-Groups: Implications for the Law of Small Numbers," *Journal of Personality and Social Psychology* 38, no. 1 (1980): 141–152.

34. Bernadette Park and Myron Rothbart, "Perception of Out-Group Homogeneity and Level of Social Categorization," *Journal of Personality and Social Psychology* 42, no. 6 (1982): 1051–1068.

35. Howard Ross, *Everyday Bias: Identifying and Navigating Unconscious Judgments in Our Daily Lives* (Lanham, MD: Rowman & Littlefield, 2014).

36. S. E. Asch, "Effects of Group Pressure on the Modification and Distortion of Judgments," in *Readings in Social Psychology*, 2nd ed., ed. G. E. Swanson, T. M. Newcomb, and E. L. Hartley (New York: Holt, 1952), 2–11.

37. Stanley Milgram, "Behavioral Study of Obedience," *Journal of Abnormal and Social Psychology* 67, no. 4 (1963): 371–378; "The Stanford Prison Experiment: Still Powerful after All These Years," press release, Stanford University News Service, January 8, 1997.

38. Cari Romm, "How We Learn to Exclude People," *New York Magazine*, April 13, 2017.

Chapter 2: The Politics of Being Right

1. John Davis, "Texas Tech Researchers: Caveman Instincts Still Play Role in Choosing Political Leaders," press release, Texas Tech University, October 19, 2011.

2. Avinash K. Dixit and Barry J. Nalebuff, *Thinking Strategically: The Competitive Edge in Business, Politics, and Everyday Life* (New York: Norton, 1991).

3. J. T. Toman, "The Papal Conclave: How Do Cardinals Divine the Will of God?," University of Melbourne, January 5, 2004.

4. Melissa Chan, "Donald Trump More Trustworthy Than Hillary Clinton, Poll Finds," *Time*, November 2, 2016.

5. "Comparing Hillary Clinton, Donald Trump on the Truth-O-Meter," Politifact, http://www.politifact.com/truth-o-meter/lists/people/comparing-hillary-clinton -donald-trump-truth-o-met, accessed May 17, 2017.

6. L. Hasher, D. Goldstein, and T. Toppino, "Frequency and Conference of Referential Validity," *Journal of Verbal Learning and Verbal Behavior* 16 (1977): 107–112.

7. The actual reference comes from *Mein Kampf,* vol. 1, ch. 6, in which Adolf Hitler writes: "The most brilliant propagandist technique will yield no success unless one fundamental principle is borne in mind constantly and with unflagging attention. It must confine itself to a few points and repeat them over and over. Here, as so often in this world, persistence is the first and most important requirement for success."

8. Emily Ekins, "The Five Types of Trump Voters: Who They Are and What They Believe," Democracy Fund Voter Study Group, June 2017.

9. "Poll: 'Obamacare' vs. 'Affordable Care Act,'" CNN, September 27, 2013.

10. "CNN Poll: Nearly Eight in Ten Favor Gays in the Military," CNN, May 25, 2010.

11. Scott Neuman, "Just How Independent Are Independent Voters?," National Public Radio, March 27, 2012.

12. Though this quote has been challenged by some, Bill Moyers affirmed in his interview with Jonathan Haidt on *Moyers & Company* on February 3, 2013, that Lyndon Johnson said this directly to him.

13. Tim Roemer, "Why Do Congressmen Spend Only Half Their Time Serving Us?," *Newsweek*, July 29, 2015.

14. *60 Minutes*, December 12, 2010.

15. R. Patterson, J. Rothstein, and A. K. Barbey, "Reasoning, Cognitive Control, and Moral Intuition," *Frontiers in Integrative Science*, December 18, 2012.

16. Jonathan Haidt and Jesse Graham, "When Morality Opposes Justice: Conservatives Have Moral Intuitions That Liberals May Not Recognize," *Social Justice Research* 20, no. 1 (2007): 98–116; Jonathan Haidt, *The Righteous Mind: Why Good People Are Divided by Politics and Religion* (New York: Vintage, 2012).

17. Definitions synopsized from www.moralfoundations.org.

18. John T. Jost, Dana R. Carney, Samuel D. Gosling, et al., "The Secret Lives of Liberals and Conservatives: Personality Profiles, Interaction Styles, and the Things They Leave Behind," *Political Psychology* 29, no. 6 (2008): 807–840.

19. Larry M. Bartels, "Partisanship and Voting Behavior, 1953–1996," *American Journal of Political Science* 44, no. 1 (2000): 35–50.

20. Marc J. Hetherington, "Resurgent Mass Partisanship: The Role of Elite Polarization," *American Political Science Review* 95, no. 3 (2001): 619–631.

21. Charles Murray, *Coming Apart: The State of White America* (New York: Crown, 2012).

22. Nate Silver, "Does Racism Affect How You Vote?," TED Talk, February 2009, https://www.ted.com/talks/nate_silver_on_race_and_politics.

23. S. Iyengar, G. Sood, and Y. Lelkes, "Affect, Not Ideology: A Social Identity Perspective on Polarization," *Public Opinion Quarterly* 76, no. 3 (2012): 405–431.

24. "The Myth of Voter Fraud," Brennan Center for Justice, New York University, https://www.brennancenter.org/issues/voter-fraud, accessed June 14, 2017.

25. Jonathan Haidt in an interview with Krista Tippet, *On Being*, October 19, 2017.

26. Atiba Ellis, personal communication.

27. Howard Ross, *Everyday Bias: Identifying and Navigating Unconscious Judgments in Our Daily Lives* (Lanham, MD: Rowman & Littlefield, 2014).

28. I am not talking here about marches in which protesters carry weapons and have an expressed intent to intimidate, threaten, or verbally abuse others. The First Amendment of the Constitution guarantees us the right to "peaceably assemble."

29. From his address in the Assembly Hall at the Paulskirche in Frankfurt, Germany, June 25, 1963, https://www.jfklibrary.org/Asset-Viewer/Archives/JFKWHA-199.aspx.

Chapter 3: Why Do We See the World the Way We Do?

1. Philippa Foot, "The Problem of Abortion and the Doctrine of the Double Effect," in *Virtues and Vices and Other Essays in Moral Philosophy* (Oxford: Basil Blackwell, 1978).

2. Peter Singer, "Ethics and Intuitions," *Journal of Ethics* 9 (2005): 331–352.

3. Philip Slater, *The Pursuit of Loneliness: America's Discontent and the Search for a New Democratic Ideal*, 3rd ed. (Boston: Beacon Press, 2016).

4. Robin I. M. Dunbar, "The Social Brain Hypothesis," *Evolutionary Anthropology* 6, no. 5 (1998): 178–190.

5. Joshua Greene, *Moral Tribes: Emotion, Reason, and the Gap between Us and Them* (New York: Penguin Books, 2014).

6. A. Laird, "Ringing the Changes on Gyges: Philosophy and the Formation of Fiction in Plato's *Republic*," *Journal of Hellenic Studies* 121 (2001): 12–29.

7. Erving Goffman, *The Presentation of Self in Everyday Life* (New York: Anchor, 1959).

8. C. B. Zhong, V. K. Bohns, and F. Gino, "Good Lamps Are the Best Police: Darkness Increases Dishonesty and Self-Interested Behavior," *Psychological Science* 21, no. 3 (March 2010): 311–314; T. Van Rompay, D. J. Vonk, and M. Fransen, "The Eye of the Camera: Effects of Security Cameras on Prosocial Behavior," *Environment and Behavior* 41, no. 1 (2009): 60–74; A. L. Beaman, B. Klentz, E. Diener, and S. Svanum, "Self Awareness and Transgression in Children: Two Field Studies," *Journal of Personality and Social Psychology* 37, no. 10 (1979): 1835–1846.

9. Dan Ariely, *Predictably Irrational: The Hidden Forces That Shape Our Decisions* (New York: Harper Perennial, 2010).

10. Mary Rigdon, Keiko Ishii, Motoki Watabe, and Shinobu Kitayama, "Minimal Social Cues in the Dictator Game," *Journal of Economic Psychology* 30 (2009): 358–367.

11. Ibid.

12. Steven Pinker, *The Blank Slate: The Modern Denial of Human Nature* (New York: Penguin Books, 2003).

13. L. J. Eaves and H. J. Eysenck, "Genetics and the Development of Social Attitudes," *Nature* 249 (May 17, 1974): 288–289; T. J. Bouchard Jr., David T. Lykken, M. McGue, N. L. Segal, and A. Tellegen, "Sources of Human Psychological Differences: The Minnesota Study of Twins Reared Apart," *Science* 250, no. 4978 (1990).

14. M. Dittmann, "Standing Tall Pays Off, Study Finds," *Monitor on Psychology* 35, no. 7 (2004): 14.

15. A reference coined by my dear friend and colleague Michael Schiesser.

16. John Searle, *The Construction of Social Reality* (New York: Free Press, 1997).

17. C. G. Jung, *Two Essays on Analytical Psychology*, trans. R. C. C. Hull (New York: Meridian Books, 1953), 19.

18. Elaine Hatfield, John T. Cacioppo, and Richard L. Rapson, *Emotional Contagion* (Cambridge: Cambridge University Press, 1994).

19. Sigal G. Barsade, "The Ripple Effect: Emotional Contagion and Its Influence on Group Behavior," *Administrative Science Quarterly* 47, no. 4 (2002): 644–675; E. Palagi, V. Nicotra, and G. Cordoni, "Rapid Mimicry and Emotional Contagion in Domestic Dogs," *Royal Society Open Science*, December 23, 2015.

20. Nicholas Christakis and James H. Fowler, "The Spread of Obesity in a Large Social Network over 32 Years," *New England Journal of Medicine*, July 26, 2007.

21. Anna Giaritelli, "Man Accused of Assaulting Protestors at Trump Rally Sues President," *Washington Examiner*, May 17, 2017.

22. "Man Accused of Assaulting Woman at Trump Rally Says President to Blame," Fox News, April 17, 2017.

23. I. L. Janis, *Victims of Groupthink: A Psychological Study of Foreign-Policy Decisions and Fiascoes* (Boston: Houghton Mifflin, 1972); Patrick Hughes and Erin White, "The Space Shuttle *Challenger* Disaster: A Classic Example of Groupthink," *Ethics and Critical Thinking Journal* 2010, no. 3 (2010): 63; Dina Badie, "Groupthink, Iraq, and the War on Terror: Explaining US Policy Shift toward Iraq," *Foreign Policy Analysis*, October 2010.

24. Jung, "The Structure of the Unconscious," in *The Cambridge Companion to Jung*, 2nd ed., ed. Polly Young-Eisendrath and Terence Dawson (Cambridge: Cambridge University Press, 2008).

25. Rupert Sheldrake, *The Presence of the Past: Morphic Resonance and the Habits of Nature* (London: Icon Books, 2011).

26. E. O. Wilson, *The Social Conquest of Earth* (New York: Liveright, 2013).

Chapter 4: Power, Privilege, Race, and Belonging

1. Alexis de Tocqueville, *Democracy in America: Historical-Critical Edition of "De la démocratie en Amérique,"* vol. 3, ed. Eduardo Nolla, trans. James T. Schleifer (Indianapolis, IN: Liberty Fund, 2010), 544.

2. James Baldwin, "The American Dream and the American Negro," *New York Times*, March 7, 1965.

3. Colin Woodward, *American Nations: A History of the Eleven Regional Cultures of North America* (New York: Penguin, 2011).

4. Katherine L. Milkman, Modupe Akinola, and Dolly Chugh, "What Happens Before? A Field Experiment Exploring How Pay and Representation Differentially Shape Bias on the Pathway into Organizations," *Journal of Applied Psychology*, May 22, 2012.

5. Roland G. Fryer Jr., "An Empirical Analysis of Racial Differences in Police Use of Force," National Bureau of Economic Research Working Paper no. 22399, July 2016.

6. D. Boatright, D. Ross, P. O'Connor, et al., "Racial Disparities in Medical Student Membership in the Alpha Omega Alpha Honor Society," *Journal of the American Medical Association*, May 2017.

7. Cody Ross, "A Multi-Level Bayesian Analysis of Racial Bias in Police Shootings at the County-Level in the United States, 2011–2014," *PLoS ONE*, November 2015.

8. C. Civile and S. S. Obhi, "Students Wearing Police Uniforms Exhibit Biased Attention toward Individuals Wearing Hoodies," *Frontiers in Psychology* 8 (2007).

9. Alice Robb, "Sunglasses Make You Less Generous," *New Republic*, March 26, 2014.

10. *2013–2014 Civil Rights Data Collection: Key Data Highlights on Equity and Opportunity Gaps in Our Nation's Public Schools*, U.S. Department of Education, Office of Civil Rights, June 2016.

11. Howard Ross, *ReInventing Diversity: Transforming Organizational Community to Strengthen People, Purpose and Performance* (Lanham, MD: Rowman & Littlefield, 2011), 6–8.

12. Sharon LaFraniere and Andrew Lehren, "The Disproportionate Risks of Driving while Black," *New York Times*, October 24, 2015.

13. Peter DiCaprio, "Why Some White People Don't See White Privilege," *Huffington Post*, July 20, 2017. The studies referred to in this passage are *Housing Discrimination against Racial and Ethnic Minorities 2012*, U.S. Department of Housing and Urban Development, 2012; D. B. Matthews, E. Rodrigue, and R. Reeves, "Time for Justice: Tackling Race Inequalities in Health and Housing," Brookings Institution, October 19, 2016.

14. Robin DiAngelo, "White Fragility," *International Journal of Critical Pedagogy* 3, no. 3 (2011): 54.

15. Adam Howard, "New 'Star Wars: The Force Awakens' Trailer Sparks Racial Backlash," MSNBC, October 20, 2015.

16. Carla Herreria, "Fox News Host Cries Because Conversation on Race Makes Her 'Uncomfortable,'" *Huffington Post*, August 16, 2017.

17. I know that many people are now using the term *micro-aggressions* to identify these behaviors. I prefer to use the term *micro-inequities*, which was originally coined by Mary Rowe at MIT in 1973. Most of these behaviors are unconscious and we almost never think of "aggression" as an unconscious act, so I find that often people are confused and unnecessarily defensive when *micro-aggression* is used.

18. Renee Stepler, "5 Key Takeaways about Views of Race and Inequality in America," Pew Research Center, June 27, 2016.

19. Tanvi Misra, "Immigrants Aren't Stealing American Jobs," *Atlantic*, October 21, 2015; Julia Preston, "Immigrants Aren't Taking Americans' Jobs, New Study Finds," *New York Times*, September 21, 2016.

20. Alexander Stephens, "The Cornerstone Speech," Savannah, GA, March 21, 1861, http://www.ucs.louisiana.edu/~ras2777/amgov/stephens.html.

21. Zack Beauchamp, "What Trump Gets Wrong about Confederate Statues, in One Chart," *Vox*, August 15, 2017.

22. John Pierce, "The Reasons for Secession: A Documentary Study," Civil War Trust, https://www.civilwar.org/learn/articles/reasons-secession, accessed July 23, 2017.

23. Noor Wazwaz, "It's Official: The U.S. Is Becoming a Minority-Majority Nation," *U.S. News and World Report*, July 6, 2015.

24. E. P. Apfelbaum, M. I. Norton, and S. R. Sommers, "Racial Colorblindness: Emergence, Practice, and Implications," *Current Directions in Psychological Science* 21, no. 3 (2012): 205–209.

25. Martin Luther King Jr., "Letter from the Birmingham Jail," April 16, 1963, https://www.africa.upenn.edu/Articles_Gen/Letter_Birmingham.html.

Chapter 5: The Social Brain

1. S. J. Suomi and H. A. Leroy, "In Memoriam: Harry F. Harlow (1905–1981)," *American Journal of Primatology* 2 (1982): 319–342.

2. H. F. Harlow, R. O. Dodsworth, and M. K. Harlow, "Total Social Isolation in Monkeys," *Proceedings of the National Academy of Sciences* 54, no. 1 (1965): 90–97.

3. F. Eyssel and N. Reich, "Loneliness Makes the Heart Grow Fonder (of Robots): On the Effects of Loneliness on Psychological Anthropomorphism," in *HRI 2013: Proceedings of the 8th ACM/IEEE International Conference on Human-Robot Interaction* (Piscataway, NJ: IEEE, 2013), 121–122.

4. N. Epley, A. Waytz, S. Akalis, and J. T. Cacioppo, "When We Need a Human: Motivational Determinants of Anthropomorphism," *Social Cognition* 26, no. 2 (2008): 143–155.

5. N. Epley, S. Akalis, A. Waytz, and J. T. Cacioppo, "Creating Social Connection through Inferential Reproduction: Loneliness and Perceived Agency in Gadgets, Gods, and Greyhounds," *Psychological Science* 19, no. 2 (2008): 114–120.

6. Julianne Holt-Lunstad, Timothy B. Smith, and J. Bradley Layton, "Social Relationships and Mortality Risk: A Meta-analytic Review," *PLoS Medicine*, July 27, 2010, doi: 10.1371/journal.pmed.1000316.

7. T. K. Inagaki and N. I. Eisenberger, "Shared Neural Mechanisms Underlying Social Warmth and Physical Warmth," *Psychological Science* 24, no. 11 (2013): 2272–2280.

8. A. E. Guyer, V. R. Choate, D. S. Pine, and E. E. Nelson, "Neural Circuitry Underlying Affective Response to Peer Feedback in Adolescence," *Social Cognitive and Affective Neuroscience* 7, no. 1 (2012): 81–92; C. G. Davey, N. B. Allen, B. J. Harrison, D. B. Dwyer, and M. Yücel, "Being Liked Activates Primary Reward and Midline Self-Related Brain Regions," *Human Brain Mapping* 31, no. 4 (2010): 660–668.

9. K. Izuma, D. N. Saito, and N. Sadato, "Processing of Social and Monetary Rewards in the Human Striatum," *Neuron* 58, no. 2 (2008): 284–294.

10. G. L. Shulman, J. A. Fiez, M. Corbetta, R. L. Buckner, F. M. Miezin, M. E. Raichle, and S. E. Petersen, "Common Blood Flow Changes across Visual Tasks: II. Decreases in Cerebral Cortex," *Journal of Cognitive Neuroscience* 9, no. 5 (1997): 648–663; M. E. Raichle, A. M. MacLeod, A. Z. Snyder, W. J. Powers, D. A. Gusnard, and G. L.

Shulman, "A Default Mode of Brain Function," *Proceedings of the National Academy of Sciences* 98, no. 2 (2001): 676–682.

11. Susan T. Fiske and Shelley E. Taylor, *Social Cognition: From Brains to Culture* (Los Angeles: Sage, 2013).

12. Matthew D. Lieberman, *Social: Why Our Brains Are Wired to Connect* (New York: Crown, 2013).

13. W. Gao, H. Zhu, K. S. Giovanello, J. K. Smith, D. Shen, J. H. Gilmore, and W. Lin, "Evidence on the Emergence of the Brain's Default Network from 2-Week-Old to 2-Year-Old Healthy Pediatric Subjects," *Proceedings of the National Academy of Sciences* 106, no. 16 (2009): 6790–6795.

14. F. Heider and M. Simmel, "An Experimental Study of Apparent Behavior," *American Journal of Psychology* 57, no. 2 (1944): 243–259.

15. Daniel C. Dennett, *The Intentional Stance* (Cambridge, MA: MIT Press, 1989).

16. G. Rizzolatti and M. Fabbri-Destro, "Mirror Neurons: From Discovery to Autism," *Experimental Brain Research* 200, nos. 3–4 (2010): 223–237.

17. Traci Pederson, "Theory of Mind," Psych Central, https://psychcentral.com/encyclopedia/theory-of-mind, last updated July 17, 2016.

18. "Autism Linked to Mirror Neuron Dysfunction," *Science Daily*, April 18, 2005.

19. Naomi I. Eisenberger, Matthew D. Lieberman, and Kipling D. Williams, "Does Rejection Hurt? An fMRI Study of Social Exclusion," *Science* 302, no. 5643 (2003): 290–292.

20. Naomi I. Eisenberger, "The Pain of Social Disconnection: Examining the Shared Neural Underpinnings of Physical and Social Pain," *Nature Reviews Neuroscience* 13 (June 2012): 421–434.

21. Kipling D. Williams, "Ostracism: The Kiss of Social Death," *Social and Personality Psychological Compass*, September 5, 2007.

22. J. L. Brown, D. Sheffield, M. R. Leary, and M. E. Robinson, "Social Support and Experimental Pain," *Psychosomatic Medicine* 65, no. 2 (2003): 276–283.

23. S. Schnall, K. D. Harber, J. K. Stefanucci, and D. R. Proffitt, "Social Support and the Perception of Geographical Slant," *Journal of Experimental Social Psychology* 44, no. 5 (2008): 1246–1255.

Chapter 6: Divinity, Division, and Belonging

1. Emo Philips, "The Best God Joke Ever—and It's Mine!," *Guardian*, September 29, 2005.

2. Thomas Jefferson, "Jefferson's Letter to the Danbury Baptists: The Final Letter, as Sent," *Library of Congress Information Bulletin*, June 1998.

3. Thomas Jefferson to Peter Carr, August 10, 1787, in *Papers of Thomas Jefferson* 12:15, cited in "Jefferson's Religious Beliefs," *The Thomas Jefferson Encyclopedia*, at Monticello.org.

4. Thomas Jefferson to Alexander von Humboldt, December 6, 1813, Founders Online, National Archives.

5. Amar Ali, "Why Do Religions Exist and What Is Their Purpose to Society?," Quora, October 8, 2011.

6. "Islam at Mount Vernon," *George Washington Digital Encyclopedia*, http://www
.mountvernon.org/digital-encyclopedia/article/islam-at-mount-vernon.

7. Craig Walenta, "Treaty between the United States and Tripoli," https://usconstitution
.net/tripoli.html, last modified January 24, 2010.

8. Andrea Stone, "Most Think Founders Wanted Christian USA," *USA Today*, September 13, 2007.

9. Heidi Glenn, "Losing Our Religion: The Growth of the 'Nones,'" *Morning Edition*, National Public Radio, January 13, 2013.

10. "America's Changing Religious Landscape," Pew Research Center for Religion in Public Life, May 12, 2015.

11. From an interview with John Danforth by Krista Tippett, *On Being*, September 14, 2006.

12. Michael Lipka, "Muslims Expected to Surpass Jews as Second-Largest U.S. Religious Group," Pew Research Center, April 14, 2015.

13. U.S. Religious Landscape Study, 2014, Pew Research Center.

14. "America's Changing Religious Landscape," Pew Research Center for Religion in Public Life, May 12, 2015.

15. Emile Durkheim, *The Elementary Forms of the Religious Life* (London: Allen & Unwin, 1912).

16. Lera Boroditsky, "How Language Shapes Thought," *Scientific American*, February 2011.

17. Lera Boroditsky, "How Does Our Language Shape the Way We Think?," *Edge*, October 31, 2017.

18. Reza Aslan, "Bill Maher Isn't the Only One Who Misunderstands Religion," *New York Times*, October 8, 2014.

19. Albert Einstein, letter to Carl Seelig, March 11, 1952, https://en.wikiquote.org/wiki/Albert_Einstein.

20. Karen Armstrong, *The Case for God* (New York: Anchor Books, 2010).

21. Tim Folger, "Why Did Greenland's Vikings Vanish?," *Smithsonian Magazine*, March 2017.

22. Richard Dawkins, *The God Delusion* (Boston: Mariner, 2008).

Chapter 7: When Worlds Collide

1. J. K. Hamlin, N. Mahajan, Z. Liberman, and K. Wynn, "Not Like Me = Bad: Infants Prefer Those Who Harm Dissimilar Others," *Psychological Science* 24, no. 4 (2013): 589–594.

2. D. Lloyd, G. Di Pellegrino, and N. Roberts, "Vicarious Responses to Pain in Anterior Cingulate Cortex: Is Empathy a Multisensory Issue?," *Cognitive, Affective, and Behavioral Neuroscience* 4, no. 2 (2004): 270–278; M. Cikara, E. G. Bruneau, and R. R. Saxe, "Us and Them: Intergroup Failures of Empathy," *Current Directions in Psychological Science* 20, no. 3 (2011): 149–153.

3. J. Decety and P. L. Jackson, "The Functional Architecture of Human Empathy," *Behavioral and Cognitive Neuroscience Reviews* 3, no. 2 (2004): 71–100.

4. F. B. de Waal, "Putting the Altruism Back into Altruism: The Evolution of Empathy," *Annual Review of Psychology* 59 (2008): 279–300.

5. M. Levine, A. Prosser, D. Evans, and S. Reicher, "Identity and Emergency Intervention: How Social Group Membership and Inclusiveness of Group Boundaries Shape Helping Behavior," *Personality and Social Psychology Bulletin* 31, no. 4 (2005): 443–453.

6. Zach Sommers, "Missing White Women Syndrome: An Empirical Analysis of Race and Gender Disparities in Online News Coverage of Missing Persons," *Journal of Criminal Law and Criminology* 6, no. 2 (2016): 275–314.

7. Daniel Goleman, *Emotional Intelligence: Why It Can Matter More than IQ* (New York: Bantam Books, 1996), 11.

8. Roper Center, "Job Performance Ratings for President Bush," March 9, 2009.

9. Bobby Caina Calvan, "Montana Governor Rejects Bill Banning Sharia Law in Courts," Associated Press, April 6, 2017.

10. Gordon W. Allport, *The Nature of Prejudice* (Cambridge, MA: Addison-Wesley, 1954); S. C. Wright, "Cross-Group Contact Effects," in *Intergroup Relations: The Role of Emotion and Motivation*, ed. S. Otten, T. Kessler, and K. Sassenberg (New York: Psychology Press, 2009), 262–283.

11. Howard Ross, *Everyday Bias: Identifying and Navigating Unconscious Judgments in Our Daily Lives* (Landham, MD: Rowman & Littlefield, 2011).

12. Kevin Schulman et al., "The Effect of Race and Sex on Physician's Recommendations for Cardiac Catheterization," *New England Journal of Medicine*, February 25, 1999; Urban Institute, Margery Austin Turner, Diane K. Levy, Doug Wissoker, Claudia L. Aranda, Rob Pittingolo, and Rob Santos, *Housing Discrimination against Racial and Ethnic Minorities 2012* (Washington, DC: U.S. Department of Housing and Urban Development, Office of Policy Development and Research, 2013). While I could easily include dozens of examples of racial bias toward people of other races, or identities beyond race, I have chosen to focus on race bias toward African Americans in this particular case to provide a more substantive set of examples. For broader examples, please check out my *Everyday Bias*.

13. Daniel M. Butler and David E. Broockman, "Do Politicians Racially Discriminate against Constituents? A Field Experiment on State Legislators," *American Journal of Political Science*, April 27, 2011.

14. Katherine L. Milkman, Modupe Akinola, and Dolly Chugh, "What Happens Before? A Field Experiment Exploring How Pay and Representation Differentially Shape Bias on the Pathway into Organizations," *Journal of Applied Psychology*, May 22, 2012.

15. Jennifer L. Doleac and Luke C. D. Stein, "The Visible Hand: Race and Online Market Outcomes," *Economic Journal*, November 21, 2013.

16. B. G. Link and J. C. Phelan, "Stigma and Its Public Health Implications," *Lancet* 367, no. 9509 (2006): 528.

17. Victoria K. Lee and Lasana T. Harris, "Dehumanized Perception: Psychological and Neural Mechanisms Underlying Everyday Dehumanization," in *Humanness and Dehumanization*, ed. Paul G. Bain, Jeroen Vaes, and Jacques-Philippe Leyens (New York: Taylor & Francis, 2014), 68–85.

18. Melvin J. Lerner, *The Belief in a Just World* (New York: Plenum Press, 1980), 9–30.

19. Rodney Coates, "The Myth of the Happy Slave and the Reality of Its Endurance," University of Miami, April 11, 2016.

20. Lasana T. Harris and Susan T. Fiske, "Dehumanizing the Lowest of the Low: Neuroimaging Responses to Extreme Out-Groups," *Psychological Science* 17, no. 10 (2006): 847–853.

21. Lasana T. Harris and Susan T. Fiske, "Social Neuroscience Evidence for Dehumanised Perception," *European Review of Social Psychology* 20, no. 1 (2009): 192–231.

22. J. Bruce Overmier and Martin E. P. Seligman, "Effects of Inescapable Shock upon Subsequent Escape and Avoidance Responding," *Journal of Comparative and Physiological Psychology* 63, no. 1 (1967): 28.

23. Joy DeGruy, *Post Traumatic Slave Syndrome: America's Legacy of Enduring Injury and Healing* (Milwaukee, OR: Uptone Press, 2005).

24. Karen Dion, Ellen Berscheid, and Elaine Walster, "What Is Beautiful Is Good," *Journal of Personality and Social Psychology* 24, no. 3 (1972): 285.

25. Alexander Totorov, Anesu N. Mandisodza, Amir Goren, and Crystal C. Hall, "Influences of Competence from Faces Predict Election Outcomes," *Science*, June 10, 2005.

26. Walter S. Gilliam, Angela N. Maupin, Chin R. Reyes, Maria Accavitti, and Frederick Shic, "Do Early Educators' Implicit Biases Regarding Sex and Race Relate to Behavior Expectations and Recommendations of Preschool Expulsions and Suspensions?," Yale Child Study Center, September 2016.

27. Michael Edison Hayden, "What We Know about the Terence Crutcher Police Shooting in Tulsa, Oklahoma," ABC News, September 20, 2016.

28. H. Mercier and D. Sperber, "Why Do Humans Reason? Arguments for an Argumentative Theory," *Behavioral and Brain Sciences* 34, no. 2 (2011): 57–74.

29. R. S. Nickerson, "Confirmation Bias: A Ubiquitous Phenomenon in Many Guises," *Review of General Psychology* 2, no. 2 (1998): 175.

30. A. H. Hastorf and H. Cantril, "They Saw a Game: A Case Study," *Journal of Abnormal and Social Psychology* 49, no. 1 (1954): 129.

31. R. P. Vallone, L. Ross, and M. R. Lepper, "The Hostile Media Phenomenon: Biased Perception and Perceptions of Media Bias in Coverage of the Beirut Massacre," *Journal of Personality and Social Psychology* 49, no. 3 (1985): 577.

32. C. G. Lord, L. Ross, and M. R. Lepper, "Biased Assimilation and Attitude Polarization: The Effects of Prior Theories on Subsequently Considered Evidence," *Journal of Personality and Social Psychology* 37, no. 11 (1979): 2098.

33. B. Nyhan and J. Reifler, "When Corrections Fail: The Persistence of Political Misperceptions," *Political Behavior* 32, no. 2 (2010): 303–330.

34. S. V. Shepherd, R. O. Deaner, and M. L. Platt, "Social Status Gates Social Attention in Monkeys," *Current Biology* 16, no. 4 (2006): R119–R120.

35. Sukhvinder S. Obhi, Jeremy Hogeveen, and Michael Inzlicht, "Power Changes How the Brain Responds to Others," *Journal of Experimental Psychology: General* 143, no. 2 (2014): 755–762.

36. D. Kipnis, "Does Power Corrupt?," *Journal of Personality and Social Psychology* 24, no. 1 (1972): 33.

37. Susan T. Fiske, "Controlling Other People: The Impact of Power on Stereotyping," *American Psychologist* 48, no. 6 (1993): 621.

38. Carl Ratner, *Cooperation, Community, and Co-ops in a Global Era* (New York: Springer, 2013), 51.

39. K. D. Vohs, N. L. Mead, and M. R. Goode, "The Psychological Consequences of Money," *Science* 314, no. 5802 (2006): 1154–1156.

40. X. Zhou, K. D. Vohs, and R. F. Baumeister, "The Symbolic Power of Money: Reminders of Money Alter Social Distress and Physical Pain," *Psychological Science* 20, no. 6 (2009): 700–706.

Chapter 8: The Media Is the Message

1. Kevin Schaul and Samuel Granados, "How Cable News Networks Reacted to Comey's Hearing," *Washington Post*, June 8, 2017.

2. T. Norretranders, *The User Illusion*, trans. J. Sydenham (New York: Viking, 1998), cited in Timothy Wilson, *Strangers to Ourselves: Discovering the Adaptive Unconscious* (Cambridge, MA: Belknap Press of Harvard University Press, 2002), 24.

3. From Dictionary.com.

4. Howard Ross, *ReInventing Diversity: Transforming Organizational Community to Strengthen People, Purpose, and Performance* (Lanham, MD: Rowman & Littlefield, 2011), 45.

5. I have seen this quote attributed to the German philosopher Johann Wolfgang von Goethe but have been unable to confirm that he actually said it.

6. S. M. McClure, J. Li, D. Tomlin, K. S. Cypert, L. M. Montague, and P. R. Montague, "Neural Correlates of Behavioral Preference for Culturally Familiar Drinks," *Neuron* 44, no. 2 (2004): 379–387.

7. R. Rosenthal and L. F. Jacobson, "Teacher Expectations for the Disadvantaged," *Scientific American* 218, no. 4 (1968): 19–23.

8. American Press Institute, "How Americans Get Their News," March 17, 2014.

9. American Press Institute, "The Relationship between General News Habits and Trust in the News," April 17, 2016.

10. Jeffrey Gottfried and Elisa Shearer, "Americans' Online News Use Is Closing in on TV News Use," Pew Research Center, September 7, 2017.

11. Amy Mitchell, Jeffrey Gottfried, Jocelyn Kiley, and Katerina Eva Matsa, "Political Polarization and Media Habits," Pew Research Center, October 21, 2014.

12. Special thanks to Gleb Tsipursky, professor of history and decision sciences at the Ohio State University, for his in-depth interview, which contributed significantly to this section.

13. Jeffrey Gottfried and Elisa Shearer, "News Use Across Social Media Platforms 2017," Pew Research Center, September 7, 2017.

14. Andrew Soergel, "Is Social Media to Blame for Political Polarization in America?," *U.S. News and World Report*, March 20, 2017.

15. From an interview with Gleb Tsipursky, June 27, 2017.

16. Ibid.

17. Amit Chowdhry, "Research Links Heavy Facebook and Social Media Usage to Depression," *Forbes*, April 30, 2016.
18. Melanie Eversley, "Study: 'Hate' Groups Explode on Social Media," *USA Today*, updated March 10, 2017.
19. E. Bakshy, S. Messing, and L. A. Adamic, "Exposure to Ideologically Diverse News and Opinion on Facebook," *Science* 348, no. 6239 (2015): 1130–1132.
20. Lee Rainie, "The New Landscape of Facts and Trust," Pew Research Center, April 21, 2017.
21. Craig Silverman and Jeremy Singer-Vine, "Most Americans Who See Fake News Believe It, New Survey Says," BuzzFeed News, December 6, 2016.
22. Jeffrey Gottfried and Elisa Shearer, "News Use across Social Media Platforms 2016," Pew Research Center, May 26, 2016.
23. Max Read, "Donald Trump Won Because of Facebook," *New York Magazine*, November 9, 2016.
24. "Conspiracy Theories Prosper: 25% of Americans Are 'Truthers,'" press release, Public Mind Poll, Fairleigh Dickinson University, January 17, 2013.
25. Jörg L. Spenkuch and David Toniatti, "Political Advertising and Election Outcomes," Kellogg School of Management, Northwestern University, April 2016.
26. Sam Sanders, "Did Social Media Ruin Election 2016?," National Public Radio, November 8, 2016.
27. Wikipedia, s.v. "Pizzagate Conspiracy Theory," accessed August 14, 2017, https://en .wikipedia.org/wiki/Pizzagate_conspiracy_theory; Ishmael N. Dao, "No, Trump Never Told People Magazine That Republicans Are 'the Dumbest' Voters," BuzzFeed News, July 21, 2016.
28. Peter C. Newman, "The Lost Marshall McLuhan Tapes," *MacLean's*, July 16, 2013.
29. "Big Data, for Better or Worse: 90% of World's Data Generated over Last Two Years," *Science News*, May 22, 2013.
30. Barry Schwartz, *The Paradox of Choice* (New York: Harper Perennial, 2005).
31. Ilan Dar-Nimrod, Catherine D. Rawn, Darrin R. Lehman, and Barry Schwartz, "The Maximization Paradox: The Costs of Seeking Alternatives," *Personality and Individual Differences* 46, nos. 5–6 (2009): 631–635.

Chapter 9: Bridges to Bonding

1. Interview with Jamil Mahuad, August 22, 2017.
2. "Peru and Ecuador Sign Treaty to End Longstanding Conflict," *New York Times*, October 27, 1998.
3. "Peru and Ecuador Sign Border Treaty," BBC News, October 27, 1998, http://news .bbc.co.uk/2/hi/americas/201442.stm.
4. Elliot Aronson, *The Jigsaw Classroom* (Beverly Hills, CA: Sage, 1978).
5. Elliot Aronson and Joshua Aronson, eds., *Readings about the Social Animal*, 11th ed. (New York: Worth, 2011).
6. Gregory M. Walton, "A Brief Social-Belonging Intervention Improves Academic and Health Outcomes of Minority Students," *Science* 331, no. 6023 (2011): 1447–1451.

7. Excerpt from a talk originally delivered at the Modern Language Association's panel "Lesbians and Literature," Chicago, December 28, 1977, first published in *Sinister Wisdom* 6 (1978).

8. Gregory Bateson, *Mind and Nature: A Necessary Unity* (New York: Macmillan, 1991).

9. Stephen Covey, *The 7 Habits of Highly Effective People*, rev. ed. (New York: Free Press, 2004), 30–31.

10. Timothy D. Wilson, *Redirect: Changing the Stories We Live By* (Boston: Back Bay Books, 2015).

11. Roger Fisher and William Ury, *Getting to Yes: Negotiating Agreement without Giving In*, rev. ed. (New York: Penguin Books, 1991).

12. Edward de Bono, *Six Thinking Hats: An Essential Approach to Business Management* (Boston: Little, Brown, 1985).

Chapter 10: Institutions Can Build Bridges to Belonging

1. From Google Dictionary.

2. M. Scott Peck, *The Different Drum: Community Making and Peace* (New York: Touchstone Books, 1987), 59.

3. Bartie Scott, "Why Meditation and Mindfulness Training Is One of the Best Industries for Starting a Business in 2017," *Inc.*, March 1, 2017.

4. Chimanda Ngozi Adichie, "The Danger of a Single Story," TED Talk, June 7, 2013, https://www.ted.com/talks/chimamanda_adichie_the_danger_of_a_single_story.

5. Jeff Stone and Gordon B. Moskowitz, "Non-Conscious Bias in Medical Decision Making: What Can Be Done to Reduce It?," *Medical Education*, July 14, 2011.

6. See our thought papers at www.cookross.com for more specifics on these interventions.

7. Carmen Nobel, "The Case against Racial Colorblindness in the Workplace," *Forbes*, January 20, 2013.

8. From an interview with George Halvorson, June 13, 2017.

9. Ibid.

10. Ibid.

11. From an interview with Jonathan Haidt by Bill Moyers, *Moyers & Company*, February 3, 2013.

12. Voltaire, "La Bégueule," in *Contes* (London, 1772).

13. Tony Schwartz, "Companies That Practice 'Conscious Capitalism' Perform 10X Better," *Harvard Business Review*, April 4, 2013.

Chapter 11: "Belonging Creates and Undoes Us Both"

1. From an interview with Pádraig Ó Tuama by Krista Tippett, *On Being*, March 2, 2017.

2. Ibid.

3. Caitlin O'Connell, "Who Is Nelson Mandela? A Reader's Digest Exclusive Interview," *Reader's Digest*, 2005, https://www.rd.com/true-stories/inspiring/who-is-nelson-mandela-a-readers-digest-exclusive-interview.

4. Jelani Cobb, "Mandela and the Politics of Forgiveness," *New Yorker*, December 6, 2013.
5. Nelson Mandela, *Long Walk to Freedom: The Autobiography of Nelson Mandela* (Boston: Back Bay Books, 1995).
6. Adapted from Loren Eiseley, "The Star Thrower," in *The Unexpected Universe* (New York: Harcourt, Brace & World, 1969).

Acknowledgments

There are so many people who have contributed in so many ways to the writing of this book, and even more to the experiences that have contributed to my thinking. First and foremost, I want to thank JonRobert Tartaglione, whose research and deep comprehension of some of the social science and neurocognitive science behind belonging gave me a new understanding not only of what to write but also of how to understand the issue in a new and deeper way. Tat, your future is incandescent.

I also want to give my deepest appreciation to Nyki Caldwell, who contributed immensely with research, editing, and a wisdom that goes way beyond her years. Nyki also helped me immeasurably in managing my life so that I could find the time to write—not an easy feat, but one that she handles with incredible grace and love.

I would also like to thank Minal Bopaiah for her wise counsel and editing support, as well as Steve Piersanti, Jeevan Sivasubramaniam, and the rest of the extraordinary team at Berrett-Koehler Publishers, who bring a dedication and sense of mission to their work that is profoundly inspiring. Thanks also to those who read and gave feedback on the manuscript and, through their critiques, made it a better work.

I am deeply grateful to those who go out every day, in various ways, to try and do their part to contributing to healing the great divide in our culture today, whether that be through community organizing, social justice work, work on legislative action, or teaching and speaking against injustice and toward belonging every day. I include in that all of my colleagues around the world who do the work of diversity and inclusion in organizations as well as organizations that I am personally connected with or support, including Operation Understanding DC, Black Lives Matter, the Southern Poverty Law Center, the ACLU, the Pro-Truth Pledge, the Children's Defense Fund, the Human Rights Campaign, and PFLAG.

I also want to give special appreciation to the dozens of people I interviewed for this book. Many were on the other side of the political divide from me and yet were willing to honestly share their experience and point of view in a way that broadened my own understanding and helped me look at my own biases and stereotypes.

I have learned, and continue to learn, from so many teachers that space is inadequate to acknowledge them all. Many of those names show up in references in these pages. I am forever grateful to live in a world in which technology allows us to learn from so many teachers if we are willing to listen.

My deepest appreciation to all of my colleagues at Cook Ross Inc., who give me an opportunity to fall in and out of belonging every day and to attempt to learn from the pain as well as the pleasure. These include, but are not limited to, Shilpa Alimchandani, Hy Alvaran, Dwight Anderson, Samiah Anderson, Sonia Aranza, Bart Bailey, Shayne Bauer-Ellsworth, Lenora Billings-Harris, Minal Bopaiah, Amanda Boucher, Dr. Tony Byers, Nyki Caldwell, Dr. Johnnetta B. Cole, Renee Collins, Johann De Castro, Peter DiCaprio, Lori Dobeus, Emily Duncan, Dan Egol, Grace Eickmeyer, Davie Floyd, Audrey Ford, Sharon Glenn, Jose Gomez, Robby Gregg, C. J. Gross, Reggie Hicks, Marsha Hughes-Rease, Arsalan Iftikar, Sally Jue, Natanya Khashan, Meg Kiernan, Cathy Kuanga, Cheryl LeMaster, Laura Malinowski, Anna Mack, Ben Mann, Allison Manswell, Melanie Miller, Armers Moncure, Chris Morin, Meena Nutbeam, Rosalyn Taylor O'Neale, Juan Osuna, Samir Patel, Dominic Perri, Eric Peterson, Kimberly Rattley, Allyson Robinson, Paige Robnett, Zunilda Rodriguez, Cory Schneider, Albert Smith, Erica Stout, Pedro Suriel, Minjon Tholen, Michael Thompson, Deanna Troust, Miguel Valenciano, Loretta Van Pelt, Isabel Varela, and Jakob Wolf-Barnett. Special thanks also to my soul brother and sister, Michael Schiesser and Neelama Eyres, for more things than can ever be listed.

My family has been incredibly loving, even as my need to travel all over the world to do my works impacts my time with all of them. Matt,

Monita, Jason, Kate, Gabe, Shauna, and Jake, I am so grateful to all of you. Hannah, Mayah, Sloane, Penelope, Davis, and Audrey, I love you so much and pray that we can leave you a future better than the world we were left with.

I don't have enough words to express my gratitude to Michael Leslie Amilcar, my friend and business partner. Michael has been instrumental in getting our work out to so many people and provides leadership where I am lacking, and grace in the face of challenge. I am forever in your debt.

And to my beloved Leslie. With you is where I most belong. You are everything to me. I adore you.

Finally, to the Great Beloved, in all of the names, my heart belongs to you.

Howard Ross
November 5, 2017

Index

Page numbers followed by f indicate figures; those followed by t indicate tables.

About the Author

Howard J. Ross is a lifelong social justice advocate and the founding partner of Cook Ross, Inc. He is considered one of the world's seminal thought leaders on identifying and addressing unconscious bias. He is the author of *ReInventing Diversity: Transforming Organizational Community to Strengthen People, Purpose and Performance* (published by Rowman and Littlefield in conjunction with SHRM in 2011) and the *Washington Post* bestseller *Everyday Bias: Identifying and Navigating Unconscious Judgments in Our Daily Lives* (published by Rowman and Littlefield in 2014).

Ross has consulted on the areas of corporate culture change, leadership development, mindfulness, and diversity and inclusion. He has taught about diversity, inclusion, and cultural integration in academic institutions, professional services corporations, Fortune 500 companies, and retail, health care, media, and governmental institutions in the United States and worldwide. In addition, Ross has delivered programs at Harvard University Medical School, Stanford University Medical School, Johns Hopkins University, the Wharton School of Business, Duke University, Washington University Medical School, and more than twenty other colleges and universities.

Howard served as the 2007–2008 Johnnetta B. Cole Professor of Diversity in Residence at Bennett College for Women, the first time a white man had ever served in such a position at a historically black college for women. His writings have been published by the *Harvard Business Review*, the *Washington Post*, the *New York Times, Fast Company, Diversity Women, Forbes, Fortune*, and dozens of other publications. He appears regularly on National Public Radio.

Howard has served on the boards of numerous not-for-profits, including the Diversity Advisory Board of the Human Rights Campaign, the Dignity and Respect Campaign, Operation Understanding, the National Council for Community Justice, and the National Women's Mentoring Network. Ross has been the recipient of many awards, including the 2009 Operation Understanding Award for Community Service, the 2012 Winds of Change Award from the Forum on Workplace Diversity and Inclusion, the 2013 Diversity Peer Award from *Diversity Women*, the 2014 Catalyst Award from *Uptown Professional*, the 2014 Catalyst for Change Award from Wake Forest University, the 2015 Trendsetter in HR from *SHRM Magazine*, and the 2016 Leadership in Diversity Award from the World Human Resources Development Conference in Mumbai, India.

Berrett–Koehler
Publishers

Berrett-Koehler is an independent publisher dedicated to an ambitious mission: *Connecting people and ideas to create a world that works for all.*

We believe that the solutions to the world's problems will come from all of us, working at all levels: in our organizations, in our society, and in our own lives. Our BK Business books help people make their organizations more humane, democratic, diverse, and effective (we don't think there's any contradiction there). Our BK Currents books offer pathways to creating a more just, equitable, and sustainable society. Our BK Life books help people create positive change in their lives and align their personal practices with their aspirations for a better world.

All of our books are designed to bring people seeking positive change together around the ideas that empower them to see and shape the world in a new way.

And we strive to practice what we preach. At the core of our approach is Stewardship, a deep sense of responsibility to administer the company for the benefit of all of our stakeholder groups including authors, customers, employees, investors, service providers, and the communities and environment around us. Everything we do is built around this and our other key values of quality, partnership, inclusion, and sustainability.

This is why we are both a B-Corporation and a California Benefit Corporation—a certification and a for-profit legal status that require us to adhere to the highest standards for corporate, social, and environmental performance.

We are grateful to our readers, authors, and other friends of the company who consider themselves to be part of the BK Community. We hope that you, too, will join us in our mission.

We hope you enjoy this BK Currents book.

A BK Currents Book

BK Currents books bring people together to advance social and economic justice, shared prosperity, sustainability, and new solutions for national and global issues. They advocate for systemic change and provide the ideas and tools to solve social problems at their root. So get to it!

To find out more, visit **www.bkconnection.com**.

Berrett–Koehler
Publishers

Connecting people and ideas
to create a world that works for all

Dear Reader,

Thank you for picking up this book and joining our worldwide community
of Berrett-Koehler readers. We share ideas that bring positive change into
people's lives, organizations, and society.

To welcome you, we'd like to offer you a free e-book. You can pick from
among twelve of our bestselling books by entering the promotional code
BKP92E here: http://www.bkconnection.com/welcome.

When you claim your free e-book, we'll also send you a copy of our e-news-
letter, the *BK Communiqué*. Although you're free to unsubscribe, there are
many benefits to sticking around. In every issue of our newsletter you'll find

- A free e-book
- Tips from famous authors
- Discounts on spotlight titles
- Hilarious insider publishing news
- A chance to win a prize for answering a riddle

Best of all, our readers tell us, "Your newsletter is the only one I actually
read." So claim your gift today, and please stay in touch!

Sincerely,

Charlotte Ashlock
Steward of the BK Website

Questions? Comments? Contact me at bkcommunity@bkpub.com.

Certified

Corporation
bcorporation.net